FIRST THINGS FIRST!

FIRST THINGS FIRST!

CREATING THE NEW AMERICAN PRIMARY SCHOOL

RUBY TAKANISHI

TEACHERS COLLEGE PRESS

TEACHERS COLLEGE | COLUMBIA UNIVERSITY
NEW YORK AND LONDON

National Association of
Elementary School
Principals
Alexandria, VA

Published simultaneously by Teachers College Press, 1234 Amsterdam Avenue, New York, NY 10027 and National Association of Elementary School Principals, 1615 Duke Street, Alexandria, VA 22314

Principals are the primary catalysts for creating lasting foundations for learning. Since 1921, the National Association of Elementary School Principals (NAESP) has been the leading advocate for elementary and middle level principals in the United States and worldwide. NAESP advances the profession by developing policy, advancing advocacy, and providing professional development and resources for instructional leadership, including specialized support and mentoring for early career principals. Key focus areas include Pre-K–3 education and advancing the development of early childhood education leaders to help every child reach their greatest potential. For more information about NAESP, please visit www.naesp.org. NAESP administers the National Resource Center, the American Student Council Association, and the President's Education Awards & American Citizenship Awards Programs.

Cover photo by Mare Kuliasz / iStock by Getty Images.

Library of Congress Cataloging-in-Publication Data is available at loc.gov

ISBN 978-0-8077-5693-5 (paper)
ISBN 978-0-8077-5694-2 (hardcover)
ISBN 978-0-8077-7408-3 (ebook)

Printed on acid-free paper
Manufactured in the United States of America

23   22   21   20   19   18   17   16   8   7   6   5   4   3   2   1

Kodomo no tame ni
For the sake of the children
Márika Takanishi and CP

Contents

ACKNOWLEDGMENTS

In the Japanese American community in Hawai'i, the Japanese phrase *okage sama de* points to the interdependence among individuals that makes any endeavor productive and worthwhile. Everything we have accomplished involves people who helped us to be who we are. The relevant translation here is, I have been able to achieve my aims because you walked with me on my long journey.

John Simon, professor at Yale University School of Law, believed in the ideas presented in this book and recommended that one of the closing grants of the Taconic Foundation, noted for its historic leadership in supporting the civil rights movement, be awarded to facilitate the writing of the book. John's belief in me and his commitment to children and civil rights spurred me to make a case for early education as a civil rights issue in the early chapters of this book. Every child's right to participate in pre-kindergarten education, as advocated in this book, is far from assured today.

The board of directors of the Foundation for Child Development (FCD) approved a grant to support the completion of this book, specifically its communications and dissemination activities. Jessica Chao, while serving as interim president and COO of FCD, remained committed to learning from its grantmaking agenda, where the central ideas of this book were incubated. Former FCD staff Mark Bogosian and Anya Bailey provided documents and other resources that enabled me to reflect on FCD's pre-K–3rd initiative, launched in June 2003.

I have been extraordinarily fortunate to have had life mentors on whom I can count for guidance. Three of them have passed away: John Gardner, Julius B. Richmond, and Docia Zavitkovsky. They were generous with their time and their advice during critical periods in my career. To have had such individuals as professional role models—*Ma ke mahalo*—my profound gratitude. Continuing in their wise steering are Michael I. Cohen, Patrick H. DeLeon, and David A. Hamburg. Through their examples, I learned how important it is have good mentors and to be one myself.

Many friends and colleagues have encouraged me on what has been a long march. Others started their emails, letters, and phone calls with, How is the writing going? I thank them without identifying all of them, because the list would be lengthy. But I do want to recognize the relentless members of my cheerleading team: Kimber Bogard, Gene Garcia, Sybil Jordan Hampton, Luba Lynch, Elena O. Nightingale, and Peggy Saika. Whenever I wanted to abandon this book for new adventures, they kept me from straying off the path.

At Teachers College Press, Carole Saltz and Peter Sciafani, who assisted Carole, have been pivotal and patient with my slow pace and even reluctance to embark on this book project. I recognize how fortunate I am that Carole advocated for this book, believed that it would contribute to the debates about American education, and firmly and gently nudged me to its completion. Marie Ellen Larcada-Smith started the ball rolling, and Carole made sure I got to the goal line. Susan Liddicoat also read an early draft and made valuable suggestions and edits for the final version.

My colleagues at New America, Lisa Guernsey, deputy director of the Education Policy Program; Laura Bornfreund, director of the Early and Elementary Education Program; and their intrepid team of Abbie Lieberman, Aaron Loewenberg, Amaya Garcia, and Conor Williams inspire me and give me confidence that the primary education field will be transformed in their lifetimes. They bring fresh insights about issues that have stagnated for too long and courage to say the things that must be said for progress to be made in both widening access and increasing the educational quality of programs. They represent the generational change that I have been waiting for.

I am also inspired by strategic advocates across the country whose efforts will move the new primary school forward: Swati Adarkar of the Children's Institute of Oregon and her team, Carla Bryant of the San Francisco Unified School District, Kristie Kauerz at the University of Washington, Laura Kohn of Education Synergy Alliance in California, Holly Miller of the City of Seattle, Arthur Reynolds of the Midwest Child-Parent Centers, and Sharon Ritchie of First School at the University of North Carolina. Like those of my colleagues at New America, their ideas and actions will make a difference in the education transformation to come.

In fall 2011, I became a member of the McKnight Foundation Education and Learning National Advisory Committee (ELNAC), which provides outside advice to that foundation as it pursues an Early Literacy Pathways Initiative in the Twin Cities area of Minnesota. I have learned so much from the participating schools and educators over the past 4 years, which has grounded my ideas on the realities of schools and districts. My thanks to Kate Wolford, Neal Cuthbert, and Ervin Gavin at the foundation; Bonnie Houck, who staffed the initiative during the first year; and fellow ELNAC members during 4 years: Linda Espinosa, Eugene Garcia, Kristie Kauerz, Tim Knowles, Kent Pekel, Sara Stoelinga, Vallay Varro, and McKnight Foundation board liaison Robert Bruininks.

The Foundation for Child Development's pre-K–3rd initiative had philanthropic partners who were crucial to its evolution: Sandra Treacy, formerly of the W. Clement and Jessie V. Stone Foundation; Huilan Yang Krenn of the W. K. Kellogg Foundation; Sylvia Yee of the Evelyn and Walter Haas, Jr. Fund; Sara Slaughter of the McCormick Foundation (now at the Stone Foundation); Luba Lynch, formerly of the A. L. Mailman Family Foundation; and Jodi Haavig of the Bill and Melinda Gates Foundation.

My thanks go to my editor, Sarah Carr, whose calm encouragement and spot-on insights about themes and ideas contributed to the entire manuscript. Lisa Guernsey was also part of the editing process, as was Laura Bornfreund. Barbara Gomez served as manuscript manager and made it possible for me to complete this book following the requirements of the press.

As an independent scholar, I could not have written this book without the New York Public Library's unparalleled resources and staff, particularly the librarians who staff the research desks and obtained the books I requested. Having worked for Carnegie Corporation of New York, I experienced my almost daily encounter with a portrait of Andrew Carnegie that hangs in my neighborhood library as a source of inspiration about the enduring impact of wise philanthropy. It was a Carnegie library in a neighboring town that introduced me to the wider world beyond Kekaha, Hawai'i, where I grew up.

I attended small rural public schools on the island of Kaua'i, and I still remember my pre-K classroom and teacher. The federal programs created in the post-Sputnik period to support new science and mathematics education and gifted and talented programs, all targeted toward developing the knowledge and skills of my teachers, enabled me to have learning experiences that have endured. Had the U.S. Congress not created these programs, I would have been on the path to being a junior high school dropout.

My parents, Misae Tokushige and Kazuo Takanishi, exemplified in their lives the Japanese phrase *Kodomo no tame ni* (For the sake of the children). Like many of their generation, especially those from families with recent immigration histories, they sacrificed so that their children would have a better life than theirs. They believed that education and lifelong learning were the pathways to a good life. And they were clear that giving back should be the highest priority for those as privileged as their children were.

For those of us who grew up knowing that our forebears had left their countries to seek a better life for their children, their unspoken aspiration was that following generations would have the freedom to pursue their true interests. They would not select professions just for economic considerations but because of their passion for learning. The late Senator Daniel K. Inouye pointed out that when my daughter, Márika, decided to become an art historian, our families achieved that aspiration.

Generations of family members labored along the way so that she could make that choice. In Márika, my professional and personal lives converge, in my hopes that all children will have the opportunities and educational experiences she has had to follow her calling.

Okage sama de! Heartfelt gratitude to all who made this book possible.

—Ruby Takanishi, New York City, December 2015

INTRODUCTION

> It is not beyond our power to create a world where all children have access
> to a good education.
>
> —Nelson Mandela, November 2010

Talent is universally distributed. Opportunity to develop that talent, sadly, is not. Leveling the playing field for American children during the first 10 years of their lives can make an enormous difference in revitalizing our nation and in fostering individual well-being (Bradbury, Corak, Waldfogel, & Washbrook, 2015). Given the disturbing and harmful social and economic inequalities in American communities today (Stiglitz, 2010), developing the talent of all our children is the civil and human rights challenge of our times.

This book calls on a broad group of organizations and individuals to join me in reimagining how American children are to be educated during the first decade of their lives. Our initial task is to reimagine how American public education can begin with 3- and 4-year-olds. Primary or elementary education, the first level of how we currently organize education from kindergarten through Grade 5 (K–5), has been oddly overlooked in recurring waves of education reform that have washed over American middle and high schools (Bornfreund, McCann, Williams, & Guernsey, 2014). Redressing this neglect is now urgent and long overdue.

Learning, now more than ever in an age of a relentlessly changing, technology-driven global economy, must be a lifelong enterprise. Skills and dispositions developed during the early years provide the launching pad for lifelong learning. Thus, we must begin with first things first.

In this book I urge policymakers, educators, reform leaders, advocates, and citizens to place the beginning years of a redesigned 21st-century public education system on a firm, stable, and coherent foundation by starting earlier. It aims to frame access to pre-kindergarten education for 3- and 4-year-olds as a basic human and civil right that requires a place in our universal public education system. Like the K–12 grades, established over a century ago, pre-K can no longer be a privilege for some.

1

Four decades of nearly stagnant measures of children's reading and math achievement at the end of 3rd grade provide compelling evidence that all is not well in America's primary schools (U.S. Department of Education, Institute of Education Sciences, National Center for Education Statistics, National Assessment of Educational Progress [NAEP], 2015). Not only are there disturbing and wide achievement gaps between groups of children; the levels of achievement for all American children are also inadequate for a good life in the 21st century. While trends have ticked slightly upward, about two-thirds of all American students do not attain proficiency in reading and mathematics by the end of 3rd grade (U.S. Department of Education, Institute of Education Sciences, National Center for Education Statistics, National Assessment of Educational Progress [NAEP], 2013). In international assessments during high school, their rankings are equally troubling (Ripley, 2013). Inequalities in education achievement related to family economic resources and to race and ethnicity are endemic. They violate America's commitment to social equality.

Starting in the late 1990s, advocates intensified their campaigns to create early learning opportunities before kindergarten because of their potential to narrow early learning gaps between children living in different economic circumstances. These campaigns have contributed to growing public awareness of the value in reducing gaps in early education, defined as pre-K programs for children from birth to age 5, and resulted in the growth of pre-K programs, typically for children 4 years of age, in states and cities. Polls indicate that public support for using federal funds to increase access to high-quality pre-K exceeds 70% (Gallup, 2014). Early education is thus framed as a bipartisan political issue.

Despite these efforts, the United States is not a leader in early education (Economist Intelligence Unit, 2012). In 2012–2013, enrollments in pre-K programs declined in the aftermath of the Great Recession, as the Congress and state legislatures cut funding for these discretionary programs. According to the National Institute for Early Education Research (NIEER, 2015) annual report, *The State of Preschool 2014*, 29% of 4-year-olds attended state-funded pre-K programs in 2014. Funding per child ranges from a high of $16,431 in the District of Columbia to a low of $1,543 in Arizona (NIEER, 2015).

Most significant to framing pre-K education as a civil rights issue, the American pre-K landscape is characterized by inequalities in access to early learning opportunities and, most important, in the quality of these programs serving low-income children (Nortes & Barnett, 2014). Inequity in access to pre-K programs is highly influenced by the economic resources of children's families, their racial-ethnic background, and state and local policies and practices regarding who is deemed eligible for public early education and at what age it begins.

Economic resources of families matter, because access to early education in America remains the private responsibility of families, and it is costly, even exceeding the annual tuition costs for public higher education. Latino children, especially, live in communities where programs are not generally available (National Task Force on Early Childhood Education for Hispanics, 2007). And states vary widely in terms of whether they provide programs for all children or just some, and in the levels of state funding (NIEER, 2015).

Inequality in early learning opportunities is a disturbing fact in America and compromises too many children's prospects in life, especially those growing up in low-income families, where early investments can result in the largest payoffs (Bartik, 2014; Raudenbush & Eschmann, 2015). Except in the few states where pre-K programs for fours (in fewer places like New Jersey and the District of Columbia for threes) are universal, low-income children are less likely to be enrolled than those from more economically advantaged households.

These inequalities based on family economic resources should no longer be tolerated, given the knowledge we now have about the early origins of inequality (Allen & Kelly, 2015) and the evidence that good pre-K programs, which are sustained by good K–12 education, can contribute to narrowing the learning gaps between groups of children (McGhee-Hassrick, Raudenbush, & Rosen, in press; Raudenbush & Eschmann, 2015; Zellman & Kilburn, 2015). And given the established connections between educational attainment, health status, and economic resources in adulthood (Marmot, 2015), pre-K education must move from being a privilege for some to becoming a basic right for all children.

The reason why I wrote this book is to point out the lack of cohesion, continuity, and collaboration between the early education and K–12 sectors, which is critical to providing a needed coherent educational foundation for young children. Greater coordination is necessary in providing the amount and quality of learning, starting with pre-K and continuing in K–12, that is critical to children's lifelong learning. Such continuity is especially important for children living in poverty and low-income circumstances and can reduce educational inequalities (McGhee-Hassrick et al., in press).

Yet prevailing assumptions, not directly expressed, are that investing in pre-K programs, typically for 1 year, is sufficient to prepare children for primary schools as they exist today and that early learning programs can have long-term benefits without changes in primary schools. That set of assumptions is not supported by the performance of most children after their pre-K experience.

Thus advocates, policymakers, researchers, and reformers, with a few exceptions, have overlooked or marginalized efforts to make stronger connections between pre-K and K–12 education. For the most part, early education and primary education remain in separate silos, even when these grades are colocated in a building.

There are, however, some small signs that this disconnect may be changing. Efforts called pre-K–3rd are beginning to emerge throughout the country as more pre-K programs are located in or near public schools (see www.fcd-us.org for a pre-K–3rd map; see also www.newamerica. org), but they remain largely local innovations, few and far apart from the more visible education reforms.

In this book, I challenge the status quo when it comes to American expectations about the education of children during the first decade of their lives. A new framework that seeks to integrate coexisting, separate early education and primary education is required to strengthen learning during the first critical decade of life and beyond. This framework is a direct challenge to those who believe that 1 or 2 years of pre-K experience can narrow the achievement gap. Reimagining primary education provides such a framework for beginning our task of reducing educational inequality in America.

Experience thus far indicates that achieving such a merger of early and primary education into a new American primary school will be a herculean effort. Structural barriers to integration are built into a byzantine maze of existing laws, policies, funding streams, and related practice. Additional barriers include the long-established agendas of various interest groups as well as deeply ingrained professional loyalties and mindsets (Karch, 2013). Later in this book, I will recommend both short- and long-term strategies to improve the likelihood of such integration. Throughout the chapters, figures and special resource boxes enhance my discussion.

This book starts with four basic questions:

- What should the United States, a country founded on values of equal opportunity and the pursuit of happiness and well-being, design as the first, widely shared educational experiences of its children?
- How can the design of that educational experience reflect demographic, social, linguistic, and cultural changes in our nation over the past 50 years and adapt to the requirements of a global economy?
- How can educators use what is known about how children learn and base their educational experiences on that knowledge?
- And, most important, how can our nation create a new primary school that educates all its children well?

END THE CHAOS AT THE SCHOOLHOUSE DOOR

As American children begin their educational experiences outside their homes—whether in kindergarten or before—they encounter wildly uneven expectations and practices in what and how they learn. Policymakers and, in some cases, advocates and reformers have created this chaos at the schoolhouse door. The addition and layering of programs without regard to what comes before and after rivals the incoherence so endemic in the K–12 grades (Cohen & Moffitt, 2009).

Most people outside the worlds of early education and primary education are not aware of the impact of a cluster of uncoordinated, incremental federal and state policies on accessibility to and the quality of early learning experiences (Karch, 2013). These policies—commonly described as fragmented and bifurcated—have created real chaos and confusion among teachers about how young children should be educated during the pre-K and kindergarten years and beyond. This confusion likely affects the instruction and learning of young children, especially in ways that are not supportive of what some children have learned in good pre-K programs.

The policies originated, in part, because of the longstanding separation of early education from K–12 education. The best known example, Head Start, a federal program for young children in poverty created in 1965, still remains outside the U.S. Department of Education and is likely to remain so. The largest federal program aimed at improving the education of low-income children in the K–12 system, originally known as the Elementary and Secondary Education Act of 1965 (ESEA), and currently known as the Every Student Succeeds Act of 2015 (ESSA), was established at the same time. Both aim to improve the educational prospects of low-income children starting from birth, but Head Start and Title I have remained largely separate in practice, reflecting the early education and K–12 divide. The passage of ESSA in December 2015 promises to bridge that divide through provisions to connect early learning programs to the primary grades.

Title I allows for funding of pre-K programs from birth, but a very small part of these funds, estimated at 2 or 3%, supports early learning programs (Pew Center on the States, 2010). Funds are used to support programs for parents of children from birth to 3 years of age, and also to augment half-day pre-K to become full-school-day programs in school districts. The best known example of Title I funds being used to support pre-K–3rd grade programs is seen in the Chicago Child-Parent Centers, created in the late 1960s, and now known as the Midwest Expansion

Child-Parent Centers in St. Paul (MN) and in several sites in Illinois, including Chicago.

To this day, both Head Start and Title I are administered by different federal agencies and have different funding streams, standards, and accountability and reporting requirements; staff qualifications; and technical support systems. And to this day, calls for greater coordination in goals, services, and outcomes between Head Start and K–12 education continue with incremental changes, largely dependent on the creativity of local innovators (Bornfreund et al., 2014; Mead, 2014). Although some school districts do run Head Start programs, most are operated by community and nonprofit agencies, which were the original settings for a program created to bypass state governments as part of the 1960s War on Poverty.

While early educators have struggled with instituting systemic changes among the many intervention, child care, and education programs serving children from birth to 5, they have not paid much attention to the heart of the matter: continuity and coherence of learning and instructional experiences of children as they progress from early education into primary education (Bornfreund et al., 2014). For the most part, system changes in early learning occur largely outside the K–12 public education system and vice versa. Advocates, educators, researchers, and legislators seem oblivious to the ripple effects of making changes in one year of schooling on the years before and after. And they are not knowledgeable about policies and practices in the early learning and K–12 sectors.

The emergence of state-funded pre-kindergarten programs, typically for 4-year-olds, in the past 2 decades, as well as changes in state policies raising the age of eligibility for kindergarten (Education Commission of the States, 2013), have led to understandable confusion among educators who have not received the curricular guidance they need and deserve as a result of these uncoordinated policy changes. One salient example is the creation of transitional kindergarten (TK) in California, which originated from increasing the age of kindergarten entry for children. Little attention was paid to the impact of TK on what comes before or after it and the resulting inequalities in amount of early education experiences based solely on the child's date of birth. TK has the unintended effect of providing 14 years of public education in California for a small cohort of children, instead of the normal 13 years of education (kindergarten plus Grades 1–12).

TK now coexists along with California's state-funded preschool programs for low-income children and the state's kindergartens with no clear direction regarding how each contributes to a coherent pathway for learning for young children. To add to the confusion, TK and pre-K are used interchangeably. Although the TK program was originally created for children too young to meet the kindergarten-age cutoff, when this group of children enter kindergarten a year later, they are not only older than the typically aged children in kindergarten, but they also have had what is essentially a pre-K experience. Children meeting the cutoff age for TK may or may not have pre-K experience, depending on what is available in their communities and the economic resources of their families to pay for the programs.

Recently, the Los Angeles Unified School District (LAUSD), the second-largest school district in the country, proposed to include younger 4-year-olds in its TK programs, using TK as an opportunity to expand pre-K opportunities for younger children. Other California school districts are following LAUSD's example, thus opening another door to expanding pre-K access for younger children in that state.

Yet another example can be found in the creation of a universal prekindergarten program in New York City, the nation's largest school district, with little discussion of its ramifications for kindergarten and the grades beyond for some 63,000 4-year-olds attending in the school year 2015–2016. Simply put, what should children learn in kindergarten and the early primary grades when they, presumably, arrive better prepared than before the expansion of New York City's universal pre-K program? How will learning in kindergarten and the following grades build on what is achieved (or not) in New York City's universal pre-K? How will teachers respond to children without pre-K experiences? These blind spots have real consequences for children and for their teachers.

This book reveals the uncertainty and confusion generated when pre-K is added without attention to the learning and curricular consequences for the later grades, both for teachers and for students. At the same time, the high-stakes testing requirements of No Child Left Behind (NCLB) that are continued in ESSA have contributed to "pushdown" effects in children's educational experiences in kindergarten. According to a national study based on the Early Childhood Longitudinal Study, Kindergarten Class of 1998–99 (ECLS-K) dataset, which supports informal observations in contemporary classrooms, kindergarten can now be characterized as "the new 1st grade" (Bassok & Rorem, 2015). These developments have raised an outcry among kindergarten educators (Diamond, 2008) and early educators but have resulted in few efforts to work together to create continuity in learning experiences for young children before and after kindergarten. The power of defending practices in pre-K and in kindergarten as separate entities remains strong.

Absent from these examples are efforts to create developmentally informed educational experiences for young children that take into account the need for a more seamless transition from pre-K to the early primary grades. Evidence from research on learning trajectories in early literacy and early math, which should guide curriculum, instruction, and assessment, is rarely acknowledged and, most tragically, not used when such continuous diagnostic and assessment systems exist to guide teaching in those content areas (McGhee-Hassrick et al., in press). The lack of attention to continuity in learning experiences can be especially deleterious to the 10% of young children called English learners or ELs, whose reading proficiency scores at the end of 3rd grade are below 20% for the entire age group (U.S. Department of Education, Institute of Education Sciences, National Center for Education Statistics, National Assessment of Educational Progress [NAEP], 2013).

At the very time in children's lives when they can benefit from a coherent set of learning experiences informed by considerable research on developmental and learning trajectories, there is no orderly progression in what and how children are taught. At the very least, this state of affairs is inefficient and a waste of scarce resources, not to mention the consequences and lost opportunities for children to learn more deeply than is now the case. Given the scientific evidence about the importance of early learning and developmental pathways, this situation must be addressed in order to have a more effective beginning for our educational system, one that addresses gaps in learning opportunities, is informed by research, and provides a sound foundation for children's lifelong education and well-being in our 21st-century global economy.

It is time for a paradigm shift (Takanishi, 2010). Our outdated K–12 education system requires fundamental changes to address inequalities in learning opportunities that start years before the current compulsory education system begins (typically at 1st grade). Instead of trying to achieve the Holy Grail of a single coordinated early learning system, one that is separate from the public education system, I propose a redesigned primary school that starts with 3- and 4-year olds.

At this point, I want to explain why I have chosen to use the term *primary school* over the more familiar term *elementary* school. Policymakers and educational administrators create and name the divisions and grade spans associated with levels of schooling. These are subject to change depending on local circumstances, including administrative and financial factors, and rarely on pedagogical considerations. While there is no uniformity across districts, generally there are three levels: pre-K–5 primary or elementary education, 6–8 middle or junior high school education, and 9–12 high school education. I have chosen *primary* to designate the new level that includes the pre-kindergarten grades or years to Grade 5—the launching pad for universal public education.

BEGIN PUBLIC EDUCATION EARLIER

I have drawn from half a century of efforts (1960s to 2015) to conclude that the education of 3-, 4-, and 5-year-olds should be a public responsibility in the United States (Guernsey & Mead, 2010; Karch, 2013). In this nation, decisions about when school begins vary among the 50 states, making the achievement of a national consensus daunting (Education Commission of the States, 2013).

Building public support for pre-K for 3- and 4-year-olds has been slow and erratic. The hard work of connecting compelling research on how and what children learn from birth to 8 (Allen & Kelly, 2015) with effective policy on when universal public education should begin has only started. In the next 50 years, we will see more and more schools that start with pre-K as the normal beginning of America's universal public education system—not a separate add-on. How soon and widespread that will occur is not clear, but the need to level the playing field for children from different family economic circumstances is an imperative one.

These schools already do exist (Ritchie & Gutmann, 2013), and their numbers are slowly increasing, but they are in no way near the norm. Such schools are highly dependent on state-funded pre-K programs, located both in schools and in community organizations, and provided by a few local urban initiatives such as in Denver, New York City, San Antonio, San Francisco, and Seattle.

Most important, except for a few states, the statutory obligations to provide state-funded pre-K are not yet in place, and therefore pre-K provision is vulnerable to competing demands on federal and state budgets, a situation that is only likely to intensify (Steuerle, 2013). At the federal level, Hahn (2015) predicts that, under current tax and budget policies, the expected increase in funding of early education and care programs will be $1 billion during the period 2013–2024. This is hardly promising for increased access to quality programs.

The American public education system, which usually starts with kindergarten (which is widely provided, but not compulsory in 34 states) and ends with Grade 12, has been basically unaltered for over 100 years. What we call K–12 education did not just happen. Education reformers created it. Universal access to high schools was introduced at the turn of the 20th century (Sizer, 2013), and kindergarten gradually became recognized as the beginning of public education after decades of struggle in the early part of the 20th century (Beatty, 1995).

Still, today, kindergarten remains unfinished business. About 25% of children attend half-day kindergarten programs of varying hours (Bornfreund et al., 2014). Kindergarten is not compulsory in most states

(Education Commission of the States, 2013). State budgetary woes have led states to increase the age of kindergarten entry, a good lesson for those who seek statutory obligations not only for full-school-day programs, but also for requirements for age of entry (Libassi, 2014).

First grade for 6- and 7-year-olds remains the beginning of America's universal compulsory education system. This made sense a century ago, but burgeoning scientific knowledge, including in the neurosciences (Allen & Kelly, 2015), about children's capacities to learn from birth and about the early emergence of inequalities in learning opportunities in families, demands new policies and practices to fulfill America's commitment to equality of opportunity.

Given what we now know about children's learning from birth, and the early emergence of inequality by age 2, the wide inequality in access to early education programs is morally unacceptable in a country based on ideals of equal opportunity. Kindergarten and surely Grade 1 is much too late for publicly funded education to begin for most American children.

Public education must begin earlier than it now does. Other countries have come to this conclusion, ironically based on American research. Pre-kindergarten is part of their educational systems to which children are legally and universally entitled, but it is not compulsory. Despite that, the vast majority of children attend on a voluntary basis.

Not only must public education in the United States begin earlier during the pre-K years, but early learning or pre-K programs must also be integrated with the following grades of kindergarten and beyond to create a firm and continuing foundation for lifelong learning. Merely providing pre-K without building on what children learn in the ensuing years or grades is insufficient for most children to continue to learn and to flourish.

INTEGRATE EARLY EDUCATION WITH PRIMARY EDUCATION

In 2003, when I was president of the Foundation for Child Development, the philanthropy launched a 10-year initiative called pre-K–3rd (www.fcd-us.org). The founding motivation of pre-K–3rd was to support approaches that aimed to build on children's gains produced by quality pre-K programs but that were not being sustained during the early primary school years. Since 2003, evaluations of the short-term effects of pre-K programs during the kindergarten and early primary grades have shown mixed results. This likely results from many factors, including inadequate implementation of the pre-K experience, poor instruction and conditions in the primary grades that do not build on what children know, and harsh life circumstances, referred to as "concentrated disadvantage," for many children in the studies. The adequacy of financial and other resources for providing a sound pre-K–3rd education, including the stability of these resources, is also a factor.

But the issue is not whether or not there is "fade-out" after a year or two of pre-K; the central issue for pre-K–3rd efforts is the nature and quality of educational experiences for children after pre-K, and whether they are designed to build on the gains made by quality pre-K programs. Thus, pre-K–3rd was based on the need for changes in both pre-K and in the primary grades. The initiative sought to overcome the finger-pointing by both fields about who was responsible for the outcomes of children's learning experiences from 3 to 8, which is an unproductive debate in light of the urgency of addressing educational inequalities.

The evidence in 2016 provides more hope that pre-K gains can be sustained during the primary school years and beyond (Allen & Kelly, 2015; Yoshikawa et al., 2013; Zellman & Kilburn, 2015) if attention is paid to the coherence of the pre-K-5 grades. What is striking, however, is that we do not understand what factors or experiences both in and outside schools contribute to sustaining children's achievement after they participate in effective pre-K. And we are clueless about those experiences that are contributing to the observed slump in children's performances, especially during the kindergarten and primary grades (Heckman, 2013).

No research has been conducted in primary classrooms with children with and without pre-K experience and into how teachers may adapt their instruction to children with different pre-K experiences and to those who have not benefited from quality programs. One hypothesis regarding the observed merging of achievement trajectories of both groups is that primary grade teachers must focus on helping children without pre-K experience to "catch up" to their peers and thus give less attention to those with pre-K experience. In some anecdotal accounts, children with pre-K experience are assigned to assist children who have not had such experience! In these ways, chaos has serious consequences for some children.

Yet it is obvious that to leverage and sustain gains from pre-K programs, we need competent teachers in the primary grades, adequate resources to support their and children's learning, and an ambitious focus on differentiated instruction in the grades or years following pre-K. Such instruction must take into account that not all children have benefited from a quality pre-K experience, while building on what some children have experienced in pre-K (McGhee-Hassrick et al., in press).

Such factors in primary schools do not exist for many children, especially those from low-income families. In fact, low-income children are likely to attend primary schools where principals and teachers are relatively inexperienced and where resources are fewer than those in more wealthy districts. Thus, children who would benefit most from continuity in early educational experiences are those least likely to receive it. The failure to provide these opportunities that could make a difference in their learning violates children's civil rights to equal education.

Pre-K–3rd was informed by existing research, but it was driven more by the goal of providing children with a primary education experience that would take maximum advantage of what effective pre-K programs can achieve after 1 year and that would build on that experience to spur further learning to the advantage of all children. The approach recognized that the preoccupation among researchers, policymakers, and advocates alike on the long-term effects of 1 or 2 years of early learning was misplaced. As part of lifelong learning, pre-K must be followed by effective K–12 education in which every grade and year matters.

In 2016, more than a decade after the Foundation for Child Development launched pre-K–3rd efforts in 2003, there are some early lessons. The first, and most heartening, has been the discovery of schools and districts that are implementing pre-K–3rd approaches and seeing good outcomes for their students (Kirp, 2013; Maeroff, 2006; Marietta, 2010b; Nyhan, 2015; Zellman & Kilburn, 2015), as profiled later in this book. The second lesson, and the one that is the most sobering, is the continuing stubborn separation of early education and primary education in the United States. Both fields have evolved separately, with their own professional cultures and associations, their own teacher preparation approaches, their own funding sources and regulations. Rarely do the twain meet (Takanishi, 2010).

Linda Wing (personal communication, September 2009) was the first to brand this stubborn status quo as "the two galaxies." Her incisive characterization of two widely separated fields existing independently underscores the power of fixed mindsets about how we organize education for young children. The form and structure—deriving from history, laws, and statutes governing American education—were socially constructed; changing those structures is fundamental to integrating early with primary education.

Those involved in creating a new primary school must engage these two galaxies and seek to forge a strong merger and genuine integration of the two for the benefit of children. Whether this approach will result in the intended outcomes remains to be seen, but evidence is emerging (Mc-Ghee-Hassrick et al., in press; Reynolds, Hayakawa, Candee, & Englund, 2016; Zellmann & Kilburn, 2015). Experience thus far indicates that this merger will not be easily achieved, but there are compelling reasons why we must begin now.

The rationale for the creation of a new American primary school is to reduce inequalities in the educational experiences and outcomes for a large group of American children. This book offers concrete strategies for how we can proceed on several fronts.

PLAN OF THE BOOK

The case for supporting the creation of a new American primary school is made in Chapter 1. Two pillars supporting this case are presented: First, I describe the robust scientific knowledge accumulated in the past 50 years about the amazing capacities of children to learn from a very early age, and the disturbing findings emerging from the neurosciences about the influence of early life conditions on the developing brain and on genetic structure. This scientific base highlights the urgency of taking appropriate action—including passing civil rights laws—to respond to the early origins of education inequality, based on current scientific knowledge. We now have a considerable body of evidence that dwarfs the studies of Kenneth and Mamie Clark that were influential in the historic Supreme Court decision *Brown v. Board of Education* in 1954 to end racial segregation in public schools.

The second pillar points to early and growing inequalities in children's opportunities to learn in the years before they enter kindergarten. Combined with evaluations that indicate that well-designed and implemented pre-K programs can influence learning of all children—especially low-income children and those whose heritage language is not English—the case for stable and adequate public investments in early learning is now stronger than ever before (Bartik, 2014; Raudenbush & Eschmann, 2015). What we know about children's capacities to learn, and what we know about documented inequalities in access to quality early learning, point to civil and human rights arguments for moving the starting line for public education to an earlier age than at present.

Chapter 2 describes the organizational or structural features of the proposed primary school, as well as the culture of these schools that are necessary for good learning outcomes for all children. These elements can be found in schools and districts throughout the country where the new primary school is already in place and where all children are learning well.

Both structural and cultural elements are essential for the functioning of the new primary school, but they cannot be implemented without the commitment and professional capital of the educators in the schools. Chapter 3 focuses on the choices regarding the recruitment, selection, preparation, and continuing support and coaching for teachers and principals in the new primary school. These challenges are as daunting as those facing middle and high schools, if not more. In this chapter, I identify both short-term and longer-term strategies to attract, prepare, and support educators for the new primary school.

Effective primary schools are partners with the families of children. Chapter 4 presents a perspective on family development and changing roles as children progress through the primary school. A long-established value in American education reform is the engagement of families and communities in their children's education. I go beyond the extensive body of work on family engagement and focus on dual-generation strategies—human capital investments in both families and children—that engage parents in their own educational and career development as a way to potentially increase the economic prospects of low-income families as their children participate in the primary school.

Efforts to enhance family economic resources, which are necessary to provide safe and healthy living conditions for families, must augment the work of effective primary schools. I also describe ways to engage parents in monitoring and supporting classroom-based instruction and the progress of their children (McGhee-Hassrick et al., in press), including the judicious use of technology in supporting that engagement.

While school and family partnerships are important, the larger society shapes and influences the effectiveness of schools and what families can provide to their children. It is fine to have a vision for a new primary school, but what will it take to make it a reality—and more significant, a widespread reality? The task, given current policies and programs in both early education and K–12 education, is herculean.

The American education governance system is multilayered, unlike those of most countries with two layers of national and local governance (Mehta & Teles, 2014), and rightly described as incoherent (Cohen & Moffitt, 2009). Chapter 5 describes roles for reformers and advocates, parents and families, individual schools, districts and cities, and states and the federal government, as well as the philanthropic sector, in creating the new primary school. Policies at each of these levels provide a context that facilitates or limits what educators can do in primary education. Form shapes function.

The final chapter reflects on the potential for growing this new primary school. I place my bet on local innovation that flourishes from the leadership of educators working with their communities (Goldstein, 2014; Kirp, 2013; Nyhan, 2015). This is the short-term strategy. Under the right conditions, schools can make a difference in reducing, even closing, educational inequalities (Kirp, 2013; McGhee-Hassrick et al., in press). But growth of such schools will be limited by laws, policies, and related practices that need to be changed in order for wider implementation to occur. Right now, innovations are tied to enterprising local leadership and the sheer commitment of wise and innovative educators.

Local innovation will provide the inspiration for changes in federal and state laws governing public education. This is the long-term strategy. Since the states have primary responsibility for children's education, they must reimagine the basic right for education to start with the pre-K years. This will be a state-by-state battle taking many years, but it can be achieved. Even after it is achieved, there is no guarantee that there will be adequate funding, but the statutory obligation will be in place and provide a more compelling basis for the new primary schools than currently exists.

Schools are but one part of the larger society in which other institutions profoundly influence opportunities for children and their families (Stiglitz, 2012). Nonetheless, inequalities in schools and in student outcomes reflect and contribute to inequalities in this larger society (Darling-Hammond, 2010). Children's well-being is also influenced by access to health care and by their families' economic resources and social networks (Crosnoe, Bonazzo, & Wu, 2015; Putnam, 2015). Luck and unexpected circumstances play their roles in the unfolding of individual lives.

That being said, in the United States today, opportunities for individuals are shaped by access to education, perhaps more than in other nations where a stronger social safety net exists for children and their families. Motivating students to believe that educational success is an important part of their future, and providing them with the support to keep them on that long, often tortuous path, is critical. This work begins in the new primary school.

Educational attainment does not guarantee a good job or a good life, but it is one of the few levers that individuals in the United States can use to enhance their own prospects and those of their children in a global economy that places a premium on competition, innovation, problem-solving, and communication skills. That is why it is urgent that we start now with first things first.

CHAPTER 1

Why Do We Need a New Primary School?

Fixing the education system is the civil rights challenge of our era. A starting point is to embrace an ethos that was born in America but is now an expatriate: that we owe all children a fair start in life in the form of access to an education escalator. Let's fix the escalator.

—Nicholas Kristof, "The American Dream Is Leaving America"

The new American primary school is one approach to give all children a ride on Kristof's escalator and set them on a path to greater equality of opportunity, starting with early education. Yet in 2016, the United States clings to a kindergarten to Grade 12 (K–12) public education structure that was created by school reformers more than 100 years ago. While there are promising innovations taking place in the transition from high school to postsecondary education, in the form of career academies and apprenticeships as well as early colleges, primary education (K–5), especially its critical connection with pre-K education, seems impervious to change.

As I pointed out in the Introduction, this K–12 structure is not responding to 21st-century demographic, social, and cultural changes in the country or to globalization (Darling-Hammond, 2010; Wagner & Dintersmith, 2015). And this public education system has not, for the most part, evolved in response to the substantial base of science about children's learning and how that learning is shaped by forces inside and outside the classroom.

Since the mid-1980s other countries have redesigned their educational systems to adapt to new economic demands (Sahlberg, 2014) and are achieving better outcomes for more of their students than is the United States (OECD, 2014). On every international comparison of education performance, whatever one might think of what is measured and how (Ripley, 2013), the United States' rankings are distressing, particularly given our status as a leading economic and global power. According to the most recent PISA study (2012), the United States ranks 27th out of 34 countries in mathematics, 17th out of 34 in reading, and 20th out of 34 in science.

The United States, once a leader in public education for the majority of its students, now lags behind most of our peer nations and prepares only a minority well (OECD, 2014). Rates of college completion have stagnated since the mid-1970s (Goldin & Katz, 2010). With changes in the global labor market and their linkages to the hollowing out of the American middle class, economic inequalities will continue to widen. The real consequences of economic inequalities for individual health and well-being are beginning to be documented (Marmot, 2015).

Most important, educational attainment has become the dividing line within American society and is now more strongly related to family economic status than to the race and ethnicity of children (Reardon, 2011). Educational attainment has cascading effects from family structure to child-rearing and, thus, has intergenerational consequences (Cherlin, 2014). And, in the American social policy context, educational attainment is highly predictive of an individual's capacity to earn a decent living and secure a job with health and retirement benefits. Within the same educational attainments, racial discrimination persists and further widens economic inequalities, especially for low-income African Americans (Alexander & Entwisle, 2014), as well as other groups of color.

The United States now has the widest income gap among the developed nations (Stiglitz, 2014). The American Dream—social mobility from one generation to the next—has become a pipe dream, not a realistic aspiration for many well beyond the time of immigration to the United States (Putnam, 2015). Stiglitz (2014) named the problem: We are a divided society. Restoring educational opportunity (Duncan & Murnane, 2013) in this age of economic inequality (Piketty & Goldhammer, 2014) must be the North Star of education reform.

Our failure to provide the educational experiences that could make a difference in children's lives may violate state and federal laws. Indeed, leaders like President Barack Obama and his former secretary of education Arne Duncan have named education as the defining civil rights issue of our time. Fundamental reforms in education will require legal strategies and new laws, including tax and budgetary reforms, to ensure that all children have equal access to a basic education, which does not now include pre-K, or even kindergarten, in the majority of the states (Education Commission of the States, 2014).

Over the past 50 years, there has been no shortage of high-profile reports calling for reform of American education. But few, if any of them, have focused on primary schools, where the gaps in achievement are clearly evident at the end of 3rd grade (NAEP, 2015), and even before (Lee & Burkam, 2002), and can have cascading consequences in middle and high schools. Primary education is Ground Zero for establishing the foundation for future educational success.

High school reform is the short-term, more immediate focus, fueled by imminent concerns about workforce quality. American policymakers are often impatient and shortsighted when they consider social policies with no immediate benefits. When high schools are deemed too damaged to repair, reformers move down to the middle schools. Primary schools, with pre-K or without it, remain the orphans of contemporary education reform. This is slowly beginning to change (Duncan & Murnane, 2013), but not fast enough. The distance between reforms in early learning (birth to 5) and in K–12 education remain vast (Bornfreund, 2015).

To be fair, the early education field (defined traditionally as spanning birth to 5 years of age but in recent years extending to age 8) has viewed the K–12 education system with trepidation, if not disdain. This has led to the isolation of the field from K–12 education, where the subject matter focus and the assumed lack of concern regarding the full development of children, specifically their social and emotional well-being, has contributed to the separation. Many early educators view an association with what they consider a failed K–12 education as undesirable. However, I consider this stance extremely shortsighted, out of date, and unproductive for transforming primary education as we know it.

If early education has sought to remain a separate field, education reformers and analysts continue to overlook the potential of pre-K education as an important contributor to children's learning in the K–12 grades, in terms of both cognitive and social development (Goldstein, 2014; Mehta, 2013). There may be a nod now and then to pre-K education, but no serious attention to it, reflecting an unfamiliarity with the field or uncertainty about its relationship to the existing K–12 system. This status quo is widely accepted, with few signs of building bridges between them. Responsibility for this state of affairs lies with both sides.

At the same time, there are encouraging new overtures among educators toward learning from each other, finding common ground, and making stronger connections (Sullivan-Dudzic, Gearns, & Leavell, 2010). The National Association of Elementary School Principals (NAESP, 2014) has issued guidelines and supporting resources for principals to initiate and make connections with early education programs in their schools and communities. Given the critical role of principals as school-site leaders in education reform (Nyhan, 2015), this initiative has the potential to contribute to more widespread change.

A small number of foundations, including the Bill and Melinda Gates Foundation, the W. K. Kellogg Foundation, the McKnight Foundation, the Foundation for Child Development, the Evelyn and Walter Haas, Jr. Fund, and the W. Clement & Jessie V. Stone Foundation, as well as community foundations in Marin and San Mateo counties in California, have supported districts to forge pre-K–3rd pathways. And the U.S. Department of Education has awarded grants to states that seek to connect their early education programs to the early primary grades. These are signs of small change, but, truth be told, these efforts remain outside discussions of K–12 education transformation and are marginal to those of early education.

From time to time, public and private organizations have convened task forces and issued reports about what should be done to reform American schools. But after a while, few even remember the recommendations. Even the powerful, moving rhetoric of *A Nation at Risk*, released in 1983 (National Commission on Excellence in Education, 1983), pointing to the mediocrity of American education and its implications for our nation's security, has not generated much change in altering the flat line of student achievement since then (NAEP, 2013).

Now, some 30 years later, the troubling issues raised by that report have only become more extreme (Goldstein, 2014). During the same time period, Americans' belief in the American Dream has severely eroded (Kristof, 2014; Stiglitz, 2010). There are, as always has been the case, schools and districts that are beating the odds. But they are too few and far between, leaving the majority of American children in jeopardy.

We must start with first things first. In this chapter, I make the case for why a new American primary school must and can educate all children better than we are doing now. Educational inequality should be a morally intolerable condition. I begin with an overview of the key scientific advances that require us to rethink when primary education begins and how children should be educated during what is essentially Ground Zero for lifelong learning.

Next, I examine the growing inequalities in young children's access to pre-K education, which is when the new primary school begins. Having documented the unacceptable inequalities in access and quality of learning experiences by children of different economic circumstances and their likely consequences for children's lives, I argue that participation in pre-K education—now framed primarily as an economic argument—should be considered a civil and human right for all young children. The dominance of the economic argument over the past 2 decades should be balanced by moral and ethical imperatives to create a society where lifelong learning and well-being are fundamental social values (Stiglitz & Greenwald, 2014).

SCIENTIFIC ADVANCES IN HOW CHILDREN LEARN

During the past 5 decades, using the creation of Head Start in 1964 as a marker, scientific advances in our understanding of children's development and learning from the time they are born have been profound (Allen & Kelly, 2015; Shonkoff & Phillips, 2000). Our understanding of how children learn over the first decade of their lives should better inform and be more deeply embedded into educational practice and social policies than is now the case.

Four organizing principles characterize these advances:

1. *Early experience matters.* The critical importance of early experience on all aspects of a child's development is firmly established. Early learning is cumulative and is the foundation for all subsequent learning.
2. *Children are active learners.* They are born ready and eager to learn. They are not passive empty vessels waiting to be filled.
3. *Learning is multifaceted.* It results from the continuing, complex relationships between and integration of biological, cognitive, social, and emotional factors.
4. *Learning is social.* It involves relationships with key adults, including family members, teachers, and other children. Through these social exchanges with sensitive and responsive adults (and sometimes older children), children make connections between what they know and what they are experiencing to deepen as well as expand their learning.

Let us explore each of these organizing principles in more detail.

Early Experience Matters

The critical importance of early experience on all aspects of a child's development is now firmly established. Previous debates over nature versus nurture are currently being informed by brain-imaging research in the developmental neurosciences, contributing to an emerging neuroscience of learning and development. As Alan Guttmacher (2012), director of the National Institute of Child Health and Human Development, concluded, the question for scientists is no longer nature versus nurture, but how both equally matter in shaping children's developmental pathways from birth.

Brain development and circuitry provide the architecture for learning, and from birth that architecture evolves from a dynamic exchange between biology and environment. Enriching experiences can support healthy brain development, and stress and disturbances can compromise the growing brain and result in behavioral consequences that are reflected in brain architecture. Children differ in their susceptibility to environmental influences, especially adversity in their families and communities. Some succumb, and others remain resilient. Understanding how and why these differences occur is still incomplete.

The growing field of epigenetics focuses on the reciprocal influences of genes and behavior. We now know that genes are not unchanging, like some heirloom passed from generation to generation. Instead, genes can be affected by what happens to a person. Children's experiences in their homes and neighborhoods can influence the configurations and changes in the DNA molecule that, in turn, affect the activities of their genes. What was previously conceived only as possibilities are now being directly studied, including the interaction of genetic variation and social and cultural influences, and how experiences modify a child's genome through epigenetic changes.

While these areas of research are just beginning and the findings are provocative, the implications for children's learning, combined with the studies of early interventions, are clear: Early experience from birth can be profoundly formative, and its influence is cumulative. A child's early experiences as part of a family and community have a "cascade of consequences" not only on cognitive, social, and emotional development but also on biological and neurological functioning (McEwen, 2012).

Neurons to Neighborhoods (Shonkoff & Phillips, 2000) was exceedingly prescient in its conclusion:

> Although there have been long-standing debates about how much the early years really matter in the larger scheme of lifelong development, our conclusion is unequivocal: What happens during the first months and years of life matters a lot, not because this period of development provides an indelible blueprint for adult well-being, but because it sets either a sturdy or fragile stage for what follows. (p. 4)

Early experiences do matter. Over time, these experiences, including those that support and those that compromise a child's overall development, affect how children learn and consequently respond and adapt to new experiences throughout their entire lives. These findings are shaping our ideas about when and how early interventions into the lives of children living in poverty and enduring other stressful conditions should take place. Research on the learning trajectories in subject matter areas like early literacy and mathematics have untapped implications for teaching and learning in schools (McGhee-Hassrick et al., in press).

Children Are Active Learners

Research has established that children, including infants, are actively engaged in their own learning, which is facilitated and extended by sensitive and responsive adults. Behavioral research with infants has overturned the previous characterization of an infant as tabula rasa. On the contrary, infants come into the world primed to learn. They possess the capacity to select complex features of their physical and social surroundings, to organize their observations into emerging conceptual frameworks, and to adapt their responses to what they have learned. These frameworks evolve over time into more complex and sophisticated guides that shape children's capacity to learn.

One of the most exciting discoveries about infant cognition is that infants can organize discrete facts and observations into a coherent conceptual system (Gopnik & Wellman, 2012). They are not passive receptacles; they are building theories that organize what they are learning about how the world of objects and people works, including causal principles and relationships.

These theories shape their daily lives and have important consequences for learning mathematics and science during pre-K and the rest of the primary grades. During these years, cognitive scientists have carefully documented trajectories on how children learn to read and understand biological and mathematical concepts, including their misconceptions. Thus, during the earliest years of life, way before schooling begins, the foundations of learning, including those relevant to the learning of subject matter content, are being established.

Infants are also capable of developing theories of mind that organize their social interactions with others. These theories influence how they respond to others and what they learn from them: what people are attending to, their feelings about their environments, and differences in perspectives about the same event. Very young children can show signs of empathy and select situations where they feel they can learn from another adult. And they are particularly sensitive to cues that alert them to the fact that someone is trying to teach them something; for example, by calling their names, pointing to an object, and establishing eye-to-eye contact.

As a report from the Institute of Medicine (now the National Academy of Medicine) concludes, implicit theories of young children have important implications for educators, including parents:

Failure to recognize the extent to which children are construing information in terms of their lay theories can result in educational strategies that oversimplify material for children. . . . To design effective materials in a given domain or subject matter, we need to know what the implicit theories are that children hold, what core causal principles they use, what misconceptions and gaps in knowledge they have—and then use empirically validated steps to help lead them to a more accurate, more advanced conceptual framework. (Allen & Kelly, 2015, p. 107)

The idea of the young child as an active, engaged learner who is naturally curious and possesses the capacity to build implicit theories or explanatory systems to organize what he or she experiences is a game changer for educational practice. Respect for and a deep understanding of the child as learner is the starting point for all educational efforts (Cohen, Stern, Balaban, & Gropper, 2016), whether through parents, teachers, and other adults. The cognitive and social capacities of young children, especially their relevance to learning subject matter in primary school, can no longer be overlooked.

Learning Is Multifaceted

The science of learning during the first decade of life can be as complex as the science of drug interactions in medicine, if not more so. This fact places a heavy responsibility on early learning programs, the teachers, and families themselves to keep these multiple factors in mind as they relate to the development and education of children. Recognizing this complexity in young children constitutes a significant advance in our evidence-based understanding of how children grow up.

In broad strokes, learning and development results from the dynamic interaction of four overlapping domains: cognitive development, socioemotional development, learning competencies, and the general health and physical well-being of the child. Elements in each domain develop synergistically with elements in the other domains and mutually support one another. As one important example, self-regulation—so central to deep learning—involves cognitive skills as well as socioemotional competence. Both domains are important in the development of learning competences of persistence and active engagement in a task. Learning specific content areas involves cognitive skills, learning competencies, and socioemotional competence, all within the context of supportive relationships with teachers and other adults. This has implications for judging the quality and effectiveness of teachers.

The upshot is that children do not learn skills in isolation from other aspects of learning, including cognitive control processes like planning and carrying out goal-directed activity, attention, and persistence. Merely providing information or facts without taking into account a range of domains and their interactions is not likely to result in deep learning that continues to build over the years, which is the goal of effective instruction.

Children may learn bits and pieces of information, but they may not be able to organize them for continuing learning. While mastering subject matter has a learning trajectory on which teachers build their instruction and assessments, generic or cross-cutting elements such as analytic reasoning, problem solving, self-regulation, positive motivations toward learning, and social exchanges are essential to learning in schools and in life.

Learning Is Social

The research on children's earliest learning during infancy and beyond points to the importance of orienting to an adult—whether a parent or another adult—as an individual from whom to learn. Learning typically takes place with others, whether through direct instruction or informal observations. Pre-K children demonstrate the ability to discern what a teacher is aiming to communicate by observing her actions (Butler & Markman, 2012). Older students in middle and high schools identify a "teacher who cares" as being an important reason for their engagement in school. Children during the primary grades are sensitive to engaging with their teachers as a condition for learning. The current education system, however, is based on the assumption that the social and emotional bond between teacher and learner is less important as the student grows older. Research challenges that assumption.

Relationships between individuals matter in how children learn from birth. They are the secure base for and the critical mediators of learning, especially when children are young and developing their theories of learning and mind (Allen & Kelly, 2015). Children are less egocentric than once believed. Instead, research indicates that they are attending to the emotional cues of others and develop theories about what adults are intending to teach. These perceptions heighten children's orientation and responsiveness to family members and later to teachers.

The growing interest in pre-K–5 primary schools as "schools for success" recognizes that executive functioning and social-emotional competence, so valued in early education, are as important as the so-called hard skills of reading and math (Bornfreund, 2015). The movement away from a hierarchical set of learning skills divided into "cognitive and noncognitive" categories, and toward seeing them as equally contributing to learning, is a welcome change and entirely consistent with the research on how children actually learn.

The development of social and emotional competence is seen as important to a child's educational success from pre-K through high school and beyond. Described by labor economist James Heckman (2013) as "soft skills," this competence includes being able to engage with teachers and with peers to work constructively with them in the classroom. In addition to interpersonal or social skills, as well as effective communicative capacities, this area includes concepts such as emotional intelligence, cultural competence, positive self-identity, and self-regulation. All these skills have a developmental trajectory that starts at birth, continue to be refined through life, and are considered essential to success in a globalized economy (Wagner & Dintersmith, 2015).

In the recent accountability climate, with its focus on tested outcomes in subject matter, these social competencies have remained in the background. However, organized efforts to include social-emotional learning in the schools and an established link between these competencies and academic achievement are leading to greater openness to social-emotional learning curricula in grades K–12. The U.S. Department of Education is now promoting "skills for success" (Bornfreund, 2015). Research indicates that the integration of social and emotional competence with subject matter learning in classrooms will be crucial for taking advantage of what is known as a lifelong task.

These findings have implications for the preparation and support of educators (see Chapter 3) and for family engagement in their children's learning during the schooling years (see Chapter 4). Adults who care for and understand children must be perceived as trustworthy, reliable sources for continuous learning. It is crucial for children to feel secure enough to explore their environment and to fail occasionally.

The big question is this: Is our current educational system, when it begins and how children are being educated, aligned with the current science of children's development and learning? The creation of the new American primary school is one effort in which teaching and learning are informed by knowledge about how children learn.

The major implication of these advances in knowledge about children's learning is that educational experiences should begin earlier than kindergarten, which most American children attend. These experiences are the shared responsibility of families and schools. As more families have parents working outside the home, and children spend more of their early years out of their homes, the educational potential of these settings looms large, and the quality of children's experiences in them is a matter of social equality.

There are, however, troubling inequalities in young children's access to programs that are based on what can put children on Kristof's escalator, mentioned in the quote at the beginning of this chapter. Such inequalities, combined with scientific advances on children's development, constitute a compelling case for early education as a civil right in America and as a basic human right throughout the world.

INEQUALITIES IN ACCESS TO QUALITY PRE-KINDERGARTEN

Universal access to pre-K has risen at least somewhat higher on the policy agenda during the past 2 decades. President Barack Obama, governors, and mayors have elevated this issue to public visibility and policymakers' attention. In the course of 2 decades, the previously "third rail" issue of early education for all children has moved into mainstream discourse. Business and military leaders have joined with child advocacy organizations to place early education on federal, state, and urban agendas.

Reports of public opinion polls indicate strong support for increasing access to early education using public funds. According to the 2015 poll of the First Five Years Fund (2015), 76% of American voters support increasing federal investment to help states provide greater access to high-quality pre-K programs for low- and moderate-income families.

Pre-K, sometimes referred to as early education, is often heralded as the solution to reducing educational inequality and poverty (Bartik, 2014). But the stark facts are that access to pre-K education is itself plagued with inequities based on the economic resources of families (Nortes & Barnett, 2014) and on the race and ethnicity of the children. And taken alone, early education is not an antidote to inequality and to racial and ethnic discrimination. Children living in poverty as defined by the federal government can also experience concentrated disadvantage in terms of neighborhood safety and resources, access to healthy food and health care, and housing conditions. Children of low-income immigrants can face additional disadvantages regarding access to health and human services, and fears about their immigration status and deportation.

Most significant, the public rhetoric does not match the private reality of children's experiences. With widening economic inequality, the idea of the "deserving poor" (Katz, 1990) is outdated, partially resulting from the 1996 welfare legislation. Which families and children are deserving of public funding of pre-K education? The hardworking middle class, left out of early education programs targeted toward low-income families, but unable to finance their children's enrollment in private pre-K programs, is slowly being recognized as also deserving of assistance (e.g., in Seattle). This change may strengthen the case for universal, non-means-tested access to pre-K in the future.

Despite the heightened visibility of pre-K, the United States is not a global leader in investing in the education of its young children (Economist Intelligence Unit, 2012). In fact, its standing is in the middle of the pack of 45 countries. Among all OECD countries, 63% of 3-year-olds are in pre-K, in contrast with 47% in the United States. The major factor in this gap is the inadequacy of public funding of early education in the United States. Even the well-known programs like Head Start, now 50 years in operation, are not adequately funded to serve all of the eligible children, and no significant changes are likely without tax and budget policy reforms.

The modest U.S. investment, averaging about $4,121 per child in 2014 for state-funded pre-K and covering less than 29% of the 4-year-olds (NIEER, 2015), reveals stark inequalities in which children are supported by public funds, in the levels of funding for the programs they attend (typically less than half of the per pupil expenditures for the K–12 grades), and the likely effectiveness of their learning experiences based on quality indicators (Guernsey, Bornfreund, McCann, & Williams, 2014). When Head Start enrollments are included, a total of 41.5% of 4-year-olds are attending some form of pre-K program.

In New York City, with its large universal pre-K program, serving more children than some entire school districts—65,000 children in school year 2015–2016—the average per child cost for full-school-day pre-K is about $10,239 a school year, one of the highest in the country (above New York is the District of Columbia, where the per child cost is about $15,372 for full-school-day pre-K). In comparison, pre-K in New York City's private elite schools, typically funded entirely by families, can cost between $30,000 and $40,000 a school year.

Researchers and advocates alike have avoided addressing what a quality early education program should actually cost if it were adequately funded. And the prospects for increased funding at both the federal and state levels are dim, given the limited availability of public funds, which are discretionary at the federal level and in the majority of states (Hahn, 2015). Consequent to our current funding streams, low-income children and their families will be most affected by the vagaries of public funding, because their family budgets do not permit them to fund their children's participation in pre-K programs.

Sustainable funding of early education must be built into the state revenue provisions for universal public education, as it now is in Oklahoma and West Virginia, as well as the District of Columbia. At present, only a handful of states fund pre-K through their state funding formula, but most of these states have caps and other limits on enrollment.

At the federal level, investments in children's learning are part of the declining discretionary investments that Congress approves annually. Unless there are changes in America's tax code governing individual and corporate taxation, in budgetary policy, and in entitlement reform (Lieberman & McCann, 2014), this shrinking part of the federal budget—slightly less than 8% (7.82%) of federal spending in 2015—is likely to be squeezed even more in the future than it already is (Hahn, 2015; Steuerle, 2013).

Thus the federal capacity for investing in American children (which is relatively small compared with state investments, but is focused on low-income children) will continue to shrink to levels that barely support what is now in place, if current laws prevail. Hahn (2015) projects that funding for early care and education programs from 2013–2024 will increase by a total of $1 billion, barring changes in the laws. This is totally unpromising for the vulnerable low-income children who are the primary beneficiaries of shrinking federal programs, which have historically sought to level the playing field for children (Takanishi, 2015).

About 10% of 4-year-olds are in Head Start, an early learning program targeted at children in deep poverty, a measure defined using the outdated federal poverty line instituted in the mid-1960s. This participation rate has been unchanged for 20 years, according to Child Trends (2015): "Between 1991 and 2005, the percentage of all children ages three to four participating in a Head Start Program remained fairly constant, ranging between 9% and 11%, and was at 9% in 2005." This constitutes clear evidence that targeted programs for low-income children have not reached and are unlikely to reach all who require such assistance (Bartik, 2014).

At the state level, investment in early education—and in K–12 education—varies widely, depending on the robustness the of state's economy, state legislative politics, and local property taxes. State funding for early education ranges from a low of $1,543 per child in Arizona to a high of $16,431 in the District of Columbia, with a national average of $4,125 (NIEER, 2015). Spending in the Abbott districts in New Jersey is $13,337 per child (NIEER, 2015). This wide variation reflects the central role of states and districts in the financing of public education—an important source of inequality in access to programs and in their quality—as well as the hours, also called dosage, of the programs, which can range from 2.5 to 6 or 7 hours a day. The amount of time available for instruction and learning—whether it involves longer school days or years, extended learning time outside the normal school day and in the summer months—is related to student achievement during the primary school years (McGhee-Hassrick et al., in press).

Low levels of public investment coexist with a private early learning system, the latter supported by family fees. Private investments by families who are not eligible for public subsidies can range from a low of $7,805 annually in Montana to $12,320 in Massachusetts for 4-year-olds in center care programs acknowledged to be of mediocre quality to close to $40,000 annually if children are attending programs in elite private schools.

Clearly, families with low to moderate incomes, even families in the lower middle class, find it virtually impossible for pay for pre-K education for their children, which on an annual basis can exceed the costs of tuition for public higher education. This likely contributes to broad public support of federal and state-supported pre-K.

Fifty percent of the 4-year-old children in the lowest quintile of family income attend public pre-K programs, this despite the fact that almost all public programs are means tested. In the top quintile of family income, 76% of 4-year-old children attend private pre-K, primarily paid for by families (Whitehurst & Klein, 2015). For the vast majority of children in the United States, pre-K education is not a public good, as is Grade 1–12 education. These inequalities are inconsistent with scientific knowledge about when and how children learn.

Thus, access to programs is highly dependent on private family resources at a time of worsening economic inequality. Enrollment in pre-K programs is also related to parents' educational levels. The more well educated the parent, the more likely is his or her child to attend some form of pre-K. There is a 32% gap in enrollment between children whose parents' highest level of education was less than a high school degree versus 4-year-old children who parents have at least a bachelor's degree (Nortes & Barnett, 2014). For 3-year-olds, the gap is slightly higher, at 37% (NIEER, 2007).

Part of the reason for this gap is the economic resources that families with higher levels of education can allocate for early education programs. For families who experience increases in income, paying for pre-K education becomes a smaller part of the family budget than it is for that of lower-income families. For hardworking middle-class families today, it is worth asking how much of a family's budget should be allocated to the pre-K education of their children. In fact, universal pre-K programs are now being proposed considering just this question, and that of how sliding fee scales can be crafted for families above the federal poverty line, which is used to determine eligibility for targeted programs. The administrative costs of this practice, as well as the cooperation of public authorities to implement billing, should also be considered.

The reality is that, despite all the political rhetoric and media attention, actual investments in pre-K education are woefully inadequate given the need and the evidence of their potential to narrow learning gaps, and increasingly so in an era of economic inequality. And they are likely to remain so, until we can break the silence on issues of universality of access, adequacy of financing and funding levels of programs, what constitutes quality and how to pay for it, and sustainability.

Importantly, current levels of funding for pre-K programs are insufficient to ensure quality. And what spending there is could be slashed at any point. In the aftermath of the Great Recession in 2008, enrollments and cost per child actually declined (NIEER, 2015). This is not a sign of progress.

The debate over targeted versus universal access to pre-K programs continues, but a targeted pre-K program has not and will never reach all low-income children (Bartik, 2014), given the funding history of these programs and the resources available. Formidable challenges confront us in achieving universal access to pre-kindergarten education and, most important, in embedding it in a public education system. But we must now engage in the long-overdue task of reimagining America public education, starting with its primary schools.

It is important to note that legal entitlements are not always compulsory, and therefore participation remains voluntary. I propose that pre-K experiences must be provided when families desire it, that is, available to all, but children not be required to attend. When full-day kindergarten becomes compulsory for children—and this is likely to be a long battle, waged state by state—the United States may be more open to compulsory pre-K education starting at 3, but not until then.

It is only when enrollment is compulsory in a state that parents must send their children to school. Except for 15 states plus the District of Columbia where kindergarten is compulsory, that grade remains completely voluntary. Depending on state law, parents must enroll their children by a specific age, typically at age 6, but also as late as 7 or 8 years.

Elsewhere in the world, a parallel situation exists between legal entitlement to pre-K, which is never compulsory, and compulsory education. In every country with high rates of pre-K participation, pre-K is voluntary. However, the important difference is that universal provision of early education results in high participation by children. I believe that voluntary pre-K in the United States is especially important in a nation that has strong values regarding the primacy of families in children's well-being, and where political battles over government/state roles over every aspect of family life remain contentious. This being said, when a compulsory education system begins in the United States is a political decision made by states that differ in cultural values.

We must insert pre-K as the new beginning of public education in America. In so doing, we will join many of our peer nations that have already moved in this direction. To achieve this fundamental redesign, early education or pre-K must also become part of ongoing debates about the transformation of American education. The long separation between early education and K–12 education *must end* (Takanishi, 2010). A new primary education system for children ages 3 to 10 years old must take its place (see Figure 1.1).

Figure 1.1. The New American Primary School: How the Pieces Fit Together

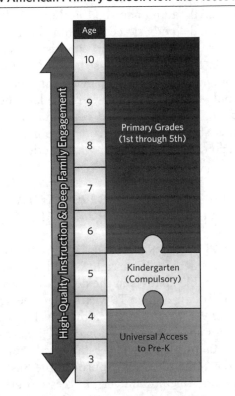

What Happens Before the New American Primary School?

The vision of the New American Primary School recognizes the need for strong support for children and families in the years from birth to age 3. That support should consist of

- Universal access to health care and preventive services
- Paid family leave for parents
- Targeted programs for vulnerable children, including home visiting and Early Head Start

Essential to this goal, we will need changes in how education is financed at the state level. As long as we retain our current system, in which pre-K is discretionary and funded on an annual basis, the case for lowering the age for public education will be stymied by the continuing battle for and lack of funds. And pre-K must be funded at least at the same levels as the rest of primary education, and for the same number of school-day hours (Bornfreund et al., 2014). Child care subsidies, for those who are eligible, can be used to augment the normal school day, instead of being used for school hours as is now the case.

One necessary but not sufficient step is to make a cogent case for universal pre-K as a civil and human right in the United States. Efforts to change state laws to redefine basic education as beginning at age 3 will hopefully follow. A related, intermediary step is to use the state education funding formula to fund pre-K based on all children who wish to participate. The long march toward achieving this goal can also provide opportunities for public debates about where to place the starting line for universally accessible, publicly financed education in the United States. This is the issue that should be at the center of our public debates about addressing social and economic inequality in America.

UNIVERSAL PRE-KINDERGARTEN AS A CIVIL AND BASIC HUMAN RIGHT

According to the 1948 United Nations Declaration of Human Rights, primary education is considered a basic right of children worldwide (Article 26). This was a reasonable goal when the declaration was written shortly after World War II. Today, almost 70 years later, the scientific evidence on the importance of early nutrition, healthy development, and environmental stimulation for children's educational and life prospects, especially during the first decade of life, is firmly established. For the first time, in September 2015, the United Nations approved the Sustainable Development Goals, which now include universal access to pre-K education by 2030. Likewise, it is now time for the United States to move its outdated goalpost of universal access from primary education to the pre-K years, starting at age 3.

This is exactly what many countries are already doing (Economist Intelligence Unit, 2012). And while many Americans are oblivious to what other countries are doing in education, it is worth monitoring how peer nations have addressed their children's legal entitlements to pre-K and what we can learn from their policies and practices (European Commission, 2014).

In the United States, states play a central role in the governance of education. The U.S. Constitution does not mention education. Some state constitutions include provisions regarding the "basic rights to education." Typically, states must provide education to children at the age specified as the beginning of the compulsory education system. It is important to understand how states define basic rights to education and how that is reflected in the provision of pre-K and kindergarten education as either voluntary or compulsory. A few states have moved to make kindergarten part of the compulsory, hence universal, public education system, but the majority of states have not done so.

What I propose is that states consider basic rights to education as beginning at age 3 with a legal entitlement that does not require attendance (i.e., voluntary) and that kindergarten at age 5 be the beginning of states' compulsory education system (i.e., attendance is required). These changes must be instituted in each state, since there is no federal role regarding school entry. Such state action would provide a framework for funding pre-K and kindergarten programs as part of the state education system and would be relatively less vulnerable to annual budget deal-making (Libassi, 2014). Funding levels would fluctuate depending on state budgets and enrollment, but the statutory obligation to fund the pre-K and kindergarten grades would be in place. This is the best we can do within the current education governance system, and we should work to achieve it.

In the United States, there is considerable evidence that investing in pre-K education improves adult health and economic outcomes, and that it generates savings by reducing remedial education rates, incarceration rates, teenage pregnancy rates, and poor educational attainment. Prominent economists are closely involved in research and policy analyses that continue to strengthen the economic case for investing in early education (Bartik, 2014). Their voices—and the fact that most, if not all, of them are men on a subject long considered a woman's issue—have proved influential in building support among the business community and policymakers as well as the public at large. But only a few, including the prominent economist and Nobel Prize winner James Heckman (2013), have yet addressed how such investments should be financed on any significant scale. And economic frameworks and arguments do have their downsides.

The case for pre-K education has shifted from a moral and ethical framework to an economic framework over the past 40 years. This change, originating to some extent in the rhetoric of *A Nation at Risk* (1983), has proved highly effective in raising the profile of the issue on policy agendas. Political analysis of the efficacy of child advocacy efforts confirms the power of economic framing of the value of early education over moral and ethical frames (Gormley, 2012).

However, we need to broaden economic arguments to embrace moral and ethical ones. Both are needed in this case, and they are not mutually exclusive. In fact, increased attention to economic inequality has brought us full circle to the moral and ethical arguments of fairness, equality of education opportunity, and social justice in creating a good society.

Despite the dominance of the economic argument, progress in achieving greater access to pre-K programs has been slow—it was so even before the Great Recession of 2008, when declines in funding, per child expenditures, and enrollment occurred (NIEER, 2015). The Catch-22 in this economic case may be that it is highly dependent on outcomes associated with poor children of color, mainly African Americans, a growing group of Hispanics, and other groups that are viewed as at risk for poor educational outcomes.

These programs are rarely universal; instead they are part of discretionary funding at the levels of federal (e.g., Head Start) and state (state-funded pre-K, but not part of state education funding formula) levels. More significant, most programs are targeted toward low-income children. As educational programs targeted to specific groups of children, they are not considered part of universal public education but as "interventions" rather than publicly supported education.

It is indisputable that the children who could benefit most from good pre-K programs are the least likely to receive it. Between 2005 and 2011, the percentage of children enrolled in pre-K programs who lived in families 200% below the poverty line actually decreased because of cuts in funding (U.S. Department of Education, 2014). Even targeted programs like Head Start do not cover more than 50% of the income-eligible children, which is restricted to those at less than 135% of the federal poverty line. But the widening economic inequalities among American families provide us with an opportunity to argue for broadening access to pre-K to children living in hardworking, struggling American families at or even over the median family income.

At the present time, the opportunity for an American child to participate in an early education program is based on the state and locality in which he or she lives. David Cohen (2011) characterizes the American way of governing education as "incoherent." Indeed, the age at which a child begins school varies between states and even between school districts (within the same state). Thus, the beginning of school can range widely. In some places there is voluntary pre-K available for all 3- and 4-year-olds (District of Columbia), in others just for 4-year-olds (e.g., Florida, Oklahoma), and in most states, very little access at all. Most states have some publicly funded pre-K, but it is not available for all 4-year-olds, and nine states do not provide state-funded pre-K at all. Pre-K and kindergarten varies from less than 3 hours to 7 hours a day.

Thus, an essential part of designing a new primary school in the United States will be to frame universal pre-K as a civil and human right. That is the first step, and the second is to enact laws that support that right with statutory obligations of governments to provide universal access to pre-K. Then pre-K will be on firmer grounds, but the battle for funding will continue.

All countries should now begin their educational entitlements earlier than the current universal compulsory education age of 6 or 7, which was set many decades ago when our knowledge was limited, especially our understanding of the early emergence of inequalities. Inequalities in family resources have also been globalized (Piketty, 2014; Stiglitz, 2014). We now know that gaps in learning opportunities can begin very early, by age 2 or even earlier, and that earlier interventions can be more effective over a lifetime and less costly to society.

A democratic society based on values of equality of opportunity must find ways by which children can begin life on a level playing field. Thus, other countries, looking at research generated in the United States, have announced plans to increase access to early education programs for their children. These countries with well-developed early education systems—including Finland, France, Germany, the Netherlands, and Sweden—are forging strong connections between early education and primary education by moving to include early education in their education agencies. Meanwhile, the Economist Intelligence Unit (2012) reports that the United States ranks 24th among 45 countries overall in early education provision—16th in affordability, 22nd in quality, and 31st in availability.

Given state and local governance of American education, the question of whether pre-K is a universal or targeted program will be solved on a district, city, and state basis—not at the federal level. Just a handful of states have instituted universal pre-K programs. Only Oklahoma and West Virginia, besides the District of Columbia, have a universal pre-K program, which is part of their public education systems.

The case for universal access to pre-K continues to gain adherents but is countered by the assumption that public investments will always be scarce, as was recently played out in Minnesota's legislature in 2015, and therefore cannot reach all but the most vulnerable children. In Minnesota, Governor Mark Dayton pushed for a universal pre-K program for all 4-year-olds but, lacking legislative and advocacy support, agreed to the expansion of Minnesota's scholarship fund targeted toward low-income families. Ironically, raising the cap on scholarship funds to families may result in fewer children being served.

The already well-established economic case for early education continues to deepen (Bartik, 2014). That case must now be tied to a moral argument that all children deserve access to quality pre-K programs. Pre-kindergarten education can and should be put forward as a civil and human rights issue in education reform. No child should be denied the right to pre-K education that is so firmly linked to wider distribution of early learning opportunities.

PRE-KINDERGARTEN:
STARTING LINE FOR BASIC RIGHT TO EDUCATION

In the United States, a child's basic right to education is delineated in state law. Legal entitlement establishes a state's responsibilities to provide education, but families can decide whether to participate in what is offered; that is, participation is voluntary. Compulsory education requires families to enroll their children in schools. Typically, in the United States, compulsory universal education begins between 5 and 8 years of age, depending on the state.

Kindergarten, which is considered part of the universal public education system, is compulsory in only 15 states and the District of Columbia. Given state responsibility for education, state legislators have sought both to increase the age of kindergarten entry, assuming that education budgets will be reduced, and to lower the age of entry, based on well-documented inequality in learning opportunities before kindergarten. As I pointed out in the Introduction, California raised its cutoff date to September 1 in 2014 and created transitional kindergarten (TK) for children who would have attended kindergarten previously. Michigan is raising its cut-off date to September 1 starting with the 2015–2016 school year. Kentucky is gradually phasing in a higher age of kindergarten entry, while Georgia is considering raising its cutoff date. In contrast, Illinois has actually lowered its kindergarten age of entry.

The proposals to lower the age are always fought, because they are projected to increase the costs of public education. Economic arguments that earlier education can or will offset or reduce the costs of education through less remediation during the K–12 grades have led to small increases of pre-K provision (Muschkin, Ladd, & Dodge, 2015). The expansion of part-day kindergartens to full-day programs is another state response when expansions of pre-K programs are not supported by the legislature; for example, Minnesota moved to full-school-day kindergarten provision in 2014–2015. New Mexico instituted full-day kindergartens as a policy choice over pre-kindergarten (Raden, 2002) and has since moved to provide wider access to pre-K.

Efforts to increase the percentage of American children who have access to pre-K have not focused on changing state laws regarding the "basic right to education." Rather, most of these advocacy efforts have relied on appropriations in state budgets, which are subject to economic and political conditions on an annual basis. Even when there are state laws for a voluntary universal pre-K program, such as in New York, access is dependent on annual, contested state budget negotiations.

Advocates are now recognizing the necessity of stable funding for pre-K based on enrollments and, in some cases, for kindergarten. Future advocacy strategies must focus on how to achieve it. Universal pre-K and kindergarten should be established as statutory obligations in each state, or as part of state funding formulas, as Grades 1–12 now are. Inclusion of pre-K and kindergarten as part of state general education aid should be a high priority for those who seek to create a new American primary school. A few states fund pre-K as part of general education, but only two states and the District of Columbia base funding on those who wish to participate.

Two states—Oklahoma and West Virginia—have universal pre-K programs that are serving about 70% of 4-year-olds and that are funded through the state education aid formula. A few other states, including Iowa, Maine, Vermont, and Wisconsin, also use state school funding formulas to finance state pre-K programs, but enrollment can be capped. While not a state, the District of Columbia also funds universal access for 3- and 4-year-olds. (See Resource 1.1.)

WHY K–5 MATTERS

Policymakers and educators create the structure of our educational systems, which are "socially constructed" and not inevitable or immutable. As such, levels of education (primary and secondary) are choices, and they can be altered.

Much of the focus in this chapter thus far has been on pre-kindergarten and why it should be the beginning of the new primary school. But the K–5 grades are equally important in sustaining the learning trajectories established in the previous years, and they must be closely connected with pre-K to create a continuum of learning experiences for children (McGhee-Hassrick et al., in press). Pre-K–5 constitutes the grade span for the new primary school in formation.

Grades K–3 are part of the emerging definition of early learning (birth to 8), but this span is rarely addressed by early educators, who have

**Resource 1.1. Incorporating Pre-K into
the Public Education Funding Formula:
Oklahoma, West Virginia, and the District of Columbia
Leading the Change**

Oklahoma: The Quiet Evolution

Oklahoma is the first state where pre-K is part of the state public education system and therefore is part of annual budget allocations to education (Dow, 2014; Rose, 2011). Thus in Oklahoma, all children, regardless
of family income, race or ethnicity, or first-language status, have voluntary access to the state's universal pre-K program; close to 70% attend.

State funding of education for all 4-year-olds has also provided opportunities for programs targeted toward low-income children, such as
Head Start, to increase access for younger underserved children to early
education. Oklahoma is a state that should be closely examined for the
lessons that can be learned by other states seeking to achieve similar
goals (Rose, 2011).

In Oklahoma pre-K is fully integrated into the public education system through the state education aid formula and, thus, has a durable
funding stream. The actual levels of funding may vary from year to year,
but there is no question of whether pre-K will be funded, and all 4-year-
olds will have the right to attend school in classrooms held to the same
standards that apply to all grades with coherent guidance from the state
department of education.

Oklahoma's pre-K is located primarily in public schools. Head Start
and other community-based programs may also offer state-funded universal pre-K, but these must comply with state education requirements,
including having a credentialed teacher. Being part of the Oklahoma
public education system, pre-K teachers have the same qualifications (a
bachelor's degree with certification in early education) and receive the
same compensation and benefits as K–12 teachers.

In contrast with rapid expansions of universal pre-K programs in
Florida and New York City, growth has taken place slowly in Oklahoma—
and without public controversy, despite the fact that it is a traditionally conservative state (Kirp, 2013). Oklahoma's program originated as
a strategy to address declining K–12 enrollments in districts during the
mid-1990s, then was bolstered by state legislation to provide pre-K in
districts that wanted to provide this grade. Oklahoma's quiet evolution
of its universal pre-K system occurred without the fanfare of advocacy
for universal pre-K or even the currently salient arguments for its return
on investments.

From its inception in 1996 until 2011, Oklahoma's pre-K had stable leadership in the State Department of Education under the late, incomparable Ramona Paul, an early educator of formidable talents who had a good sense of what an appropriate pre-K curriculum should look like. Paul exemplified the power of long-term state-level leadership in the development, expansion, and refinement of a state pre-K system. She had a clear vision that 4-year-olds were the starting line for public education in Oklahoma and, with her strong background as an early educator, of what an education-based pre-K experience, informed by research on children's development, should be.

Thus, Oklahoma is the poster child for a new primary school, in this case beginning at age 4. Over the years, efforts have been made to extend Oklahoma's universal pre-K to 3-year-olds, but growth has been slow because of the lack of legislative support. Factors include funding constraints and the visibility of the program, which has drawn the attention of groups opposed to publicly funded programs for young children in a political milieu decidedly different from that of the 1990s. But in its initial evolution, pre-K education flew under the radar of typical opposition.

Oklahoma is also a leading example of how a state universal pre-K program for 4-year-olds can have a cascading effect on enhanced provision for children younger than age 4. Because 4-year-olds are served in the Oklahoma universal pre-K programs, Tulsa's Head Start, for example, a program that is required to serve 3- to 5-year-old children living in poverty, is now able to serve a larger proportion of such vulnerable children from birth to 3 (Dow, 2014). Early Head Start, a federal program created to serve infants and toddlers living in poverty, reaches less than 5% nationally of the eligible children.

Thus, the potential impact of a state-funded universal pre-K program is that younger, low-income children may gain greater access to targeted programs than is presently the case. Given the science of early development, particularly from birth to 3 years, and the early emergence of learning inequalities, more targeted funds should be directed toward vulnerable, low-income children and their families before the children are 3 (Allen & Kelly, 2015).

West Virginia: Ample Time for Planning Implementation

Like Oklahoma, West Virginia is an unlikely state to have a universal pre-K program for 4-year-olds. And as in Oklahoma, the rollout of the program has been deliberate and undramatic. Led by the West Virginia Department of Education, the West Virginia universal pre-K is, like Oklahoma's program, part of the state school aid funding formula. In fiscal year 2015, total state aid funding was over $91 million, in addition to federal Head Start and child care funding. For a state with high rates of poverty, it is a prime example of sustained state commitment to early education with ample time to plan for statewide implementation to achieve higher-quality programs.

The West Virginia universal pre-kindergarten program now enrolls the majority of 4-year-olds (about 70%) in a mixed delivery system of public school- and community-based settings in a state that is largely rural. About 79% of the programs (2014–2015 school year) are offered in non–public school sites, including community-based programs such as child care centers and Head Start programs. West Virginia is the only state to offer targeted pre-K to all 3-year-olds with special needs, thus combining a targeted and universal approach before kindergarten, a move that should be considered in other states.

When the West Virginia legislature passed the law for universal pre-K in 2002, it provided for 5 years of planning before implementation, which likely resulted in higher overall levels of program quality at the outset. According to the annual benchmarks of NIEER, West Virginia met all ten benchmarks in 2015–2016, which includes a bachelor's requirement for the head teachers. Thus, it is an important state for making comparisons with the high-profile and large-scale implementation in Florida and New York City. While Florida and New York City serve much larger numbers of children, West Virginia provides a model for many rural areas of the country where poverty is high and access to pre-K is limited because of those two factors.

District of Columbia:
The School District in the Nation's Capital Leads the Country

The District of Columbia, the site of our nation's capital, leads the country in the provision of universal pre-K, serving 69% of its 3-year-olds and 99% of its 4-year-olds in the DC public pre-kindergarten program in 2015–2016. Children attend classes in public schools, public charter schools, community-based programs, and Head Start. The district's program has a long history, having its origins in the 1970s and moving to providing spaces for most of its 3- and 4-year-old children during the past decade, with the leadership of DC mayors.

The DC program is funded as part of the district's school funding formula. District funds are blended with Head Start funds to provide full-day, school-year programs staffed by credentialed teachers. As in Oklahoma and West Virginia, universal pre-K in DC is followed by full-day kindergarten (Garcia & Williams, 2015).

focused on the status quo of birth to 5. I have chosen K–5 to reflect the prevailing grade span for primary education, which is followed by middle or junior high schools (typically Grades 6–8), depending on the school district. To this grade span, I have added pre-K.

Pre-K–5 includes the first decade of life and ends with the beginning of adolescence (Carnegie Council on Adolescent Development, 1996). In fact, districts have created permutations within the pre-K–5 grade span, including pre-K–3 in Lansing, Michigan (Ritchie & Gutmann, 2013), depending on local leadership and managerial considerations. Given local control of education, variations on pre-K–5 will be in place, but what is essential is that pre-K become an integral part of the primary education system whatever the last grade is.

The reason why K–5 matters is that good outcomes from quality pre-K programs cannot be sustained, leveraged, and maximized without strong connections with the primary grades and beyond (McGhee-Hassrick et al., in press; Zellman & Kilburn, 2015). The scientific foundation for quality pre-K and quality K–5 is that learning is cumulative, that it builds on previous learning, and that the early years are the basis for lifelong learning (Allen & Kelly, 2015).

While continuity of learning experiences is important for all children, it is especially important for children who require larger amounts of learning time (McGhee-Hassrick et al., in press), those who are learning a second language, and those with disabilities. Under current conditions, children who come to school speaking a heritage language other than English require 5 to 7 years to achieve academic literacy in a second language. And the demands for that literacy only increase as they continue into middle and high school. When educators aim to create a continuum of learning experiences (Sullivan-Dudzic et al., 2010), the potential for educational success is enhanced. Such continuity of experiences is currently far from the norm. The new primary school has the potential to create such conditions for learning.

WHAT COMES BEFORE—AND AFTER—THE PRIMARY SCHOOL

I will briefly touch on what should be in place from birth to age 3, and what middle and high schools can be like when well-educated children enter them after their primary school experience. Such policies and supporting practices are not now in place for the vast majority of American children.

One obvious outcome of more effective primary education would be less costly remediation and catch-up for children in middle and high

schools, and more opportunities to build on and enhance skills that enable adolescents to deepen their learning and to connect with their choices
for the future and the workplace. Given the considerable costs of such
remedial efforts, the pre-K–12 education system may become more cost-
efficient and effective should there be sound primary schools.

A study of two early intervention programs in North Carolina (Smart
Start and More by Four) showed that such programs can significantly reduce special education placements after the 3rd grade for children without
genetic or physical disabilities (blindness, deafness). The cost savings to
the state is considerable for children with preventable disabilities. At 2009
funding levels, Smart Start reduces placements by 10% and More by Four
by 32% (Muschkin et al., 2015).

As of the most recent (2012) PISA results, American high school students score below average on mathematics and average on reading and
science (Kelly et al., 2013). Nearly 32.8% of first- and second-year undergraduates took a remedial class (Cascio & Schanzenbach, 2014), and the
percentages are greater when students have not been adequately educated
in their local schools. This is not only costly to public coffers, but it is
also costly to students in time and money as they seek to complete their
postsecondary education.

The economic impact of inadequate primary education in terms of
the costs of remediation in middle and high schools should be an important part of a case for redesigning primary education. But what may be
equally costly, if not more so, are the consequences of being inadequately
educated when it comes to the motivation and identity of adolescents as
they encounter the demands of postprimary education, which require the
application of reading and math literacy and more complex demands of
problem solving and analysis. The consequences can range from discour-
agement to despair, as Alex Kotlowitz (1991) captured so painfully in his
book on two brothers as they moved through the Chicago public schools
from primary into middle and high school.

For all these reasons, and above all in terms of individual lives, focusing on and investing in creating effective primary schools should be a
much higher priority than it now is.

Before the Primary School

Recognizing the research on the remarkable learning capacities of infants
and toddlers from birth to age 3 described earlier in this chapter, I will
briefly describe what policies and practices should be in place during
the earliest years of life. First, we must acknowledge prevailing American values about the private rights of families over their children. These

values align with conservative rhetoric regarding the primacy of families, parents' responsibilities to their children, and the alleged intrusiveness of public policies during these years.

Patrick Buchanan's text in support of President Richard Nixon's veto of the Comprehensive Child Development Act of 1971 affirmed the primacy of families and parents over the state or government in the development of children before their entry into the public education system. The current state of affairs in early education policy today bears the legacy of that turning point in American social policy (Karch, 2013; Schulte, 2014).

A few school districts in California, taking seriously the crucial birth to 3 years, are cobbling together funds from federal programs and philanthropic funds to provide programs for infants and toddlers. But the currently available levels of funding are insufficient to make this a widespread or even sustainable practice. While Title I funds can be used for programs serving infants and toddlers, it is unlikely that they will be used, given the needs and stronghold of the K–12 system on using these funds for low-income students even under the Every Student Succeeds Act of 2015.

From birth to age 3, three specific policies and programs are desirable, in addition to universal health insurance for children and their families: paid family and sick leave, programs and services for children with disabilities and special needs, and targeted home visiting and Early Head Start programs for children from low-income families.

Paid family and sick leave. The United States remains one of the only countries in the world that does not have a national paid family leave policy after the birth of a child. Paid family leave would enable American families to join families throughout the world in having the opportunity to be with their infants for some period after birth. The organized business community has successfully opposed family leave provisions thus far. Only California, New Jersey, and Rhode Island have mandated paid family leave laws, and it is unclear whether advocacy for national paid family leave will have legs (Sandler, 2015). Washington state passed a paid family leave law in 2007, but it has not been implemented.

In 1993, President Bill Clinton signed national legislation for family and medical leave, but it did not require employers to pay parents if they took leave, and provisions of leave are discretionary. As with much of American social policy, employers can choose to provide paid family leave of varying lengths to their employees. Typically, the beneficiaries of such privately paid family leave are more highly educated professionals, working in more highly compensated positions. Low-wage workers do not typically benefit from family leave or even sick leave. This practice contributes to inequalities in family supports based on family income, can have consequences for child and parental well-being (Ochshorn, 2015), and can lead to possibly wider social inequities.

Despite being an outlier, the United States is unlikely to join the ranks of countries that provide paid family leave to parents anytime soon. Of note, studies of paid family leave in California and New Jersey indicate that employees are more likely to return to their jobs, and turnover and replacement costs are reduced. At the national level, proposed paid family leave is a strictly partisan issue with only Democrats supporting the Family Act, based on a proposed fund within the Social Security system.

Children with disabilities. The Individuals with Disabilities Education Act (IDEA) provides for services for infants and toddlers with disabilities, regardless of family income. However, families with greater economic resources are more likely to avail themselves of these services than are poor families, and funding varies by state and is not sufficient to meet the current needs of all eligible children; thus this is what is commonly described as an unfunded mandate. Given that children with disabilities are likely to experience more challenges as they enter school, stronger connections between areas of special education, which is now segmented into infants and toddlers, early education, and K–12 grades, are highly desirable.

Targeted programs of home visiting and Early Head Start. From birth to age 3, home visiting and Early Head Start programs should focus on children up to least 200% of the federal poverty line at first, and gradually move to 300%. Currently, these programs serve less than 4% of the eligible population, because of insufficient funding. Given what we now know about the influence of these first 3 years, especially for children growing up in poverty, access to and funding of these efforts is woefully inadequate (Muschkin et al., 2015).

Programs and services for children during the first 3 years of life should be targeted to low-income children and families and followed by universal access at age 3. Few countries, even those with universal access to pre-K at age 3, provide early learning programs for all children younger than 3. As states provide support for pre-K programs, federal Head Start funds for 4- and 5-year olds can be used for low-income children from birth to 3. As I pointed out in Resource 1.1, this is occurring in Oklahoma, which has a state-funded universal pre-K program for 4-year-olds.

We should seriously consider reinventing Head Start to focus its resources on low-income children from birth to 3 (Zigler, 2011). This targeted approach is consistent with growing evidence that inequality in learning experiences occurs as early as 8 months, and that earlier interventions can be helpful. This is unfortunately not likely to take place anytime soon.

Too many programs and constituencies would be destabilized, and well-prepared adults to serve younger children are not now available. And bottom line, funds to support these programs are not currently available.

And What Comes After

In the past 50 years there has been no dearth of proposals about how American middle and high schools should be changed. Concerns about dropouts, low graduation rates, remedial education in post-secondary institutions (Ortiz, Oakley, & Burdman, 2015), and workplace preparation have fueled this fervor for reform of education during the second decade of life or adolescence (ages 10–18).

Given the inadequate levels of learning for many children in our primary schools, these reform efforts have focused on remediation. The cost of grade retention is $11,000 per student. West (2012) reports that the direct cost of retaining 2.3% of the 50 million students in American schools is over $12 billion annually, and notes that primary schools have been overlooked as a source of student retentions.

The new primary school sees its mission as educating children during the first decade of life, so that they are able to take on new challenges in postprimary education that provide them with options for higher education and workforce opportunities. As such, middle and high schools will ultimately need to be redesigned, since students will arrive with better preparation and increased motivation.

Every year counts. The new demands of adolescence, and broader socioeconomic inequities, must be addressed no matter how good the outcomes of primary education become. Such supports, which address new demands on students during middle and high school, can be more easily provided when most of the students have a strong foundation from primary school.

Three approaches described below illustrate the need for greater flexibility in how we structure high schools. More attention should be focused on the last 2 years of high school in particular. The opportunities to engage in postsecondary education through early colleges, and in aligned workforce development for specific industry sectors, are examples of the kinds of change that need to be considered in the 21st-century redesign of high schools.

Early college for all. The economic benefits of a college education versus high school completion are well documented. In 2013, median earnings for young adults with bachelor's degrees were $48,500, compared with $23,900 for those without a high school credential, $30,000 for those with a high school credential, and $37,500 for those with an associate's degree (U.S. Department of Education, Institute of Education Sciences, National Center for Education Statistics, 2014). The pay gap between college-educated and high school–credentialed individuals was significantly smaller in previous generations (Pew Research Center, 2014).

At early college, high school students can attend community colleges or other higher education institutions prior to high school graduation. This practice is a win-win option for those who are ready for college-level courses and for those who are disengaged in high school.

Similar efforts are called dual-enrollment, dual-credit programs at, for example, South Texas College, where high school students combine high school and community college completion by being enrolled in both institutions, with career and technical education courses that enable them to work at good jobs while continuing their higher education.

It is important to note that 4 years of high school is not a worldwide standard. In many countries, students are tracked into vocational, business, technical, and higher education pathways during early or mid-adolescence. The United States has resisted these approaches in principle, while in practice, de facto tracking in high schools is commonplace. Early college approaches are one strategy to add flexibility for students with different needs; other strategies should also be tried.

Apprenticeships tied to "high-demand" jobs. The value of a college education in the United States is attenuated by the absence of comparably valued pathways to careers and workplaces. In Germany, for example, an apprenticeship system provides a path to employment in decent-paying jobs and with appropriate status. The lack of high-quality apprenticeships that are closely tied with employment in high-demand, decent-wage jobs requires that American youth earn a college degree as a basic credential required in a competitive job market. However, the value of a bachelor's degree has been eroding.

Despite efforts in the 1980s to promote an apprenticeship approach (Hamilton, 1990), schools and companies were unable to cooperate effectively, largely because of a lack of commitment on the part of industry. Recently, there has been a small revival of apprenticeship programs, which bears close watching and possible emulation.

PRIMARY SCHOOLS: THE START OF LIFELONG LEARNING

In this chapter, I provided a framework for thinking about public investments in children during the first decade of their lives. This framework places the new pre-K–5 primary school into a continuum that supports lifelong learning from birth (see Chapter 2). While this book centers on what should take place in publicly supported primary schools educating children from 3 to 10 years of age, even the most effective primary education experience for children requires continuing investments during the postprimary years, as well as during the previous years from birth to 3.

Unlike middle and high schools, the new primary school is on unstable financial footing, specifically with respect to the pre-kindergarten and kindergarten years, which are not yet part of most state education laws and state education funding. Working for predictable financial sustainability provides an opening for revising state education laws to include pre-K and kindergarten as part of the state's definition of basic rights to education. Establishing statutory obligations to pre-K and kindergarten should also be considered by state policymakers. This is one of the unexplored frontiers of education transformation and policy change.

Done right, primary education can play an important role in reducing inequalities that begin early, and in reducing the need for costly remediation of academic skills in middle and high schools, as well as in higher education.

Viewing primary education as constituting the critical years for establishing the foundational mindsets and skills for lifelong learning will be required. This is not the case now and would be a significant change from our current situation, where too many students continue to falter in the years during and after primary education. How that new primary school will effectively educate children is the subject of Chapter 2.

Nicholas Kristof eloquently expressed the main argument of Chapter 1 in the opening quote; children's opportunities to participate in early learning experiences before kindergarten is an urgent civil rights issue. The research of psychologists Kenneth and Mamie Clark on African American children was pivotal in the 1954 Supreme Court ruling in *Brown v. Board of Education* that reversed racial segregation in public schools. We now have much more evidence to support public investments to provide education programs for all children as a basic human and civil right in America.

This book offers one approach to start all children—who have enormous talent and potential—on a path to greater equality in their opportunities to learn. This is the responsibility of our public education system. How children are integrated into the workplace and into their communities during adulthood is the joint responsibility of organizations outside the schools. Promoting and shaping that mindset will not be easy. Starting on that journey begins in the new primary school.

CHAPTER 2

WHAT DOES THE NEW PRIMARY SCHOOL LOOK LIKE?

> One fact remains immutable: the default setting of every form of government . . . is the status quo. Overcoming resistance and simple inertia is hard, all the more so because what exists is real and familiar while the proposed change is imagined and novel, unfamiliar and therefore threatening. Although the details vary, it always takes energy and sustained commitment to move the status quo.
>
> —William A. Galston and Elizabeth McElvein, "Institutional Innovation: How It Happens and Why It Matters," April 22, 2015

New primary schools already exist (Maeroff, 2006; MinnCAN, 2014; Ritchie & Gutmann, 2013). Led by strategic and committed educators at the district and school levels, schools integrating pre-K into the traditional K–5 primary grades are being established across the country (Ritchie & Gutmann, 2013; Sullivan-Dudzic et al., 2010; www.fcd-us.org).

These schools are place- or site-specific efforts, scattered throughout the country, educating children well. The sustainability of these efforts, often referred to as systemic change, is proving to be highly dependent on local leadership and conditions.

Heroic leaders are leading the pre-K–3rd movement in districts and school sites with almost no direction or incentives from states (Bornfreund et al., 2015). The 2015 reauthorization of the Elementary and Secondary Education Act, now called the Every Student Succeeds Act (ESSA), contains enabling provisions that encourage states, for the first time in the 50-year-old education legislation aimed at narrowing achievement gaps, to forge stronger connections between their early education and K–12 grade experiences.

Authentic implementation is the big elephant in the room. When educators say they are already "doing pre-K–3rd," they sometimes take a piece of this approach by making stronger connections between pre-K programs and kindergarten (MinnCAN, 2014), but, at best, this is only the beginning of what is required to move the needle on the stubborn trajectories of children's educational success, that is, a comprehensive strategy, not only school-based but also in partnership with families (see Chapter 4).

At the center of the authentic integration of pre-K into the existing primary grades is what takes place every school day in classrooms between teachers and students, and among students themselves, starting with pre-K and every year through the primary grades. In this chapter, I aim to capture what is at the heart of learning taking place in the new primary school, which is based on a growing consensus from separate areas of research about the development of children and the conditions that contribute to well-educated, independent, thoughtful individuals with a sense of social responsibility.

Research on children's learning and development during the first decade of life (Allen & Kelly, 2015), aligned with instructional strategies (Goldman & Pellegrino, 2015), is converging and can inform the ways in which children can be more effectively educated than they now are. The divide between early learning and K–12 education need not continue to be the typically identified divide between developmentally informed practice with its premium on social-emotional learning, on the one hand, and content knowledge, on the other. Both are integrated in the new primary school (see Figure 2.1).

This integration requires the recognition of key structural and cultural factors described in this chapter, and demands heavy lifting at the district (Nyhan, 2015) and school levels. The opening quote of this chapter refers to institutional change and innovation in government agencies (Galston & McElvein, 2015), but it also captures what has long been the case in the education sector. Tyack and Cuban (1997) analyzed the high barriers to education reform as being embedded in the stubborn "grammar of schooling."

None of the features of the new primary school are original, except for the connection with early learning, which is new. In fact, education reformers have been trying to institutionalize them for at least the past 50 years under the rubric of "effective schools." These schools have the elements for creating new American primary schools, but in most cases, pre-K remains separate from, or loosely connected with, the K–5 grades, as is the case in New York City, which served over 68,000 4-year-olds in its full-day universal pre-K program in school year 2015–2016 but has no plan for how that program aligns with the K–12 grades. In the few states and districts where pre-K is now the beginning of public education, pre-K classrooms are typically located in or on the grounds of a primary school, but making that connection between pre-K and K–5 does not

Figure 2.1. Bridging the Early Education and K–5 Divide: Points of Convergence

Convergence	Early Education	K–5 Grades
Education aims to develop cognitive and social competencies to engage in and to relish lifelong learning.	The purpose of education is to develop all aspects of children's well-being.	The purpose of education is to develop deeper learning and 21st-century competencies.
Teachers require deep understandings of what children know to design and adapt instruction.	Children are not blank slates; they are naturally curious and select opportunities to learn.	Students bring prior knowledge and beliefs to new situations.
Children are active learners who seek to learn in ways that build on and cut across adult-created subject matter divisions.	Children are not vessels to be filled up; they learn by being actively engaged in what is meaningful to them.	Learning is organized around thematic units, to which teachers integrate content knowledge learning and skills.
A trusting relationship between student and teacher is essential for deeper learning to occur.	Children learn from individuals with whom they develop trusting relationships.	Students learn from teachers whom they trust and respect.
Learning is inherently social and benefits from spirited exchanges between students and teachers.	Children's learning is essentially social; children learn with and from other children and adults.	Children learn best in small groups, where they are deeply engaged in discussing and solving problems.
Both families and schools contribute to children's educational success.	Families must be strong allies in supporting children's learning at home and in the classroom.	Families and teachers must be partners in the educational success of students.

Sources: Goldman & Pellegrino (2015); Gordon & Rajagopalan (2016).

occur naturally and requires strong intentionality by district and school leadership. Colocation of pre-K programs in schools is not enough.

Creating the new American primary school requires a mindset shift in how educators think about how children learn and how they should be taught (Takanishi, 2010), and then engaging in the arduous task of altering longstanding policies, beliefs, and practices to support a continuum of learning that is not yet widely in place. As it now stands, pre-K, kindergarten, and the other grades of the primary school exist as separate silos without much attention to the benefits to both teachers and students of creating a seamless, continuous set of learning experiences for children that begins with pre-K and ends with Grade 5, followed by middle or junior high school. On this fundamental dimension of continuity of goals, curriculum, and instruction, our current education system is dysfunctional in terms of supporting even children's basic learning.

Changing the status quo to create a new American primary school will require strong and stable leadership from the managerial ranks of districts combined with the slow and steady work of educators at the school and classroom levels (Sullivan-Dudzic, et al., 2010; Nyhan, 2015; Reynolds et al., 2016; Ritchie & Gutmann, 2013). Current experience, based on schools and districts nationwide that seek to create this new primary school, shows that it can be done and that, as an approach, the results for student outcomes and closing achievement gaps are promising (Lindholm-Leary, 2015; Reynolds et al., 2016; Zellman & Kilburn, 2015).

Those experiences, however, demonstrate that the creation of new primary schools is a herculean effort and requires a long-term perspective, at minimum 5 years and more often 7 to 10 years to implement even in optimal conditions (Nyhan, 2015; Ritchie & Gutmann, 2013). To launch a movement for these schools, we must first address the question of what our purposes are for primary education. What are we trying to accomplish in terms of what and how children should learn during the pre-K–5 grades? After we articulate our purposes, how do we design schools that achieve these purposes? What are the basic foundations—structural and cultural—on which such schools rest? And then, most important, what does teaching and learning in these schools look like? Purposes of education, school structure and culture, and classroom life must all become aligned, consistent, and coherent. And these efforts must be designed, from their inception, to be sustainable and widespread.

PURPOSES OF PRIMARY EDUCATION

The purposes of primary education, typically viewed as Grades kindergarten–4/5, sometimes to Grade 8, have aimed to establish the fundamental skills of reading, writing, and mathematics in preparation for learning content or subject matter beginning around grade 4. The most egregious example of the divide between the primary and the middle and high schools is the misleading mantra "Learning to read; reading to learn." This divide has had damaging consequences for young learners, and has been especially contentious in the education of Dual Language Learners whose first language is not English. The separation of learning the elements and mechanics of literacy from learning subject matter violates our substantial understanding of the conditions and processes by which all children learn. Children learn by addressing topics that have meaning for them, and reading literacy is a pathway to acquiring knowledge about the world and contributing to its further expansion. Mastering the mechanics of reading is not a goal of education.

Under the influence of No Child Left Behind (NCLB) during the administration of President George W. Bush, the focus on 3rd-grade reading performance (actually measured in the 4th grade) became a national obsession. Coupled with high-stakes testing of children and efforts to use test outcomes of children to evaluate teacher performance, the purposes of primary education unfortunately narrowed to reading performance with less attention on other content areas, with the exception of a rising focus on mathematics. There has been less time for social studies and even science. Arts and music became rare. These developments have restricted the educational experiences of many children, particularly those who are at risk for poor educational outcomes.

Common Core State Standards (CCSS), voluntarily adopted by states and now in the process of weakening in some of these states, was a worthwhile effort to create higher standards for learning and for cultivating analysis, thinking, and what are called higher-order skills in language and math literacy. These standards are welcome for raising the bar for deeper learning in American schools, but CCSS have become a political minefield. Inadequate support for teachers to prepare children to meet these standards, coupled with the premature testing of students before they and their teachers had sufficient time to respond to desirable higher standards, have meant that conditions for learning have been compromised, creating stressful situations for both teachers and students.

Nonetheless, some schools and teachers have responded positively to these new standards and are achieving promising results. What distinguishes these schools is that they have a clear sense of what the purposes of their educational efforts are seeking to achieve. And test outcomes are not the North Star of what happens in their classrooms.

If reading test performance at end of 3rd grade is not the purpose of primary education, what is? To be clear, we want all children to be highly literate, to be able to communicate well with peers and with adults. This means being able to read and understand the meaning of texts, and to communicate orally and through the written word. But literacy provides the skills to make meaning out of what children are learning about the world, and being able to work with others to solve problems, resolve differences, and live together in a civil society. These competencies are often referred to as "deeper learning and 21st-century skills" (e.g., Goldman & Pellegrino, 2015), including students' being able to use what they know and to apply knowledge in new situations.

The purpose of education should be to develop individuals who are eager to learn, enjoy inquiry, are curious about their world, can work with others, and can develop the capacity to focus their attention on the matter at hand, avoid distractions, and persist when things are difficult. Whether these attributes are called grit, executive functioning, or cognitive flexibility (Tough, 2012), they point to the desirability of a self-directed individual who loves to learn, in the classroom and everywhere else. One highly promising approach, the pre-K–3rd Sobrato Early Academic Language (SEAL) model, piloted to serve low-income dual-language Hispanic children, expresses this best: Is there joy in children's learning? (See Resource 2.1.)

Leading education reform gurus expound on these purposes or goals for education in the K–12 education system (Robinson & Aronica, 2015; Wagner & Dintersmith, 2015). The consensus is clear: communication, creativity, critical analytic skills, and collaboration. These goals are not new or unique, but making them explicit is necessary to guide and to evaluate whether primary schools are achieving their purposes.

Third-grade reading proficiency is an important and basic purpose of early primary education, but it is only one of a host of other equally important goals. The vision of a new primary school is aptly captured in this phrase: "moving from filling buckets to lighting fires" (Gordon & Rajagopalan, 2016, p. 76). Thus the goal of primary education is not to fill children's heads with information, but to spur them to love learning throughout their lives, reflecting a "fundamental shift in the learner's role from passive recipient of knowledge to active participant in learning processes." Our goal is to foster the development of a person who is able to apply his or her knowledge in different contexts in creative ways (Goldman & Pellgrino, 2015, p. 36).

To achieve its goals, the new primary school requires two essential foundations. First, certain structural elements must be in place. These elements include the provision of sound full-day pre-K educational experiences and of full-school day kindergarten. Principal leadership is critical to establishing aligned curriculum and instruction, which is created by collaborating teams of teachers, working on a regular basis, optimally daily, but certainly weekly or at least biweekly, to plan, implement and reflect on their instruction. However, what we now have in districts throughout the country is the presence of some of these structural elements, but not the complete array of these elements. The new American primary school has all these elements in operation at the same time.

The second foundation is the cultural elements that represent the core values of the school, an idea associated with the late Seymour Sarason (1996), a community psychologist and educational reformer. In the

RESOURCE 2.1. WHY PRE-K–3RD APPROACHES ARE CRITICAL FOR DUAL-LANGUAGE LEARNERS: THE SOBRATO EARLY ACADEMIC LANGUAGE MODEL

Sobrato Early Academic Language (SEAL) is a pre-K–3rd model designed by Laurie Olsen, a leader in the education of English learners (ELs). It aims to build rich language and early literacy skills as a foundation for the educational success of both dual language learners (DLL) and English-only children. The model was piloted in three primary schools (and their feeder pre-K programs) serving children from low-income families in the San Jose and Redwood City school districts in California, resulting in promising outcomes (Lindholm-Leary, 2015). At the end of 2015, SEAL was being implemented in 12 school districts involving 69 schools and reaching more than 39,000 students. Most of the replication sites are located in the greater Silicon Valley region of California.

The SEAL model is based on "foundational understandings" that connect teaching and learning during the pre-K–3rd grades:

- The development of language and literacy for dual language learners takes time, and requires a systematic, articulated approach throughout the pre-K–3rd years that is widely shared and faithfully implemented. This requires the joint participation of and collaboration among early education and the K–3 grades. Strong leadership at the school site and district levels is essential.
- The SEAL model aims to produce strong language skills through students' active engagement in theme-based units in science and in social studies aligned with Common Core State Standards. Language learning is fully integrated with content or subject matter using high-leverage instructional strategies with high expectations for students' learning and their engagement.
- The authentic implementation of pre-K–3rd instruction requires intensive professional development, regular coaching of teachers, and time for grade-level collaboration involving joint planning and reflection among teachers on their instruction and its improvement. Replication sites must commit to 3 years of professional development in order to implement SEAL consistently.
- The development of biliteracy in all children is viewed as an asset. Building on the primary or home language of young children can play an important role in their literacy development, including the learning of English.
- SEAL engages families in supporting their children's language and literacy development in their homes and in their classrooms. Although many of the parents have low levels of education, 50% report reading to their children at least twice a week, which is the norm for college-educated parents.

Lindholm-Leary (2015) evaluated SEAL in the San Jose and Redwood City school districts after 4 years of implementation. Three cohorts of children who experienced 1 year of a SEAL pre-K program and then moved to a SEAL kindergarten through 3rd-grade program were compared with one cohort of partial SEAL students who did not experience the SEAL pre-K. Students were assessed with five measures of language, literacy, math, and cognitive and social development in English and Spanish.

Lindholm-Leary (2015) found that teachers implemented the SEAL instructional components at a high level. While SEAL students entered pre-K and kindergarten with low levels of language and literacy measured in both English and Spanish, these students at all grade levels showed statistically significant progress on all five measures. Students who had received the full pre-K–3rd SEAL experience scored significantly higher than partial SEAL students, particularly in the second and third grades. While there was significant variation among the three sites in parental education levels and in rates of student growth, all sites showed significant student growth on the outcome measures.

These SEAL evaluation findings provide support for bilingual two-way programs that foster the primary or home language while developing English language competence during the pre-K–3rd years. By the 3rd grade, students participating in bilingual instruction scored the same or higher than students receiving English-only instruction on the California English Language Development Test (CELDT), the California Standards Test in both language arts and math, and the Standards Test in Spanish in both language arts and math. Moreover, students who were fluent Spanish speakers scored higher than limited Spanish speakers in the 2nd and 3rd grades on all assessments measured in English. These results are consistent with the body of research on dual-language programs showing that students in bilingual programs show as strong or stronger progress than their peers in English-only programs (Genesee & Lindholm-Leary, 2011). A large-scale evaluation of SEAL replication sites, using Common Core assessments, is now under way.

Starting with the pre-K year with a focus on language and literacy provides children with a strong base for sustaining their learning in the K–3 years through the SEAL model, which shows the value of a pre-K–3rd approach to effective education of DLLs at the beginning of their schooling. The model attests to the fact that learning is a cumulative process, and it requires a period of years, guided by coherent instructional strategies, to master high standards for educational success.

But the highest aspiration for SEAL learners is what designer Olsen sees as an essential: "confident, motivated, engaged and joyful learners."

For more information, contact Laurie Olsen, SEAL director, at lolsen@sobrato.org.

new primary school, the continuity of shared learning experiences is valued within grade levels (horizontal alignment) and from one grade level to another (vertical alignment), pre-K through Grade 5. Collaboration and teamwork among teachers and among students are core values, and both are essential to achieve horizontal and vertical alignment among the grades levels.

In the next two sections I examine more deeply the foundations of structure and culture of the new primary school.

THE STRUCTURE OF THE NEW PRIMARY SCHOOL

The structure of the new primary school provides a framework for what can take place between teachers and students and among students themselves in classrooms. Three essential elements of this structure include (1) voluntary, universally available, full-school-day pre-kindergarten beginning no later than age 4, and preferably at age 3; (2) compulsory full-school-day kindergarten at age 5; and (3) strong principal leadership and responsibility for creating and sustaining an organized continuum of curricula and instruction from pre-K to Grade 5 developed and implemented by stable, collaborating teams of teachers. Let us examine each of these elements in turn.

Voluntary Universal Pre-Kindergarten

The new primary school begins no later than at age 4, and preferably at age 3. It is available to all children regardless of the economic circumstances of their families; that is, participation is not based on family income or means tested. Some places may choose to levy fees for families above an income threshold, as the city of Seattle is doing. Given the income distribution of American families and the high costs of pre-K programs relative to their annual incomes, such a threshold should be set at the median family income or, ideally, higher. The median family income of $50,000 for a family of four does not leave much discretionary income, which now includes pre-K education for the children.

I highly recommend that when states provide universal pre-K starting at age 4 that they consider targeted access at age 3 or even earlier for children who are likely to benefit from early learning programs such as children with learning disabilities, those who are learning a second language, and those who live in concentrated poverty. Local sites may choose, as in the state of West Virginia, to start with a targeted pre-K at age 3, followed by universal access at age 4. In that state, all children with an Individual

Education Program (IEP) qualify for pre-K at age 3. In a few states where universal access for 4-year-olds has been attained, enrollment of 3-year-olds has followed. In the District of Columbia, close to 70% of 3-year-olds participate in the universal pre-K program, building on a 4-year-old pre-K program that is universally accessible, with 99% of the age group attending in school year 2015–2016 (Garcia & Williams, 2015).

In states and localities that have already achieved universal provision of serving more than 65% of the age group (Florida, Georgia, Oklahoma, West Virginia, and the District of Columbia), there will always be families who choose private education or to raise their children at home until kindergarten entry. So universal access does not mean 100% voluntary attendance in the public education system. Throughout the world, no nation, even any with universal provision, requires pre-K attendance before the beginning of compulsory primary education. However, when pre-K is universally provided, whether in a state or locality or nationally, the majority of children in the age group participates, indicating that families value pre-K experiences for their children, and that paying for pre-K out of the family budget is out of the reach of at least 50% of families, based on family income distributions.

An important issue for the new primary school is whether pre-K is a half- or full-school-day program. Research has established the value of full-school-day provision on a range of child outcomes (Reynolds et al., 2015), and longer hours are also more supportive of deeper learning, including small groupings and activity- and project-based learning, among children. However, moving from half- to full-day programs is currently (and for the foreseeable future) constrained by inadequate funding, lack of appropriately trained teachers, and the shortage of facilities for young children. Thus the typical default position is to serve more children for a shorter period of time versus fewer children in a full-day program that is more likely to have the beneficial outcomes documented in research. The new primary school provides pre-K for the same hours as it does for kindergarten–Grade 5 (Bornfreund et al., 2014).

School and district policies should support stable pathways for children from pre-K to kindergarten and the grades beyond. This is low-hanging fruit. District policies do not now reflect the importance of continuity of learning experiences from pre-K to Grade 5. Thus, children in pre-K programs in a school, reflecting pre-K's status as an "extended learning time" program, can enroll in any primary school in the district. This is just one of several indicators that pre-K programs, even those located in public schools as they have been in California since the end of World War II, are add-ons and not considered part of a coherent primary education system.

To be a *new* primary school, parents should enroll their children in pre-K programs with the clear expectations that, barring housing and other factors not under their control, their children are expected to continue in kindergarten and the rest of the primary grades in that school. In the same way that some districts give priority to children who enroll in a school where their siblings are enrolled, districts should create pathways from pre-K to kindergarten in the same school. In the rare districts where there is a common or shared curriculum in all schools, enrollment in other schools is less of an issue because of the likely continuity in learning experiences for the child regardless of whether he or she continues in a specific school in the district. In these cases, however, the continuity of peer groups and the social networks among families are likely to be disrupted by moving to another school.

Pathway policies aim to build a sense of community among families and schools, with joint responsibility for student learning. Parents and teachers get to know each other over the years. Perhaps as important, when children in a classroom have a common experience of pre-K, the teacher is able to focus more on individual differences and less on differences because of early learning experiences. She or he gets to know children well, which is the starting point for engaging them in learning. This is a win-win situation in which the instructional work of the teacher is facilitated, and in which children experience continuity and coherence in their learning experiences. The uncommon practice of looping—where teachers remain with groups of children over a period of years, typically in early primary education—should be considered as a more regular practice in primary schools than it now is.

Thus, in the new primary school, pre-K is not an add-on to the K–5 school or an extension of potential learning time in the same bucket as summer and after-school programs. It is a new beginning for public education, and on the same footing as K–5 with the same policies applying and the same compensation packages for the teachers with similar qualifications. Hence, all policies, particularly those that aim to protect the well-being of children such as disciplinary and suspension practices in Grades 1–5, as well as civil and legal rights protections for English learners, should also apply to pre-K and kindergarten. The current example of Indiana's barring undocumented children from attending pre-K is another reminder that early learning programs are not part of our public education system.

Advocacy campaigns in states and localities to increase access to pre-K programs should be organized to take into account the features of pre-Ks that increase the likelihood that they are the gateway to universal public education. This means that pre-K programs should be full-school-day offerings staffed by lead teachers with the same education, credentials, and compensation as those of K–12 teachers (Allen & Kelly, 2015). The pre-K educational experiences of the children should be the first year of a coherent foundation for literacy and social development that is part of a continuum of learning into later primary education. Pre-K teachers should be involved in joint professional development and collaboration with those staffing K–5 grades. Whether pre-K programs are community based or in the school building, the principal should include them as an integral part of the professional learning community of the new primary school (NAESP, 2014).

Compulsory Full-School-Day Kindergarten

Most people assume that kindergarten is the starting point of America's universal public education system, thus referred to as K–12. The fact is that kindergarten provision varies by state and districts. What is not widely known is that kindergarten is compulsory in only 15 states and that entry ages vary according to state law. In 2014, 35 states did not require attendance in this grade. Only 12 states (the majority of them in the southern region of the United States) require their school districts by law to provide full-day kindergarten. In 2016, Washington and Rhode Island are moving toward providing full-day kindergarten. What is important, regardless, is that when kindergarten is provided, most eligible children attend, and few families are aware of kindergarten's voluntary nature.

Because kindergarten is not part of our compulsory education system, it is not protected in the same ways as are the compulsory Grades 1–12. Funding can be reduced for these grades, but they are protected from certain state legislative actions. However, kindergartens can be reduced from full-school-day programs to part-school-day programs, threatened with reductions in hours, or eliminated all together as occurred in Arizona after the Great Recession when state revenues plummeted (Libassi, 2014). Parental fees or tuition, especially for full-day offerings, can be instituted, another indicator that kindergarten is not seen as part of our public education system.

States have also raised the kindergarten entry age, again partially as a cost-reduction measure in state budgets for education. These measures are shortsighted, given the preponderance of research pointing to the value of starting public education earlier than we now do, and especially since more young children attend state-supported pre-K programs, some of which can be full day. Attending a part-day kindergarten after such experience does not make educational sense, in terms of time for teachers to sustain and extend students' previous learning. What these legislative moves indicate is that when budget cuts in education occur, the noncompulsory grades like kindergarten and pre-K are obvious targets when they are not required by state statue. And little attention is paid to the ramifications of these cuts on what comes before or after these grades.

Most important for equal learning time, about 25% of children in the United States still attend part-day kindergarten for hours varying from 2.5 to 4 hours in contrast to the normal K–12 school day, which ranges from 6 to 7 hours. Only 27 states set a requirement for full-day kindergarten to be equivalent in hours to 1st grade (Bornfreund et al., 2015). In some sites, parents must pay for full-day kindergarten attendance, which advantages higher- over lower-income families and contributes to inequalities in access to an important set of early learning experiences.

Certainly more controversial than offering universal pre-K on a voluntary basis is the requirement of compulsory kindergarten. When public education begins with voluntary pre-K at age 3 or 4, kindergarten is no longer the starting gate for schooling. It is another grade or year of schooling between pre-K and Grades 1–5, and it cannot be considered optional or reduced in hours.

When a grade level is not compulsory, district policies and regulations may not apply in the same way they do to Grades 1–12. This can be especially important in policies and practices related to suspensions and truancy, which can be very high during pre-K and kindergarten years and disproportionately affect African American and Hispanic young children, especially males (Gilliam, 2008).

Perhaps the most compelling reason for making kindergarten compulsory is that it signals to all—families especially—that in the 21st century kindergarten is an integral part of our educational system and is an experience where regular attendance is required. Because of family and community stressors, kindergarten absences in lower-income communities can be very high (Attendance Works & Healthy Schools Campaign, 2015), and thus children do not have the opportunity to benefit from a quality educational program because their attendance is sporadic. This can add to their disadvantage as they move up the grades. Efforts to increase attendance in kindergarten may be strengthened by making it part of the compulsory education system and subject to the same responsibilities of parents for their children's attendance with appropriate sanctions. For all these reasons, making kindergarten compulsory is long overdue. State legislatures should move to include full-school-day kindergarten as part of a state's responsibility for publicly supported education.

Principal Leadership to Support Alignment of Curriculum and Instruction

Strong principal leadership is a critical structural element of truly implementing a new primary school. Without this leadership and responsibility for understanding early learning and for organizing and sustaining collaborating teacher teams in the school, such a school cannot exist. Collaborative teams are necessary to create continuity, that is, alignment, in the learning experiences during the school year itself from one year to the next. This cannot be accomplished without the shared commitment of a principal and the teaching staff in a school to allocate the time to this work. Time for collaboration and reflection among teachers is typically in very short supply in most American schools and should be a high priority for improved work conditions when teacher unions negotiate their contracts (see Chapter 5).

Alignment of standards, curriculum, instruction, and assessment across the pre-K–5 grades is core to new primary schools. Without it, the learning experiences of children are chaotic, hit or miss, and highly dependent on whether they have got a good teacher that year. This state of affairs is unfortunately more the norm than it should be, given what we know about the optimal conditions for children to learn. The extent to which this chaos contributes to lowered levels of student achievement has not been investigated, but cross-national comparisons indicate that it may be considerable (Tucker, 2016).

Pre-K and kindergarten have typically operated separately from the rest of the primary grades. Part of the reason is that both are not part of the universal compulsory public education system, which starts in most states with Grade 1, as I explained above. Both pre-K and kindergarten have been added to primary education in fits and spurts without consideration of how they relate or affect children's learning before or after. This contributes to the lack of continuity in learning experiences for children and constitutes a formidable challenge to teachers in designing their instructional programs to foster the continuing learning of their students based on what they have learned before.

Early education or pre-K and kindergarten have evolved as separate educational sectors, although they are more alike in their child-centered focus than the subject- or content-centered focus of Grades 1 and above. This separation is based on the decisions to make kindergartens part of the public schools while the largely private non- and for-profit sectors providing pre-K programs remained apart from public education and, with that stance, separate from the content and academic orientation of public schools. This position among early educators to view the K–12 schools as potentially overwhelming the play- and child-led early education programs (Kostelnick & Gracy, 2009) remains a barrier to expansion of state-funded pre-K programs even in a mixed delivery system, which is the case in the vast majority of state-pre-K programs.

Shifting from adult concerns to the potential impact of the pre-K–early primary grades divide, the expansion of pre-K programs has changed the skills, behavior, and dispositions with which children with pre-K experience now enter kindergarten and resulted in uneven adaptations in kindergarten curricula and teaching methods (Bassok & Rorem, 2014). Kindergarten and 1st-grade teachers find that they are faced with educating children with different pre-K experiences from those they had prior to the recent expansions in pre-K access. Because of the lack of universal access to pre-K programs, some children in the same classrooms have had no pre-K experiences at all. The uneven access to pre-K experiences among children contributes to a wider range of competencies with which children enter 1st grade and presents large challenges to teachers in using differentiated instruction in the primary grades.

Teachers must adapt their curriculum and instruction to this fact, as well as to the normal range of individual differences among young children. For example, one of the reasons cited for the lack of sustained gains in kindergarten and beyond of pre-K attendees is that the kindergarten teacher is understandably focused on bringing non-pre-K students up to similar levels of learning as those who attended pre-K. Differentiated instruction in such a classroom could build on what children with pre-K experience bring to kindergarten, but may not take place as widely as it should depending on the teacher, who may be attending to other students without such experience. In some cases, those children with pre-K experiences are harnessed to work with groups of children who do not have that experience. The opportunities to build on what they bring to the kindergarten milieu are squandered.

The times have changed, and primary education must be reimagined. The new primary school seeks to create a seamless learning continuum for children starting with the pre-K years through kindergarten and continuing until the end of primary education. When all children have similar opportunities to learn from age 3, they are more likely to benefit from good educational programs later on. For children who are learning English (as noted earlier, referred to as English learners or ELs, and sometimes as dual-language learners or DLLs), this continuum can be especially advantageous, given the 5 to 7 years required to foster the development of academic literacy in their second language of English (Olsen, 2014). A longitudinal study in the Los Angeles Unified School District found that children who entered kindergarten with high levels of both first or home language proficiency and English proficiency were more likely to be reclassified as proficient in English than children who had low levels of both home language and English proficiency (Thompson, 2015).

In the new primary school, teachers will have a better sense of what can be expected of the students from year to year, and how they can organize educational experiences with appropriate scaffolding and sequencing. As one desired outcome of a new primary school, teaching itself may become a more coherent process (Cohen, 2011), not to mention children's learning.

The biggest challenge in implementing genuine pre-K–3rd alignment of curriculum and instruction is the piecemeal approach, which is rooted in the structure of education, how educators are prepared, and their working conditions, which typically do not provide time for professional reflections on practice with their fellow teachers. Most energy has focused on the pre-K–kindergarten nexus. That is a necessary beginning, but what happens throughout the pre-K *and* the rest of the primary grades has not been widely tackled. A national survey of states on birth–3rd-grade policies to support strong readers found that the connection of pre-K and kindergarten to Grades 1–3 is acknowledged to be in its infancy (Bornfreund et al., 2015).

The single most important reason for this partial alignment of curriculum and instruction is the limited numbers of principals, supported ideally by district supervisors, who can initiate and lead teams of teachers in these grades to work on creating and implementing a seamless continuum of learning experiences for children (Sullivan-Dudzic et al., 2010). To be fair to the current workforce, principals have 24/7 jobs, and they are not prepared in their training programs to be instructional leaders, although this may be changing (NAESP, 2014). At the same time, teachers are not prepared to work as teams and cannot do so without appropriate managerial leadership at the school site and the time to do so. So both structural and cultural changes are involved and need to be thoughtfully implemented over time.

Some states like California have established pre-K–3rd offices within the state education agency. Similar offices at the district level to support pre-K–3rd approaches are desirable. At the school level, especially those that are serving large numbers of children, directors of early learning with responsibilities for pre-K–3rd should be considered (Maeroff, 2006). At the South Shore School in Seattle, Washington, an assistant principal for the pre-K–3rd grades with experience in early learning works alongside the principal to show this school's longtime commitment to integrating pre-K classes into the larger primary school (Nyhan, 2011). This approach is being scaled up in Seattle's new expansion of pre-K programs, funded by a special levy approved by the voters in November 2014.

Professional development institutes for principals and their supervisors at the district level are beginning to address this lack of capacity in several states, as I will describe in Chapter 3. Much more attention must be focused on creating a pipeline of educators in transformed educator preparation programs to sustain pre-K–3rd efforts and, in the long term, to build new well-functioning systems of education. The only sure way to build such systems is to ensure that they are led by large numbers of educators who share different ways of thinking about primary education from those we have now. And that journey begins in our educator preparation programs.

THE CULTURE OF THE NEW PRIMARY SCHOOL

The structural elements of the new primary school must be in place, but how well these elements work together depends on the cultural values of the school. These values, in turn, reflect the school's identification of and shared understanding of the purposes of education, that is, what kinds of students and outcomes schools are seeking to develop.

Three cultural values of the primary school are essential, recognizable, and most often found in the classrooms of the school. They are at the heart of the new primary school enterprise:

- Continuous learning is prized and practiced by educators (see Chapter 3), students, and their families (see Chapter 4). Students are not the sole learners in schools. There is a culture of shared, joint learning by students, families, and all adults in the school.
- Learning involves active engagement by students, by which they are constructing knowledge, individually and together with other students and adults. The norm is not the orderly, silent classroom, but the classroom that hums with purposeful activity and quiet conversations.
- Respect for human diversity—recognizing common humanity—is exemplified by educators, families, and students. Becoming bi- and multilingual is viewed as a strategy for developing individuals with dual-language capacities, affirming the home and cultural value of the primary language, and creating individuals with global perspectives and respect for other cultures and individuals.

Everyone Is Learning!

Learning in the new primary school is not only what students do. The unifying ethos is a commitment to lifelong learning, not only for children but also for educators and for families. Perhaps at no time in our history are the capacity and commitment of individuals to acquire knowledge and skills over their lifetimes so crucial for their survival and well-being. In the education reform literature, we see references to "professional learning communities," or PLCs, as well as "continuous improvement" for teachers (Ritchie & Gutmann, 2013). But the commitment to learning by children, teachers, and families goes much deeper than these terms would imply.

Our current thinking about education reform tends to be child-centric, but slowly shifting, to recognize the needs, development, and support required by key adults such as teachers and families in fostering educational success of children (Schulman, 2000). These shifts are promising for children, who cannot succeed on their own. Children require caring families and caring teachers, who themselves require the support we now mainly give to children. Focusing on adult development and supporting the exceedingly demanding work of being a parent and a teacher is an integral part of the culture of the new primary school, which I focus on in the next two chapters.

Active Engagement in Learning

One deep divide between early education and kindergarten–5, often cited by teachers, is whether children's learning is based on play and their own activity, guided by a sensitive teacher, or whether it is largely structured and directed by the teacher. In practice, this divide has shifted over time, with kindergarten becoming more like the upper primary grades (Bassok & Rorem, 2014). At the same time, forms of activity-based learning find expression in Grades 1–5 in project-based learning and in the use of thematic units that seek to connect the separate subject matter under a theme such as modes of transportation and communications, or focusing on environmental issues. These forms of organizing learning are based on similar ideals of early educators who value free play and following the child's interests. Indeed, there is acknowledgment that across the pre-K–5th-grade span, a balance of child- and teacher-initiated activities is desirable.

What is most important is how teachers organize classrooms and learning experiences for children that value and facilitate the active engagement of children in learning from each other, from engaging in solving real-life problems with others. Thus, a distinguishing characteristic of the classrooms is a high level of intentional activity among the children, working with others and individually, with the teacher as guide. Children are talking with one another, involved in problem solving and other forms of inquiry. The classroom where there is the typical premium on quiet or little noise, reflecting effective classroom management, should change to a classroom where there is a level of quiet, respectful conversation among students and with their teachers.

Dual-Language Learning for All

In designing a new primary school, educators should seriously consider dual-language learning for all children, starting with pre-K and extending into the other primary grades. This is not as radical an idea as it may seem at first glance.

More individuals throughout the world are multilingual than are monolingual. Furthermore, there are more speakers of English who are multilingual than there are those who speak only English. The appeal of children learning what are called world or global languages from the beginning of their school-based education is evident in the marketing strategies of private schools, including those that are established explicitly to prepare children for a global world. In some districts, dual-immersion language programs starting from pre-K are seen as a way of attracting and retaining middle-class and affluent families in changing neighborhoods in the public schools (e.g., District of Columbia; Fairfax County, Virginia; and Montgomery County, Maryland; all of which experienced increases in numbers of children in immigrant families) and in areas undergoing gentrification (e.g., District of Columbia and Harlem, New York).

There is a growing trend among a certain segment of educated, striving families to value multilingualism as a desirable asset for their children's future. In a few states, such as Utah, dual-language immersion from the beginning of public education is part of state law, because political leaders view biliteracy as providing an economic advantage to students of their state in a globalized economy. Indeed, 12 states and two cities (Miami, District of Columbia) award the Seal of Biliteracy at high school graduation to recognize the bi- or multilingual competence of high school graduates. The seal is seen as a way of recognizing the home or first language competencies of students who learn English in the schools, and connecting that recognition with the separate world of foreign languages. Small steps to connect foreign language learning with bilingual education for low-income children whose first language is not English are promising.

Aside from the potential economic advantages of bilingualism (speaking) and biliteracy (reading and writing) in two languages or more, learning multiple languages can have important social and cultural consequences.

These include development of empathy and tolerance through learning about other cultures, and ways of perceiving and understanding the world as the basis for relating to and working with individuals who are different in racial, ethnic, and language origins. There is growing evidence that bilingualism is related to cognitive flexibility or executive functioning and also to the delay of dementia and Alzheimer's in late adulthood, but these latter benefits have not been firmly verified.

CLASSROOM INSTRUCTION: THE HEART OF THE MATTER

What and how children are taught in their classrooms is at the heart of the new primary school. But how do we know that the structures in place, the cultural values that are conveyed, really contribute to sound instruction leading to deep student learning? This question is not easily answered, but such a classroom exemplifies the following key dimensions:

- A learning environment that supports student planning, choice, and reflection on what and how students have learned
- Teachers who serve as resources for students as students engage in classroom activities
- Opportunities for students to work together in pairs and in small groups
- Parents who are systematically prepared for supporting roles in the classrooms and at home

Whenever viewed in this way, the classrooms of the primary school can no longer be seen as having the imprint of early education *or* K–12 education. Rather, what the classroom represents is a setting in which the learning sciences constitute the guiding principles of pre-K–5 grades. Goldman and Pellegrino's (2015) "first overarching design principle is that learning environments should promote agency and self-regulated learning" (p. 36).

The principles used for the design of instruction begin in pre-K, then continue into kindergarten and all grades to postsecondary education and continuing education (Goldman & Pellegrino, 2015). These principles are based on research from the learning sciences on the cognitive, motivational, and sociocultural dimensions in different content or subject areas. Thus viewed, the divide between early education and K–12 and beyond, articulated by educators on each side, recedes and can be replaced by a unifying vision of instruction. (See Resource 2.2.)

RESOURCE 2.2. GROWING THE ORIGINAL PRE-K–3RD APPROACH: MIDWEST EXPANSION CHILD-PARENT CENTERS

The Child-Parent Center (CPC) is the original education reform model for publicly funded pre-K–3rd approaches in the United States. Four CPCs were established in 1967 in the Chicago public schools serving low-income students, mainly African American and a small number of Hispanic students. With the leadership of Assistant Superintendent Lorraine Sullivan (1917–2013), the pre-K grades of the CPCs were the first in the nation to be funded by Title I of the Elementary and Secondary Education Act (ESEA) of 1965.

The longitudinal studies of the Chicago CPCs are unique in documenting the long-term benefits of a pre-K plus K–3 intervention experience into adulthood (Reynolds & Robertson, 2003; Reynolds, Temple, Robertson, & Mann, 2001). Starting in 1985, the Chicago Longitudinal Study followed a cohort of about 1,500 children born in 1980 and living in high-poverty neighborhoods who participated in the CPCs. Participation beginning with pre-K closed achievement gaps in school readiness and educational performance, and reduced rates of child maltreatment and special education placement.

Findings also showed that the CPC children were more likely to graduate from high school and were less likely to be involved in criminal activity. During young adulthood, they have better health outcomes, including higher levels of health insurance coverage based on employment and lower rates of substance abuse. Cost-benefit analyses indicate that for every dollar invested from pre-K–3rd grade, there is a return of $8.

In 2012, the U.S. Department of Education's Investing in Innovation (I3) funds were awarded to support the expansion of the CPCs in three additional districts, including suburban Evanston and Normal, Illinois, and St. Paul, Minnesota. Stanford Research Institute (SRI) is evaluating the implementation of the CPC pre-K–3rd approach as well as charting children's progress from pre-K through 3rd grade in these sites. The four school districts involving 24 schools serving children living in poverty now constitute the Midwest Child-Parent Center (CPC) Education Program. The program model was adapted to address the needs of more diverse children and low-income families living in suburban, rural, and urban communities at a different time from when the CPCs were established in 1967.

CPCs today are characterized by six core program elements aimed at strengthening the continuity of learning experiences for participating children:

- The curriculum aims for mastery in multiple domains, including language and literacy, math, science, and socioemotional development, using a balance of teacher-directed and child-initiated activities. All teachers have bachelor's degrees and are certified in early education.
- Within a balanced literacy approach, curriculum and instructional practices are aligned and sequenced based on research on children's development in those domains starting with pre-K at age 3, followed by every grade until Grade 3.
- A head teacher and two family coordinators direct the CPCs. The parent-resource teacher leads the family-support activities, and the paraprofessional school community representative conducts home visits and outreach to families involving health and nutritional services.
- A collaborative leadership team, including the principal of the elementary school and head teacher of the pre-K program, facilitates continuity of children's learning experiences from pre-K until grade 3, through curriculum alignment and parent engagement.
- Pre-K to K–3 continuity and stability are facilitated by colocation in or close proximity to the primary school.
- Professional development includes online resources and follow-up to support classroom instruction, working with parents, coaching of teachers, and site mentors.

Preliminary findings from the SRI study indicate that compared with matched children attending Head Start or state pre-K programs, CPC children are scoring higher on school readiness, literacy, and math skills and social-emotional development at the end of pre-K. Parent engagement was also higher in the CPC schools (Reynolds et al., 2015). Evaluators are following the children who entered pre-K in 2012 into kindergarten through 3rd grade. When the longitudinal evaluation of the Midwest CPC Education Program is completed, the findings will address whether they replicate those of the Chicago CPCs in the 1980s, as well as variations among sites and the impact of the CPCs on children who differ in race/ethnicity, dual-language status, and school experiences. The evaluation will also address challenges to scaling up this model with high levels of fidelity in multiple sites and sustainability (Reynolds et al., 2016).

For more information on the Midwest Child-Parent Center (CPC) Education Program, contact Arthur Reynolds (ajr@umn.edu).

PROSPECTS FOR NEW PRIMARY SCHOOLS

Our prospects for increasing new primary schools are encouraging, but daunting. These schools are at the leading edge of what are likely to be more widespread changes in the structure and in the culture of public education by starting early and drawing from a substantial knowledge base in the developmental (Allen & Kelly, 2015) and the learning sciences (Goldman & Pellegrino, 2015). For reasons described in this chapter, these schools remain highly dependent on visionary leaders at the local level. When those heroic leaders move on, and on average they often do, these schools may not be sustained. Schools and districts can revert to what existed before if thoughtful succession planning is not instituted prior to changes in superintendents.

Our dependence on individual educational leaders to create new primary schools is a major barrier to systemic change. Being able to imagine, develop, and sustain schools must be baked into the professional preparation of educators who are supported by enabling policy levers in their schools. One strategy to diminish the dependence on a few individuals, although not the sole one, is to change how teachers, principals, and superintendents are prepared for their positions in the future. This strategy, focused on the supply side of education reform, should be pursued more strongly than it now is. Meanwhile, estimates are that states and districts spend between $4 and $18 billion a year for professional development of the existing workforce. And there are serious concerns about the effectiveness of these programs in supporting teachers to better educate students (The New Teacher Project [TNTP], 2015). These challenges in developing the human capital for primary schools are addressed in the next chapter.

CHAPTER 3

WHO ARE THE EDUCATORS FOR THE NEW PRIMARY SCHOOL?

> What makes a good teacher? Ideally, teachers design environments
> where students can construct understanding in social, active, personally
> meaningful ways. Teachers can help students build on the knowledge,
> values, customs, and language they bring to school from home and
> community. Intellectuals themselves, exemplary teachers create just,
> trusting, caring, ethical, collaborative, democratic, interactive classroom
> environments. Exemplary teachers model self-efficacy, intellectual and
> critical agency, problem-solving, compassion, courage, flexibility, grit,
> persistence, resilience, and all the other traits we hope to cultivate in our
> children.
>
> —Inda Schaenen, *Speaking of Fourth Grade:*
> *What Listening to Kids Tells Us About School in America*

The new primary school will require a different breed of educator, one who spans the galaxies of pre-K and primary education and integrates them into one continuous whole. Teachers, to be sure, are at the core of this enterprise, but principals and superintendents and central office administrators provide the leadership and necessary instructional infrastructure that are critical to support teachers working as a team.

In the powerful quote that opens this chapter, Schaenen misses one crucial characteristic of teachers' work conditions: Often laboring alone in their classrooms, teachers must be able to join with other educators on a daily basis to establish collaborative teams of teachers and school staff focused on the development of well-educated students. Heroic, individual teachers by themselves cannot produce high levels of learning from pre-K to Grade 5.

For there to be an effective primary school, all educators in the school must share a sense of common purpose and an understanding of children's learning and development combined with content knowledge. All must be committed to reflecting on and continuously improving their practice as part of a collegial team. While this description seems straightforward, in practice, creating such schools under current policies and conditions is formidable (Goldman & Pellegrino, 2015; McGhee-Hassrick et al., in press).

As I have earlier pointed out, the fractured governance and weak instructional infrastructure endemic to American education are powerful forces working against such schools. Creating these schools will be arduous (Cohen, 2011; Klein, 2014), and success is thus far limited to a small number that are beating the heavily stacked odds.

This chapter has the audacity to describe what it will take to prepare and support educators for a new primary school that combines the best in early education and primary education. Both forms of education are now separate enterprises with distinct programs of teacher preparation—with some notable exceptions (Allen & Kelly, 2015; National Council for the Accreditation of Teacher Education, 2010).

Currently, there is no agreed-upon core set of competencies for early education and for elementary or primary education. Teacher preparation programs are "doing their own thing," following only the credentialing and licensing requirements of their states. This fact contributes to the incoherence of an educational system in which teachers do not share common experiences of preparation that can be the bases for reflection on practice and improvement with fellow teachers.

This chapter is being written during a time of heightened attention to how educators should be recruited, prepared, supported, and evaluated (Cohen, 2011; Goldstein, 2014; Green, 2014; Klein, 2014), so that many more children will experience the primary education proposed in this book. We know enough about how children learn to design thoughtful systems and processes for preparing primary teachers (Allen & Kelly, 2015; National Council for the Accreditation of Teacher Education, 2010). However, too few teacher education programs are making use of this established knowledge base.

The reasons are many and varied, including the following:

- The scarcity of teacher educators who are knowledgeable about developmental processes and pedagogical content knowledge (Goldman & Pellegrino, 2015), and can prepare new teachers with this combined knowledge and related competencies
- The relative costs of providing teacher education that is more intensively focused on teachers as developing adults, such as teacher residency programs and clinically oriented programs that can include apprenticeships and longer induction processes, especially after new teachers graduate from these programs

- The lower status and recognition accorded clinical faculty, especially in research colleges of education
- The financial incentives for training programs to certify too many teachers on the cheap, giving them limited experience in classrooms

Educator preparation on the cheap is, in fact, expensive. The Alliance for Excellent Education (2005) estimates that the annual cost of turnover of educators for grades K–12 ranges from $4 to $7 billion, including lost state and federal investments in teacher preparation and professional development. According to the National Commission for Teaching and America's Future, the average national cost of replacing a teacher in 2014 dollars is $9,540 for urban schools and $4,090 for rural schools (2007). The rate of turnover in schools—whether of teachers, principals, or superintendents—is especially high in schools that serve children living in poverty.

But it is not only the financial costs to the district. Unfortunately it also means starting over again with new leadership seeking to forge new directions, and often new teachers in classrooms starting once again to be part of professional development efforts on curriculum, instruction, and assessment approaches adopted by a school or district. And the churning in our education systems is unsupportive of growing the professional capital needed for children's learning.

Currently, early educators (birth to 5) and primary teachers (kindergarten to Grades 5 or 6) are trained, for the most part, in some 1,000 colleges or schools of education, governed by 50 different state requirements for educator preparation, licensure, and certification (Whitebrook, 2014). Preparation of early educators also occurs outside schools of education in community colleges, colleges of human development, and psychology departments. As with K–12 education, we are likely to see new teacher preparation programs outside the traditional schools of education as charter school networks establish their own teacher preparation programs to staff their schools.

A longstanding lack of articulation between 2-year community colleges, where early educators start their preparation, and 4-year colleges makes it difficult to transfer applicable course credits toward a bachelor's degree, making it more costly for students who start off in community colleges, as do many who do not have the financial resources to attend more costly forms of higher education. Alternative teacher preparation programs such as Teach for America, The New Teacher Project (TNTP), and teacher residency programs are emerging and may become more dominant in preparing teachers. However, they now prepare very few teachers compared with the colleges of education.

For educators already in teaching in schools and districts, professional development becomes essential to creating new primary schools. An enormous body of literature on professional development exists, and research and evaluation studies all point to a discouraging fact: Effectiveness is uneven (TNTP, 2015). Too often, professional development is used as remediation for poor teacher preparation and lack of collegial support when teachers are isolated in their classrooms. Teacher turnover, including in the early education programs, requires professional development to start anew each school year. And the alignment between what professional development seeks to change in teacher behavior and the work conditions and policies that prevail in the schools is often weak.

None of these observations are original. Many have made similar observations about the status of teacher education and continuing professional development (Hargreaves & Fullan, 2012; Klein, 2014). But what is unique in this chapter is its taking up the daunting task of integrating K–12 teacher preparation with the preparation of early educators, the latter self-described as being even more in a crisis than K–12 and seeking to establish an identity apart from elementary and secondary education (Goffin, 2013). This aspect of teacher preparation must be addressed to prepare a teaching force for the new primary school.

OUR PREDICAMENT

Almost all the staff members in early learning programs are women. In primary schools, 89.3% of the teachers are female and 81.2% are white (Goldring, Gray, & Bitterman, 2013), even as the students become more ethnically diverse across America. The staff of early education programs is more diverse; about one-third are individuals of color (Park, McHugh, Batalova, & Zong, 2015). When compared with teachers in the K–12 grades, their level of education is mixed, based on different state requirements, ranging from high school graduation to post-bachelor's degrees. Generally, the younger the students, the more feminized the teaching ranks and, accordingly, the lower professional status accorded the teacher—regardless of education and credentials. While almost 90% of primary school teachers are women, 72.6% of middle school teachers and 58.3% of high school teachers are women (Goldring et al., 2013).

Teachers of young children below kindergarten are the only group for whom attainment of a bachelor's degree is not related to increases in compensation (Bassok, Fitzpatrick, Loeb, & Paglayan, 2013). For example, on average in school-based programs, pre-K teachers with a bachelor's degree earn 80% of what kindergarten teachers do (Whitebrook, Phillips, & Howes, 2014). When this is seen in the context of relatively low salaries for K–12 teachers in general, given their educational attainment and the demands and responsibilities of their work, teachers of young children (like pediatricians in the medical hierarchy) are at the bottom of the pay schedule.

In early education, a debate continues about whether those who staff programs for children from birth to age 5 should be required to have a bachelor's degree (Allen & Kelly, 2015). Research in early education continues to focus on this issue, aiming to determine whether programs with teachers holding bachelor's degrees have better child outcomes. That this requirement is still debated is revealing. Suffice it to say, if there is to be any progress to achieve equal compensation for pre-K teachers with that of K–12 teachers, a bachelor's degree with appropriate credentials will be required, research evidence notwithstanding. And this is essentially the conclusion of a consensus committee of the national Institute of Medicine (now National Academy of Medicine) report on the educator workforce for children from birth to 8 (Allen & Kelly, 2015).

In the case of Head Start, the attainment of bachelor's degrees, required in the last reauthorization of Head Start, has led to only minor increases in teacher compensation in these programs. The reasons include the lack of allocated funds to reward increased education of the workforce and the fact that the number of children served by Head Start would decline if the current level of funds were used to reward teachers' increased level of education. Meanwhile, Head Start teachers working in public school systems with bachelor's degrees and certification can receive compensation and benefit packages similar to those of teachers in other grades.

In brief, the teaching staff of the primary school is overwhelmingly feminized and accorded lower status than that of their peers in middle and high schools. And teachers in pre-K grades typically earn lower salaries even when they have education credentials similar to those of K–12 teachers. These are not attractive features to individuals who are concerned with professional status and earnings, not to mention basic needs for housing in high-cost-of-living areas. These facts point to a greater challenge for preparing educators for a new primary school than for the middle and high schools.

Addressing the preparation of educators for the new primary school is to step into a minefield. First, teachers in the primary grades tend to see early educators, and even kindergarten teachers at times, as babysitters who supervise the play of young children and are not seriously involved in teaching content knowledge (Fromberg, 2003). Early educators see primary school teachers as focusing on subject matter or content and on tests that are used as indicators of their effectiveness, and ignoring the "whole child," especially the social and emotional development of students.

In actual practice, this divide is not always as rigid as each side tends to characterize it. Primary teachers can be mindful of the life experiences children bring to their classrooms (Schaenen, 2014), especially when supported by knowledgeable principals, and early educators are not always as concerned with the social and emotional well-being of their students as they claim to be. Findings based on CLASS, a widely used classroom observation instrument in early education and primary grades, indicate a wide range of scores on the CLASS emotional support scale in classrooms (Burchinal, Vandergrift, Pianta, & Mashburn, 2010).

The second issue is that researchers and teacher educators, both within the traditional schools of education and in alternative programs, continue to struggle with how to prepare individuals to teach students well, not only for test performance but also for them to be productive workers and engaged members of their communities (Green, 2014). The best means of preparing teachers—not only to teach reading and mathematics, but also to cultivate creativity, critical thinking, and teamwork skills—remains contested territory

Most significant, as Green (2014) asserts, can all who wish to teach be prepared to be effective teachers? It is worth noting that in other countries with high international achievement—Finland, South Korea, Singapore—candidates for the teaching profession are selected by competitive national tests, and many who wish to be teachers are not able to enter training programs.

The preparation of educators is a reflection of how the American education system is now organized. Each level, including higher education, has its own requirements for its teaching force. Higher education itself is acknowledged not to have systematic processes for preparing scholars steeped in their disciplines with the pedagogical strategies to impart that knowledge to their students (Zimmerman, 2014). The many efforts to reform teacher preparation are based on the current, bifurcated K–12 system (Greenberg, Walsh, & McKee, 2015; Mehta, 2013; Tucker, 2011). Efforts to reform the preparation of early educators, birth to 5, remain separate from those addressed to the K–12 grades.

Part of the strategy to create a new primary school is to change teacher preparation in both early and primary education and to rethink age and grade spans for teacher certification. For the new primary school, the ideal grade span would be pre-K–Grade 3 (Bornfreund et al., 2014), with separate certification for Grades 4 and 5. Teachers prepared for these grade spans are more likely to know what children are like through this grade span, as well as what children are expected to learn before and after the specific grade in which they are teaching. Such preparation could contribute to greater continuity in children's learning from one grade to the next.

As one example, the French teacher education system prepares teachers in two 3-year primary grade spans. The pre-primary education provided by the *écoles maternelles* spans ages 3 to 5; the primary grades span ages 6 to 8. French teachers are prepared to teach children across these two age spans in an educational system—one that is admittedly more centralized than in the United States— that has greater coherence than that in the United States and that is highly selective of teacher preparation candidates through a nationally competitive examination.

A compromise can be certification from birth to 5/kindergarten, pre-K–3, and Grades 3–8. Many states have pre-K–3rd certifications in place. However, they coexist with pre-K, pre-K–2, K–3, and other grade span certifications, which have been added over the years. In general, principals and superintendents favor the broadest grade spans for certification, which allow them to assign teachers to the widest possible grade levels. As one telling example, a pre-K–3rd certification, which was put into place in Texas during the early expansion of its pre-K program in the 1980s, was overturned, with superintendents leading the change, but is now being revived. Principals, however, still favor wide grade spans to preserve flexibility in assigning teachers to grades. Such practices may not be beneficial to children's learning.

Early childhood education is striving for greater professional legitimacy even as it suffers from an identity crisis (Goffin, 2013). For the most part, its leaders do not see their field as part of primary education and instead focus on birth to age 5. Its leadership seeks to develop a unified teacher education preparation system based on what it sees as a fragmented landscape of programs for children from birth to age 5 that have different purposes, funding streams, regulations, and requirements for staffing (Allen & Kelley, 2015).

Unfortunately, the early education field does not directly address the increasing role of public education in providing early learning programs, and the implications of such a change for increasing the professional status and compensation of those who educate our youngest children. This blind spot must be recognized and addressed.

At the same time, those concerned about K–12 teacher education pay no attention to pre-K or early educators (e.g., Goldstein, 2014; Green, 2014). In most states, early educators teaching pre-K in public schools are required to have a bachelor's degree and state certification in early education and can be compensated like K–12 teachers. There is typically an earnings gap between those in publicly funded programs and those in the private nonprofit and for-profit early learning programs that receive state funds (Whitebrook et al., 2014). In New York City's universal pre-K program, as one example, teachers in the same programs in non–public school settings are compensated differently from those in public schools, depending on whether the classroom in which they are working is a designated New York City pre-K program and whether they have an appropriate teaching credential. The inefficiencies and associated costs of such diverse practices, not to mention the understandable tensions between teachers, have not been calculated, but they are likely to be considerable.

It is unlikely that in the foreseeable future, the United States will evolve toward "one best system" in teacher education. The fraying of Common Core State Standards (CCSS) consensus is yet another example in a long line of efforts to create a common set of standards, curriculum, and assessments around which the preparation of educators can take place.

At this time, the preparation of teachers to meet the requirements of the CCSS, both pre- and inservice, is insufficient to enable teachers to provide the educational experiences and instruction necessary for students to meet these higher aspirational standards. And the Obama administration's proposals for teacher preparation and accountability clearly assign the responsibility to the 50 states. As a result, there will be no common teacher preparation to implement the CCSS, which itself is a voluntary initiative.

If I have accurately characterized our predicament in preparing educators for a new primary school, how do we address it? Can some order be created out of considerable chaos? How do we connect and integrate the best of early education and primary education into a more coherent whole that enables teachers to be more effective, and children to learn more deeply than they now do? And how do we begin to do this when the two sectors, or galaxies, continue to be worlds apart (Whitebrook, 2014; Wing, personal communication, September 2009)?

The best description of our current predicament is stalemate. The leadership needed to span the two galaxies of early education and K–12 education has not yet emerged with sufficient strength. What I will argue in the next section is that there is more light ahead than what we now can see. Existing, but neglected, ideas, combined with the current interest in how to "build better teachers" (Green, 2014; Klein, 2014), provide some potentially productive solutions that should be debated and tested as we redesign how we prepare teachers for new primary schools that span pre-K through Grade 5.

TOWARD CONVERGENCE: MORE LIGHT THAN WE SEE?

The timing is right to bring together the best in early education and in primary education to prepare educators for the new primary school. The focus on addressing the preparation of educators (Goldstein, 2014; Green, 2014; Klein, 2014), combined with the basic research, especially from the cognitive sciences, on how young children learn, including in content areas like reading and mathematics, provides an opening to redesign educator preparation for the new primary school and to improve its effectiveness. Recent syntheses of research on learning and instruction—focused on K–12 education—are remarkably consistent with long`standing values in early education in their understanding of the child as learner and how instruction is aligned with what is taught, how it is taught, and how it is assessed (Goldman & Pellegrino, 2015).

This convergence is heralded by core ideas that are part of the traditional canon in early childhood education and that are gaining ascendancy in analyses of teacher preparation for primary and secondary schools (Green, 2014). The central tenet of early childhood education is to know—and care deeply—about the social, emotional, cognitive, and physical capacities of the young child. Early education is fundamentally child centered: focused on the idea that the child should lead and be a full participant in his or her own education (Allen & Kelly, 2015). This mindset among early educators is entirely consistent with research that shows that from infancy, the child is an active participant in her own learning. Thus, teachers must know each child's developmental path and progress based on in-depth, sensitive observations of the child (Cohen et al., 2016) and adapt their instruction to "where the child is" and should be going.

On the face of it, this tenet is straightforward. But it is extremely intellectually and emotionally demanding to prepare teachers to become astute observers of children, to prepare teachers who can make accurate observations across settings, including in the home, and adapt their instructional strategies accordingly. Just as not all of us can become surgeons, not all may become teachers who are skilled practitioners of their profession.

In allied professions such as health, social work, and clinical psychology, entrants have many more years of education and supervised practice, take licensing examinations, and are required to participate in continuing education programs as a condition for keeping their license current. There are no comparable experiences required of teachers to maintain their licenses and credentials, even though as David Cohen (2011) has argued, teaching, like these helping professions, is also aimed at the complex task of human improvement. Emerging programs of teacher preparation, such as the Harvard Teaching Fellows (described later in this section), provide untested, promising examples of teacher preparation as a long-term effort in the personal and professional development of teachers before they become full-time teachers—and during their early years as new teachers.

Often overlooked is the requirement that the teacher have a level of self-understanding and awareness that enables her or him to understand where each child is developmentally, and to devise appropriate activities aimed at fostering both cognitive and emotional learning. The characterization of teaching as a technical act does not consider these profoundly complex human processes and engagement between adult teachers and child students in real time (Hargreaves & Fullan, 2012).

Teachers of young children have highly complex, demanding jobs, physically, mentally, and emotionally, which challenge the notion that anyone can be prepared to teach young children. We certainly do not make this assumption when we train doctors, airplane pilots, and members of other selective professions where lives are at stake!

But what is referred to as "child development knowledge" and a respectful relationship with the student—while a necessary foundation for learning—is not sufficient for learning subject matter or what Lee Schulman (2000) called "pedagogical knowledge of content." This requires the teacher to have deep knowledge about the history and structure of the content area as well as an understanding of how the discipline identifies key questions and goes about answering them (Zimmerman, 2014). Thus, to teach content well, the teacher him- or herself must engage in deep intellectual inquiry and analyses.

Advances in the cognitive sciences over the past decades now provide a firm foundation for the teaching of content knowledge (Allen & Kelly, 2015; Horowitz et al., 2005). The teacher's task is to align the structure of knowledge in a discipline with how children learn that knowledge, and to adapt his or her instruction to where a child is at the moment.

The central tenet of primary education is to know pedagogical content or subject matter such as reading, mathematics, science, art, and social studies, often referred to as content knowledge. Traditionally, there has been less emphasis on the social and emotional characteristics of learners. Primary school teachers are generalists. They are required to have knowledge of many subjects, in contrast to teachers in middle and high schools, who tend to specialize in one subject. And the work of the primary school teacher can be even more critical in establishing the foundations of knowledge for children as well as nurturing their motivation to learn. Thus, all teachers in the new primary school will be required to have both knowledge of how children develop and learn (Allen & Kelly, 2015) and content knowledge to be effective pedagogues. And they have the awesome responsibility to build on the natural curiosity and eagerness to learn characteristic of young children.

These characterizations of the early educator and primary teacher are not as stark in actual practice, but they do serve as a dividing line that has been drawn by and now exists between the two groups. The educator preparation system for the new primary school, therefore, must closely link knowledge of the student and how he or she learns over time, knowledge of the content to be taught, and how to teach content, combined with the teacher's self-knowledge and capacity to reflect on practice and to improve instruction. The intellectual, cognitive, and emotional demands on the individual teacher at every stage of preparation are considerable. Thus, social support of the developing teacher is a requirement of our teacher preparation programs.

Such a foundation will require a different breed of teacher educators and different models of financing teacher preparation, including changes in higher education and its expectations for the revenue generated by current teacher education programs. And it raises the question of who should be recruited and selected to prepare to be a teacher, and what criteria should be used to certify or license a teacher. By definition, the preparation of teachers would be a longer and more intensive process of induction than currently exists.

Forms of this preparation for teaching occur in places like Bank Street College of Education (New York), the Erikson Institute (Chicago), and specialized teacher education programs at the University of California–Berkeley (National Council for the Accreditation of Teacher Education, 2010). However, they are not implemented at any scale at this time. They are labor intensive in terms of time and effort on the part of teacher educators, more costly to the teachers in training, and therefore, more expensive than producing large cohorts of teachers with a few weeks or months of practice teaching, as is the common practice.

Schools or colleges of education have been referred to as cash cows for higher education. That revenue stream would have to change, and teacher education would have to be seen to be as worthy an investment as that of health professional training and preparation. Public subsidies for teacher education, such as exist in the health professions, and loan forgiveness programs, such as exist in legal education for public interest law, should be enhanced to include preparation of teachers for children from birth to age 5. The reauthorization of the Higher Education Act does address the needs of teachers of young children through loan-forgiveness programs. But given the number of teachers required and in training at any one time, public subsidies for those in training, which are discretionary items in the federal budget, are not likely to be sufficient anytime soon.

We must start now and build for the future. The declines in individuals entering teacher preparation programs and the resulting shortage in prepared teachers in some states (Aragon, 2016) should be a sufficient wake-up call that teacher preparation is an issue that can no longer be overlooked.

The Harvard Teaching Fellows program at Harvard University, which prepares middle and high school teachers, provides a case in point. The design of this new teacher preparation program is based on analyses of what other countries with high-ranking achievement scores do to recruit and select teachers. Assuming that Harvard undergraduates are at the top of the nation's higher education institutions, seniors will be selected and begin their coursework in the last year of college. They will continue their coursework during the summer after graduation, and start part-time teaching under close supervision for a full school year, starting in the fall after graduation. Finally, they will complete their requirements during the summer after their first year of supervised teaching, becoming full-time teachers in urban schools. They will receive continuing support and induction in their early years as teachers.

As described, this teacher education program for 50 students will be free of charge and supported by private donations. As it offers this experimental teacher education program, Harvard University's leadership, in trying a more selective, intensive, well-supervised first-year teaching experience followed by continuing professional support, will be closely watched in terms of teacher effectiveness. It will take a number of years before the results are in on whether this approach is one that should be adopted more widely. A similar investment in the preparation of teachers for the new primary school is highly desirable.

However, the financing of a relatively long teacher education experience at an elite private university producing only 50 teachers a year raises questions about how similar programs can be supported at other institutions, including the public institutions where the vast majority of new teachers are now prepared. There are 3.3 million teachers in the United States. Teach for America represents just 1% of these teachers, annually generating 6,000 teachers, most of whom leave the classroom after 2 or 3 years. If our health organizations were staffed in this way, dependent on churning or turnover in the workforce, we would be in deeper trouble than we are now in terms of health care delivery.

CAN ANYONE TEACH (OR WANT TO)?

George Bernard Shaw's patronizing and dismissive assertion, "Those who can, do. Those who cannot, teach," is well known. In contrast to Shaw's sentiment, countries like Finland, South Korea, and Singapore, which post top rankings on international assessments of education achievement, are highly selective when it comes to teacher training, drawing from the top third of their college graduating classes for their teacher education programs (Mourshed, Chijioke, & Barber, 2010). In the United States, teachers are more likely to come from the bottom two-thirds of their college graduating classes. Whether such competitive selection procedures matter for student learning is highly contentious in the American context.

Unlike these countries, there is no consensus in the United States regarding how teacher candidates should be selected. Some people believe that anyone can teach. Others believe in natural-born teachers. Still others believe that teaching is a skill that can be taught (Green, 2014). In the absence of consensus, it is unlikely that those who want to prepare for teaching will be denied that opportunity in the United States, even though they may decide never to enter the classroom, which many do.

The numbers of individuals entering teacher preparation programs is dropping significantly. According to the U.S. Department of Education (2014), national enrollments in university-based teacher preparation programs have fallen by 10% from 2004 to 2012. It is not clear why teaching appears to be a less attractive profession than in the past, but explanations include teacher evaluation and accountability regulations based on standardized tests, the work conditions and status of teachers, the rise of anti-teacher rhetoric, and strapped education budgets that led to layoffs during the Great Recession. It is noteworthy that in a preparation system that is not highly selective, and in a time of economic inequality, individuals are not opting to prepare to become teachers. What is clear is that teaching is no longer a route to a middle-class life, itself being more elusive as the United States moves deeper into the 21st century.

As explained earlier, effective teachers must have deep knowledge of children's development, deep knowledge of their content or subject matter, and the pedagogical capacity to teach based on that knowledge of the child and the content area. Whether anyone—regardless of aptitude and personality—can be well trained in these capacities is not yet known. This being said, we must at least try to produce more teachers with this knowledge and these skills and to learn how to do so more effectively.

In their book on transforming teaching, Andy Hargreaves and Michael Fullan (2012) describe the "professional capital" that should be at the core of teachers in the new primary school. In contrast to the "business capital view" of teaching, which assumes that teaching is simple and not intellectually demanding, the professional capital view assumes the following:

- Good teaching is technically sophisticated and difficult.

- Good teaching requires high levels of education and long periods of training.
- Good teaching is perfected through continuous improvement.
- Good teaching is a collective responsibility and accomplishment.
- Good teaching maximizes, mediates, and moderates online instruction. (p. 14)

We are far from achieving this ideal in our teacher preparation today, and achieving it in the new primary school will be difficult. Putting the recruiting and preparing of teachers aside—no easy enterprises themselves—school districts today do not have the structures in place to support continuous improvement, a sense of collective responsibility for student learning, genuine collaboration with peers, and purposeful instruction based on individual students' needs. The missing and critical factor is the absence of an instructional infrastructure that provides leadership and time for teachers to develop their professional capital (McGhee-Hassrick et al., in press).

In fact, a report from the OECD (2014) noted that teachers in Japan spend about 30% of their time and in South Korea about 40% of their time teaching students, using the rest of the time to reflect on instructional practices in exchanges with their peers and master teachers to improve their effectiveness. In contrast, American teachers spend 55–80% of their time in classrooms with students. Not all this time is involved in instruction. How teachers spend their time during the school day—especially whether they are engaged in collegial conversations about teaching—is an important work condition that is addressed in Chapter 5.

Compensation is also an issue. American teachers earn 68% of what the average college-educated worker earns, while in the OECD countries, teachers earn 88% as much. In the leading countries in education achievement, teachers earn as much as doctors and lawyers and have similar professional status.

How to provide the necessary conditions—time to plan and reflect, to work with colleagues to improve practice, and adequate compensation—for primary school teachers to develop and demonstrate their professional capital has not been systematically addressed in education policy efforts. Some schools, such as the University of Chicago charter schools (McGhee-Hassrick et al., in press), have extended the school day to provide time for teachers to prepare and reflect on instructional practices on a daily basis. In the Pittsburgh school district, contract hours have been negotiated to provide regular time for teachers to collaborate and improve their effectiveness. Increasing weekly professional development hours for teachers should be a priority in union negotiations so all teachers could have time to reflect on their practice, ideally with their principal and fellow teachers. (See Resource 3.1.)

RESOURCE 3.1. HOW PRE-K–3RD COLLABORATION IN RURAL MINNESOTA ACHIEVES ACADEMIC SUCCESS: KING ELEMENTARY SCHOOL

It's no secret. King Elementary School in Deer River, Minnesota, posts tremendous academic results for its 525 students and ranked third in 2013 for American Indian student performance among all elementary schools in the state. Educators at this north-central Minnesota school, which is next to the Leech Lake Reservation, have been laser focused and disciplined in helping students succeed. And now, focusing heavily on pre-K–3rd grades, King teachers are changing the odds for their youngest learners too.

King Elementary serves children and families living in concentrated rural poverty with incarceration and drug use as salient community concerns. In 2014, 40% of the children at King were American Indians. From 2008 to 2014, free or reduced-price lunch rates have jumped from 15% to 77%. Responding to student needs, the school's mental health services have quadrupled. During the same period, the percentage of Deer River's 4-year-olds on target in developing their language skills has risen from 38% to 72%.

Educators attribute much of the school's remarkable success to robust academic and behavioral interventions. Joining King in 2008, principal Amy Starzecki aimed to boost oral language skills among kindergarteners by starting these interventions even earlier and increasing results-oriented teacher collaboration across grade levels. Starzecki has emphasized how high-quality language instruction in pre-K sets students on the path to greater success in later years. She has been intentional about developing teacher leaders and community partnerships, all to ensure continuity beyond her tenure. Starzecki has since moved to another district.

The key elements of Deer River's pre-K–3rd approach include the following:

- Almost 100% of Deer River children attend formal pre-K programs, all of which collaborate around curriculum and instruction, ensuring that children come to kindergarten with similar skills and knowledge. Children's participation is financed by state scholarships, Race to the Top grants, Head Start, and Invest Early. To help children from various programs make a good transition, King Elementary hosts monthly events for all 3- and 4-year-olds, including those who do not attend pre-K in the school building. King also worked with the Minnesota Department of Education to create one single application form for parents to access different sources of funding for pre-K.

- Teachers have high expectations of all students and their capacity to achieve at high levels.
- Teachers communicate regularly about students' progress. Pre-K teachers meet monthly to review individual student data and adapt their instruction to the data. In Grades 1–3, teachers meet bimonthly solely to review student data. Data-driven instruction across the continuum from pre-K to Grade 5 uses Response to Intervention on a systematic, schoolwide basis.
- Teachers collaborate within and across grade levels to share accountability for student learning. King Elementary has all-staff and multigrade meetings annually, during which pre-K–5th grade teachers analyze schoolwide benchmark data and develop an individualized instructional plan for every child.
- Teachers develop their professional capital by receiving regular peer observations within and across grade levels, demonstrating their commitment to ongoing evaluation and improvement of their instruction. A commitment to developing professional capital is made real by the practice of students' leaving school one hour early every Wednesday so that teachers can participate in professional learning communities regularly, as part of their contract day.
- Families are involved in their children's learning on a regular basis through a backpack system—a homegrown intervention in which teachers send children home with instructional activities so that they can do additional work in areas where they require more practice. Parents report progress in a journal, which teachers track.

King Elementary School demonstrates that demography and geography are no limits to educational opportunity for children. Building professional capital combined with strategic partnerships with state and community programs can make a difference in ensuring that all children reach their potential.

Source: Adapted with permission from MinnCAN (2014). *Starting Strong: Pre-K Through 3rd Grade Success Stories from Across Minnesota*. Minneapolis, MN: MinnCAN: The Minnesota Campaign for Achievement Now.

PRINCIPALS FOR THE NEW PRIMARY SCHOOL

Principals are key to effective schools, and they are especially critical to creating schools that integrate pre-K with the primary grades (Mead, 2011; NAESP, 2014). Without principals' instructional and managerial leadership, pre-K classes, even those located in primary schools, will continue to be separated from the rest of the school enterprise (NAESP, 2014). But creating a strong instructional infrastructure for effective learning is not the principal's responsibility alone. She or he must assemble a team of colleagues who focus on working with and supporting families and who recognize the social, health, and economic needs of families and their children (McGhee-Hassrick et al., in press).

For decades, pre-K programs have operated in the basements of primary school buildings and, less often, in portable units on school playgrounds. The well-known Perry Preschool Project was located in the basement of Perry Elementary School in Ypsilanti, a racially segregated school in a small town next to the University of Michigan at Ann Arbor (Weikart, 2004).

Since already overstretched principals rarely have authority over the early learning programs, they do not feel responsible for them. But that is changing as more pre-K grades are located in public schools, as in New York City, and principals are becoming responsible for this grade and for the evaluation of pre-K teachers, as in the San Francisco Unified School District (Nyhan, 2015). These new responsibilities require principals to learn about pre-K programs and how to provide leadership in integrating pre-K teachers and staff with the rest of the primary school. When principals themselves have early education experience, that job is made easier. Most often that is not the case. Only one in five felt prepared to supervise pre-K programs and teachers (Superville, 2015).

Not only must principals adhere to requirements that currently evaluate pre-K teachers differently from other primary teachers; principals must also be knowledgeable about play- or activity-based learning and child-centered activities that are an essential part of pre-K education so that they can appropriately evaluate instructional activities when they see them. It bears repeating that understanding how activity-based learning and child-centered activities contribute to the learning of young children is not a natural or easy task. Since principals rarely have training in early learning, whether through their teacher or principal preparation, their new responsibilities require relevant professional development.

Recognizing the importance of principal leadership, a small but growing number of professional development efforts engage primary school principals in early learning efforts in the states of Delaware, Illinois,

Maryland, New Jersey, Pennsylvania, and Washington (Brown, Squires, Connors-Tadros, & Horowitz, 2014). Yet most states do not require early childhood content as part of principal preparation or professional development, even when principals are responsible for pre-K programs (Brown et al., 2014).

Illinois is the only state in which legislation (PA 96-0903) requires that principal preparation programs include early childhood content, as part of an effort to improve the instructional leadership of principals. This requirement is part of Illinois's licensure and accreditation process. The legislation is based on the recommendations of a state task force and informed by the principal education program at the Urban Education Leadership Program at the University of Illinois–Chicago. These initiatives were supported by the McCormick Foundation, which supports leadership in early education, including connecting early childhood programs and primary schools. More states can learn from the Illinois law and experiences thus far and can craft similar requirements in their states.

Since the 1990s, the National Association of Elementary School Principals (NAESP) has provided leadership to assist principals in forging strong connections between school- and community-based pre-K programs and primary schools (NAESP, 2014; see Figure 3.1). In its national task force report the NAESP Foundation (2011) stated,

> What elementary and middle level principals know from decades of experience and from their day-to-day work with children is that we need to re-think, re-orient and re-work our approach to early childhood education and now focus on the child's perspective and their many developmental needs.

In sum, principal leadership today requires creating a joint sense of purpose among all school staff, not only teaching staff, but also allied health professionals, social workers, and specialists. This means principals ensure that there is time for such collaboration to occur on a regular basis, toward the goal of building stable instructional and interprofessional teams that become stronger through the years. All adults, including families, must commit to sharing joint accountability for the educational outcomes of the students (McGhee-Hassrick et al., in press).

SUPERINTENDENTS AS ADVOCATES FOR THE NEW PRIMARY SCHOOL

Whether in Union City (NJ), Bremerton (WA), East Lansing (MI), San Francisco (CA), or Montgomery County (MD), the pivotal role of district superintendents in connecting pre-K classes and programs to the primary

Figure 3.1. Six Competencies and Strategies to Guide Principals in Leading Pre-K-3 Learning Communities

1. Embrace the Pre-K–3 Early Learning Continuum

- Engage your learning community in understanding the importance of the early learning continuum and the transitions along it.
- Set expectations that the continuum of learning from age 3 to grade 3 is fundamental to your school's mission.
- Expand the concept of "learning community" to include collaboration among external, as well as internal, stakeholders.
- Articulate the long-term value of early learning and the benefit of inclusive early learning to parents and all learning community stakeholders.
- Align funding, resources and governance to support the pre-K–3 framework.

2. Ensure Developmentally Appropriate Teaching

- Align ambitious standards, curriculum, instruction and assessments to create a consistent framework for learning from age 3 to grade 3.
- Provide a comprehensive curriculum inclusive of, but not limited to, language arts and math.
- Work with teachers and teacher leaders to develop an interactive and engaging early learning curriculum.
- Create professional communities of practice to empower teachers to learn from each other and to improve instruction.

3. Provide Personalized, Blended Learning Environments

- Promote environments that blend face-to-face and technology-enhanced learning and that are rigorous, are developmentally-appropriate and that support individual learning.
- Facilitate the use of technology tools for learning and provide instructional leadership in schools to use technology effectively.
- Support instructional use of appropriate technology and interactive media to support learning and development—through work and play—in school, at home and in community settings.
- Integrate technology directly into curriculum, student learning and outcomes.
- Help teachers develop their understanding and ability to use technology effectively to individualize and differentiate instruction for each student.

4. Use Multiple Measures to Guide Growth in Student Learning

- Build understanding throughout the learning community of the various purposes and appropriate uses of different student assessments to improve teaching and learning.

Figure 3.1. Six Competencies and Strategies to Guide Principals in Leading Pre-K–3 Learning Communities (continued)

- Support teachers in using multiple forms of assessments, along with observation, portfolios and anecdotal records, to guide student learning and growth all along the pre-K–3 continuum.
- Support open and collaborative discussions about assessment data with parents and community.
- Share information about program effectiveness among schools and other providers.

5. Build Professional Capacity Across the Learning Community

- Build principal professional knowledge about what is age- and developmentally-appropriate across the continuum.
- Support ongoing, job-embedded professional learning opportunities for teachers all along the continuum.
- Support professional learning communities that focus on authentic work.

6. Make Your School a Hub of Pre-K–3 Learning for Families and Communities

- Develop a welcoming environment and sense of belonging, and cultivate a shared responsibility for children's learning from age 3 to grade 3.
- Provide meaningful transitions between preschool and elementary school.
- Develop out-of-school and summer learning opportunities for children age 3 to grade 3.
- Blend and braid funding to maximize resource opportunities.

Source: Quoted with permission, NAESP, 2014.

grades has been well documented (Marietta, 2010a, 2010b; Marietta & Marietta, 2011; Nyhan, 2015; Ritchie & Gutmann, 2013). Building integrated pre-K–12 learning systems starts with them and their central office teams.

Superintendents' reaching out to early educators in and outside schools signals to school boards, teacher unions, families, and community organizations that early learning is an important part of the public education system, and that strong relationships benefit everyone. This effort by superintendents is especially important in smaller school districts, which constitute the vast majority of districts in the United States. But districts in which superintendents engage in such outreach remain the exception, not the rule.

Few programs are in place to prepare superintendents to take steps to work with community and early learning leaders to forge connections with early learning programs inside schools and in the community. However, more targeted professional development opportunities for superintendents and district administrators can contribute to stronger connections that strengthen achievement for children as they move from pre-K into the primary grades. District leaders play crucial roles in working with school boards and with teacher unions, both essential to district-level policies that forge stronger connections between early learning and the traditional K–12 grades.

Superintendents are important in articulating to boards and communities why such connections are important, and why transforming primary education will benefit both students and the districts. The first step is to recognize the educational potential of pre-K programs to support and enhance learning during the course of the K–12 grades. In districts where there are significant numbers of dual-language learners (DLLs), a pathway that begins early with pre-K and provides continuous dual-language learning in the primary grades can provide students with a firm grounding in English, while fostering bilingualism in English speakers. And in fundamental subjects such as reading and mathematics, teaching and learning based on developmental trajectories for learning these subjects will rest on a strong, continuous foundation.

WHAT ARE THE PROSPECTS?

Some superintendents and principals are now leading efforts to connect early learning programs—located both in and outside the school building—with the existing primary grades (NAESP, 2015; Nyhan, 2015). They are doing so without systematic preservice professional preparation themselves, demonstrating creative leadership based on their personal experience and values (Marietta, 2010a), and in the absence of district and state policy incentives (Bornfreund, 2015) to do so. Teachers in their schools are working together within and across grade levels from pre-K into the primary grades to build a coherent continuum of learning, especially in reading literacy and in mathematics. Some efforts include school board members, community-based organizations, the philanthropic sector, and business leaders.

These primary schools represent a movement from the base. They break the top-down mold of federal and state policy that influences what districts and schools do at the local level. Jal Mehta (2013) has referred to this change as inverting the pyramid: Practice in the districts and in schools influences policy (see Resource 3.2 about the Children's Institute in Oregon as a prime example).

RESOURCE 3.2. DEMONSTRATING THAT EFFECTIVE PRACTICE CAN INFLUENCE POLICY: THE CHILDREN'S INSTITUTE IN OREGON

The Children's Institute in Oregon is part of a new breed of a state child advocacy organization. Founded in 2003 to improve the lives of Oregon's children at risk for poor health and educational outcomes, the institute's early work (2003–2010) as a traditional policy advocacy organization centered on advocating for increased state investments in early education for low-income children. Achieving success in expanding funding for early learning, including Head Start, the institute sought to ensure that early learning is part of Oregon's educational continuum from birth to postsecondary education.

The Children's Institute recognized that isolated program interventions were not sufficient to ensure that low-income children and children of color would meet the key developmental milestones during the first 8 years of life. In 2010, the institute took the bold step of engaging directly in the implementation of policy by establishing two flagship sites to be "learning laboratories for policymakers, school districts, and communities statewide all aiming to align early learning programs with the primary grades."

The Early Works Initiative was launched in 2010 at the Earl Boyles Elementary School, a community school in southeastern Portland serving low-income and immigrant families (see Resource 4.1), in partnership with the David Douglas School District, the Mount Hood Community College Head Start, and Multnomah Early Childhood Program.

A second site was created in 2012 at Yoncalla Elementary School, a rural site in southern Oregon, as a partnership between the Ford Family Foundation, the Yoncalla School District, and the Children's Institute.

Through independent developmental evaluations of the two sites, conducted by researchers from Portland State University, the institute aims to learn from its direct engagement in implementing a strategy directed at birth to Grade 3, and to leverage what it learns to inform state and national policies. The evaluations of both sites collect consistent child- and family-level outcome data and qualitative data that track system-level changes over time in the two communities.

A high priority in staffing and resources is allocated to site-level capacity building, communications to key stakeholders, and the identification of actionable steps based on what is being learned. This strategy contrasts with the standard top-down approach of shaping policy, with little subsequent attention to how policy is actually implemented in communities and how policy can be continuously improved as a result.

Children's Institute president and CEO Swati Adarkar states:

We wanted to create a new vision for education that connects early learning, the primary grades, and health. This vision was conceived as community driven with deeply engaged families, and based on new partnerships to leverage public funding. Data-driven decision making and a culture of continuous quality improvement are central to our efforts.

The Children's Institute of Oregon is a values-driven advocacy organization. As Adarkar affirms:

We strongly believe that focusing on both policy formation and implementation results in more informed and effective advocacy. We are now much closer to understanding how to better achieve desired outcomes. The design of the Early Works Initiative has allowed us to bring key on-the-ground lessons to our state policy and advocacy work. Parents are now among our most effective advocates. Our work has been a catalyst for new private and public funding to support communities connecting the early years and early grades. We are committed to sharing what we have learned through an array of communications tools, including blog posts, published reports, and videos, in addition to our evaluation reports.

For a detailed account of the David Douglas School District and the Children's Institute partnership, see Williams & Garcia, 2015.

Source: Children's Institute, www.childinst.org

What is most significant, then, is the sustainability of these efforts once a superintendent or principal leaves the district or school. And given the short tenures of school leaders, the vulnerability of the new primary school model is obvious. When principals and superintendents have long tenures, the likelihood of successful primary schools is enhanced.

It is not yet possible to quantify the growth of this movement, given its emergent nature and the need for field building that is only now occurring (Bornfreund, 2015). Without a national survey, a state survey in Minnesota (MinnCAN, 2014) and the mapping work of New America (www.newamerica.org) and the Foundation for Child Development (www.fcd-us.org) provide data on progress toward new primary schools.

Unless America's educator-preparation systems can be changed to produce more individuals who have the knowledge and skills to lead the new primary schools, this instructional system model will reach limited numbers of children. Public schools with pre-K programs will continue to increase, but those programs will remain unconnected to the K–5 grades without strong central office and principal leadership that understands not only early learning, but also how to create a continuous learning experience as children move up the primary grades. The fact that some primary school principals are taking a leadership role in what is already happening in their schools is encouraging (NAESP, 2014), but it has only just begun.

Professional development for school leaders can be helpful in spurring the creation of new primary schools by educators already working in districts and schools. Some of these schools have outcomes for children that should be more widespread. Case studies of Union City (NJ) by Kirp (2013) and of Montgomery County (MD) by Geoff Marietta (2010b) show the crucial role of superintendent leadership, working with school boards, teacher unions, and local government to create a coherent educational experience for students, from pre-K into high school. These examples demonstrate that it is possible to narrow the achievement gaps between rich and poor children, especially those who are dual-language learners. But such district examples are still few and far between. Sustainability of such effort during leadership change remains unresolved.

The elephant in the room is this: Will teacher educators in early childhood education be willing to work with those in primary education to prepare educators for pre-K through Grade 5 and vice versa? Or will the early childhood education field continue to see its own profession as distinct from primary education and seek its own path outside the public education system (Goffin, 2013)? Are the key players in both fields willing to begin the dialogue and make the trade-offs to create a new and different educational experience for young children beginning with pre-K and continuing through the primary grades? Will the research base that provides common ground for curriculum, instruction, and assessment from pre-K to at least 3rd grade provide the leverage needed to redesign educator preparation programs?

At this time, I see no efforts on either side to reach over the divide between early education and K–5 primary education. Early educators who work with children from birth to age 5 are deeply concerned about the future of their field (Goffin, 2013; Whitebrook, 2014). K–12 reformers are equally concerned about the state of teacher education and seek to fix it (Klein, 2014). As a telling indicator of the divide, neither side has yet to address the issues in this chapter, and the indexes of their books are proof of this conclusion. The huge divide between two galaxies (Wing, personal communication, September 2009) remains a powerful image of our dilemma.

Is our predicament a failure of will or of vision? Does it reflect an underlying mistrust of each field? I believe the situation reflects the prevailing assumptions of two fields that have not seriously considered the creation of a new primary school, starting at age 3. If there is greater support for this primary school, the preparation of educators for this school is likely to follow to supply the school leaders and teachers needed. At least, that is the strategy and the hope.

In considering these questions, we should remember that educational systems, and when they begin for children, are created by historical and national considerations, not by some immutable principle that is universal. But the very nature of existing institutionalized practices makes the status quo very hard to change (Klein, 2014). And it is particularly challenging for change to occur during a time when public investments in education are constrained by how education is currently governed and financed (local property taxes and state revenues) and the seemingly limited flexibility in generating new sources of funding for education.

The costs of inaction or faulty action can be calculated, but we need to also examine the return on investments for current practices. We should consider the expense of professional development for teachers who have not been adequately prepared and the costs of turnover in the superintendent, principal, and teacher ranks for school systems. When teachers are better prepared, it may be more costly up front, but it is less costly in the long term.

The best approach to training teachers for the new primary school would be to draw from both the child and developmental focus of early education and the content/subject matter focus of primary education. Stating that and doing it remain worlds apart. As I have argued in this chapter, there is more light shining on what we can do to prepare new primary school teachers than we now are able to see. But will we choose to act? What will it take for us to do so?

Leadership from outside education will be required to move an agenda for preparing educators for the new primary school. Foundations can play a role (as I will discuss in Chapter 5), as well as a National Academy of Sciences, Engineering and Medicine consensus committee, which has recommended a bachelor's degree for all lead teachers in early education programs from birth to age 5 (Allen & Kelly, 2015). That report, *Transforming the Workforce for Children Birth Through Age 8: A Unifying Foundation*, acknowledged that attaining that goal is likely to be a long-term effort. Most significant, the report did not address how the professional preparation of that workforce could be financed and implemented within the current policies and practices based in 50 states in several state agencies with oversight of early learning.

CHAPTER 4

How Are Families Engaged in the New Primary School?

Finding support for early childhood education is relatively simple (although funding it is a different matter). As much as we as a nation are inclined to punish children for what many see, or are persuaded to see, as their parents' failings, we also like the idea of helping the innocents who "didn't ask to be born," and haven't yet failed to pull themselves up by their bootstraps. In helping them, we're not "rewarding" their parents for things like their inability to get a steady job, or to support them with the minimum wage job they have—or having children at all.

But many of those parents were themselves the target recipients of programs just like these two decades ago (or even less). Somewhere along the road from Head Start to high school, the investment stopped, and the adorable children . . . became complicated teenagers and young adults, looking to their parents and communities to see what they could expect from their adult lives. The children who could see, and thus imagine, steady jobs, lives and partnerships were and are far more able to achieve those for themselves.

When those stable lives are out of reach for parents, their children are more likely to find themselves on the same merry-go-round. The ultimate goal of every one of these programs and initiatives and foundations should be obsolescence. Getting there will require an understanding that investing in children requires investing in families. The too small to fail can't succeed on their own.

—K. J. Dell'Antonia. "'Invest in Us,' and Our Parents, Too," *New York Times*

Dell'Antonia posted the preceding text on her blog on the day of President Barack Obama's White House Summit on Early Learning in 2014. Reflecting on an event infused with economic metaphors, she argued for a dual-generation strategy that invests not only in the educational success of children but also in the human capital development of their parents and families. Given the administration's plan to target public funding of pre-K education toward low- and moderate-income families, Dell'Antonia made a strong case for improving the economic prospects of these struggling working families with incomes below the median family income—not just the early education of their children.

Supporting families to be economically secure, Dell'Antonia argued, would demonstrate parents' commitment to the value of their own education and workforce skills, or as economists express it, in their own human capital, and inspire their children's engagement in learning. Children who saw their own family members benefiting from education and workforce development programs would be more likely to invest in their own education and skills. And families would have more opportunities and resources to invest in their children, including during the crucial out-of-school and summer hours.

A few attending the summit may have remembered that when Head Start was first created as part of President Lyndon B. Johnson's War on Poverty in 1964, it was seen foremost as a career mobility program for low-income mothers. Over time, it evolved into one more focused on the developmental needs of young children living in extreme poverty (Zigler & Muenchow, 1992). The goal of economic mobility for families receded into the background. Fifty years later, a national evaluation of Head Start made the news with findings that parents of Head Start children were more likely to continue their own education than parents of non–Head Start children (Sabol & Chase-Lansdale, 2015). Nonetheless, the influence of early childhood programs on children's outcomes dominates the evaluation studies. Very little is known about how children's participation in these programs can influence parents' socioeconomic prospects (Suarez-Orozco, Yoshikawa, & Tseng, 2015).

Americans have always valued family engagement in education because they believe that families are primarily responsible for their children's educational success (Spero, 2015). This belief, undoubtedly, has its roots in American ideals of the primacy of the private sphere of the family in the lives of children. However, as Dell'Antonia and others have noted, American policymakers are, at best, ambivalent about how best to support families in that role—so much so that this value is rarely examined or questioned (Russakoff, 2009).

The research support for this American cultural belief in the primacy of the family in children's educational success originates in the landmark Coleman study, which concluded that families and structural factors have a stronger influence than school resources on children's educational outcomes (Coleman, 1966). This pivotal study, appearing at the height of the civil rights movement, bolstered existing beliefs in the primacy and responsibility of parents for children's educational outcomes, especially before the age of compulsory education, but also during Grades 1–12.

Teachers and principals strongly believe that parents are the most important influence on children's learning (Ripley, 2013). But educators guard their professional autonomy and school territory, leading to tensions between educators and parents regarding their appropriate roles in educating children. The tensions can be racial and economic and cut across the economic backgrounds of families. Middle-class parents can be viewed as overly intrusive in school affairs. Low-income families, on the other hand, are often faulted for lacking interest in education or not transmitting a culture of behavior and skills that enables their children to benefit from instruction.

The enduring legacy of the 1966 Coleman report is that since that time, debates about education reform have centered on the primacy of poverty in influencing children's educational outcomes. One camp claims that educational disparities cannot be solved without addressing poverty and economic inequalities that are part of the daily experiences of families (Rothstein, 2004). Another camp asserts that poverty is an excuse to let the schools off the hook for educating children of families living in concentrated disadvantage (Klein, 2014). Both camps have a partial claim to the truth, but the reality is more complicated.

Seeking to bridge that divide, combining support for families' economic mobility as well as their children's learning, has been tried with limited success thus far (Boots, 2015). Drawing from decades of experience beginning with Head Start in the 1960s and the Family Support Act in the 1980s, dual-generation programs are once again being redesigned and evaluated.

These programs, labeled Two-Generation 2.0, such as Career Advance in Tulsa (OK) and the Jeremiah Project in Minnesota (Chase-Lansdale & Brooks-Gunn, 2014), represent recent efforts to connect the "child" and "family" policy camps (Boots, 2015) in recognition of the joint roles of schools and antipoverty policies in narrowing achievement gaps. These efforts connect access to early education for children to participation in workforce development programs for families. These "whole family" interventions recognize that child and parent development must be linked to address both family poverty and low educational achievement, starting when children are young.

Despite its primacy in America, the value placed on family engagement in children's education is not shared globally. In some cultures, roles for teachers and for parents are sharply defined and distinct; the home and school are considered as separate domains. Parents are expected to cultivate their children's interest in learning, and to provide experiences that augment that learning, but not be directly involved in the school in the ways that are familiar to American parents (Ripley, 2013). In countries like France and Finland, there is more trust in teachers and schools and subsequently less family engagement activities in schools. Parents are assumed to be strong allies with the schools' mission without their visible and active engagement in school activities.

In the United States, the belief in the importance of family engagement in schools is reflected in a large body of resources and campaigns about how families can be more effectively involved in their children's schools (Epstein, 2011; Henderson, Mapp, Johnson, & Davies, 2007). The website of the U.S. Department of Education features frameworks and resources to promote family engagement. Any challenge to this central American belief would be considered heretical.

In spite of the value placed on it, family engagement in schools is widely considered to be weak or ineffective, especially in schools serving low-income and low-income immigrant families. The changing demography of American families requires us to rethink our approaches to family engagement, particularly in light of diverse family structures in which children now grow up (Gadsden, 2013).

As of 2012, 20% of American households were married couples with children under 18 (Vespa, Lewis, & Kreider, 2013). Real-time constraints on families, especially those with variable work schedules and multiple part-time jobs, make it difficult to engage in the desired reading of books and conversations with young children that are called for by research (Talbot, 2014), not to mention time for volunteering in the schools. Many very-low-income families have members who work long hours with unpredictable work schedules that disrupt stable routines and times to be with their children.

Family engagement can be successfully achieved with appropriate respect for and understanding of parents' needs (Hong, 2011; Kirp, 2013; Olsen, 2014; Williams & Garcia, 2015), but such engagement is still far from the desired norm. Wide variations in family-engagement practices exist. Research is only beginning to specify what forms of parent engagement matter for educational outcomes. Educators are not well trained in their professional preparation and development programs to engage families in schools, and family disengagement tends to increase in upper elementary through high school (Epstein, 2011). The chasm between values and practices remains wide.

Given our changed and still-changing context for thinking about the relationship between families and schools, the new American primary school aims for the simultaneous enhancement of the human capital of both children and their parents. The intended focus of the school is on dual-generation strategies starting when children are young and during the early childhood years when the impact of poverty is especially harmful (Duncan & Chase-Lansdale, 2001).

This approach is a significant departure from the almost exclusive focus on parents as a child's first teachers to one that places equal attention on the human capital development of parents, which includes enhancing their skills, knowledge, and experiences that can create economic value for themselves and their communities. Thus, parents with enhanced human capital can more fully nurture the human capital of their children, directly through their daily interactions and through providing a more economically secure family life. Parental development and child development are closely related.

In this chapter, I make a case for why we must invest in families to increase their capacity to provide economic necessities for the healthy development of their children—food, shelter, regular access to health care—as a basic foundation for their educational success. I address why family engagement can be particularly powerful for low-income newcomer or immigrant families as they take on powerful roles in planning and implementing educational programs and in advocating for them at the local and state levels (Williams & Garcia, 2015).

I then turn to two strategies to involve parents more closely in what their children are learning in classrooms, which may benefit parents' own learning, especially their literacy and, for immigrant parents, their English skills. I conclude by urging attention to how family roles in their children's education evolve as children grow up (Henderson, Mapp, Johnson & Davies, 2007).

INVEST IN FAMILIES TOO!

The new American primary school connects children, their teachers, and their parents and families in a culture that is committed to lifelong learning not only of students, but also all the adults. In describing the new American primary school in Chapter 2, I argued that children's learning is enhanced when their teachers see themselves as learners engaged in ongoing professional development and collaborating with fellow educators throughout their careers. Similar influences and processes also apply to families.

Dual-generation approaches that invest in children as well as in their parents and families should be a priority in the transformed primary school. Such approaches aim to address directly the established relationship between a family's economic resources, including parental education, and children's outcomes (Reardon, 2011) by enhancing the education and work skills of their parents (Chase-Lansdale & Brooks-Gunn, 2014). For many low-income parents, programs that build their intellectual capital and skills—whether through completion of high school or a GED, learning English, participating in postsecondary education, apprenticeships, or workforce development—can result in benefits for their children through their daily parent-child interactions as well as improved family economic prospects.

Given the pervasive economic framing of education and its benefits in recent decades—especially return on investments (ROI) in early education (Bartik, 2014)—it is puzzling that such framing does not extend to investments in the human capital of parents and families. This is surely a blind spot that must be addressed.

In 2014, separate White House summits were held six months apart: on families in June and on early education in December. The White House Summit on Families issued a wide-ranging agenda that focused on "supporting working families" and enabling them to achieve "middle-class status," including early education for children and workforce development programs for parents. What was missing in both these summits—and will be addressed in the new primary school—is how to connect programmatic strategies to foster human capital development of children with that of their parents.

ROIs in parents' education and training can be assessed sooner than for young children and have more immediate impact on family life and to society than ROIs for children, which typically manifest themselves, at the earliest during adolescence, but primarily during adulthood as they become productive workers, taxpayers, and parents themselves.

When parents successfully complete postsecondary education or workforce development programs, they have the chance to increase the economic resources of their families. While there is no guarantee that this will occur, increased resources can stabilize family life, including in housing, and contribute to greater optimism and enhanced well-being among family members. This can occur within a few years, whereas the investments in children at age 3 or 4 cannot be assessed until 2 to 3 decades later (Putnam, 2015). At least as much attention, therefore, should now be paid to ROIs for increasing educational capital of parents as there has been to their children.

Dual-generation approaches should be seriously considered as part of reimagining American primary education. The relationship between family economic resources and children's achievement is well established (Reardon, 2011). This gap based on family income is currently larger than the black-white achievement gap of 50 years ago.

Families with greater financial and time resources have more to invest in their children during the 78% of the time children spend outside school. Their families are less likely to be stressed in terms of time and resources. They are more likely to talk with their children and read books. All these factors extend children's vocabulary, comprehension, and interpretation of text, thus contributing to rich literacy development. While such "quality time" is by no means guaranteed, the conditions and parental capacity for engaging in such activities with their children is potentially enhanced, whereas currently it is clearly constrained.

These activities and interactions can augment classroom learning, especially during the 3-month summer vacation. Parents may also be able to allocate resources for summer enrichment activities that counter the "summer slump" in achievement associated with low-income children and attributed to the lack of enrichment experiences that middle- and higher-income parents provide for their children. Overall, the time for learning inside and outside formal programs is likely to be enhanced.

It is imperative to recognize the influence of the economic conditions of families on parenting behavior while not making judgments about the quality of the behavior. The notions of "toxic stress" and the medicalization of poverty are sensitive subjects for many who are rightly dubious about another wave of deficit models and denigration of family practices in low-income families, which are not biologically determined, as these terms suggest.

Low-income parents are not inadequate parents. Their behavior reflects responses and adaptations to their circumstances and to intergenerational poverty. Suffice it here to say that when parents experience economic adversity, they may contribute to their own children's adversity and stress, which can compromise their children's learning.

Concepts of concentrated disadvantage, which capture the conditions of low-income families to include difficulties in their regular access to adequate food and shelter, and living in dangerous neighborhoods with inadequate public services, are important to understanding the daily lives of families and their children and how these conditions compromise opportunities to learn. The 20% of young children growing up in poverty live in families, many with lone mothers, where low-wage jobs make it exceedingly difficult to provide for basic needs such as food and housing. Assisting adults, especially lone parents, to improve their educational attainment and workforce skills can increase the economic resources of these families and potentially contribute to better outcomes for the children, if not for the adults.

Evidence from interventions globally shows that increasing mothers' education and economic resources through microloans improves children's outcomes in education and in health (Björklund & Salvanes, 2011).

Levels of mothers' literacy skills are a critical factor in narrowing the achievement gap between children living in low-income and those in affluent neighborhoods (Sastry & Pebley, 2010). Mothers with more education tend to provide a rich and supportive home learning environment that helps their children succeed in school. They are more likely to have hope for their future, to transmit this optimism to their children, and to urge them to succeed in school.

Dual-generation strategies for narrowing economic and social gaps are re-emerging (Chase-Lansdale & Brooks-Gunn, 2014) after some earlier attempts in the 1980s and 1990s, which did not result in expected outcomes for both parents and for children. Two-Generation 2.0 programs build on the lessons learned from earlier Two-Generation 1.0 programs in the 1980s and 1990s (Chase-Lansdale & Brooks-Gunn, 2014).

These earlier programs did not focus on the quality of programs for children, specifically on appropriate opportunities to learn. To be fair, the current focus on quality pre-K programs evolved as a salient policy issue during the late 1990s and first decade of the 21st century after the creation of Two-Generation 1.0 programs. As a result of concerted advocacy campaigns (Watson, 2011), the idea of quality early learning programs and their indicators has risen on the policy agenda.

The earlier programs provided a package of services to parents, largely adolescent mothers, to increase their literacy skills, attain GEDs, and support their job search activities in a period predating the 1996 welfare reform, which required work first. Parents were not prepared to enter high-demand work sectors, and hence the mismatch between training and availability of positions proved to be an important dimension that current workforce programs now directly address (Searcey, Porter, & Gebeloff, 2015).

The lessons learned from these 1.0 efforts are now incorporated into current "sectoral workforce development programs," which aim to train individuals to enter and advance in workplace sectors that are expected to grow (e.g., health care and information technology) and that are likely to provide decent or middle-class wages and benefits. The work-first strategy of earlier welfare reforms in the 1980s and in 1996 has proved not to enhance the economic security of families. Instead the result has been to keep them in the low-wage sector during a historical period of wage stagnation without the education and skills to advance potentially into higher-wage sectors.

Chase-Lansdale and Brooks-Gunn (2014) describe four kinds of Two-Generation 2.0 programs: adding adult programs to child programs, adding child programs to adult programs, merging child and adult programs in an existing organization or agency, and residential-based mergers (see Figure 4.1). The new American primary school is the fifth setting to co-ordinate dual-generation programs, where connections with workforce

Figure 4.1. Connections to Workforce Development for Parents: Dual-Generation Strategies

Program	People served	Platform	Services	Background of group leaders	Assessment evaluation
Adding adult programs to child programs					
Career Advance Community Action Project (CAP) of Tulsa, OK	Low-income parents and their children	Early Head Start and Head Start	Stackable training in nursing and health information technology at community colleges; incentives; career coaches; life skills training; peer support; center-based and home-based early childhood education	University faculty; antipoverty agency; workforce intermediary	Implementation and outcomes study
College Access and Success Program (CAASP); Educational Alliance	Low-income parents and their children	Early Head Start and Head Start programs	College and GED prep classes; ESL courses; case management; mental health counseling; financial supports; center-based and home-based early childhood education	Nonprofit organization university and college faculty	Implementation and outcomes study
Adding child programs to adult programs					
Dual Generation and Green Jobs, Los Angeles Alliance for a New Economy (LAANE)	Low-income parents and their children	Job-training program and apprenticeships for existing jobs	Employment training in public utility for power and water; relevant courses in community colleges; online learning; peer supports; coaches; early childhood education	Antipoverty advocacy organization; coalitions of community organizers; labor union; government leaders; workforce intermediary	None
Adult and child programs merged within existing organizations or agencies					
AVANCE Parent-Child Education Program	Low-income families and their children, ages 0–3	Early childhood programs and elementary schools	Classes on parenting, toy making, and community resources; volunteer opportunities in early childhood classrooms; home visits; ESL courses, GED prep, and postsecondary education; early childhood education	Nonprofit organization; university graduate students and faculty; early education teachers	Outcomes study

Program	Target population	Setting	Services	Partners	Study
The Annie E. Casey Foundation Atlanta Partnership	Low-income parents and their children	Early education programs and elementary schools	Workforce development; entrepreneurship opportunities; subsidized housing opportunities; asset-building programs; subsidized child care	Private foundation; elementary schools; neighborhood development agencies	Implementation and outcomes study
Garrett County Community Action Committee (GCCAC)	Low-income parents and their children	Head Start and child care services	Homeownership education; financial literacy classes; support for savings accounts; access to affordable rental units; case management; Head Start and child care	Nonprofit agency	Implementation and outcomes study
Adult and child programs as residential programs					
Keys to Degrees Program at Endicott College	Single parents and their children	Residential college	Housing in dorms; scholarships and financial support; courses toward a bachelor's degree; mentoring partnerships; life skills; Montessori early education	College president, faculty, and staff	None
Housing Opportunity and Services Together (HOST) at the Urban Institute	Head of household and his or her children	Housing authorities	Public or mixed-income housing; financial literacy; management; self-sufficiency workshops; incentives; youth support groups and service projects; after-school programs	Housing authorities research think tank	Implementation and outcomes study
Jeremiah Program in Minneapolis and St. Paul, MN	Single mothers and their children	Housing near community colleges	Housing in apartments; education and workforce training; life skills training; partnerships with employers; peer meetings; early childhood education	Community leaders and professionals	Designing a pilot study

Source: Chase-Lansdale & Brooks-Gunn, 2014

development can be offered to parents of children in or through the primary school. This will require closer connections between primary schools and postsecondary institutions. Building such connections will require changes in the roles and responsibilities of school staff and at the district central office, and such change will require deep commitment from all parties.

Career Advance is an example of a dual-generation program intentionally connecting postsecondary education, job training, and career skills for low-income parents at the same time as their children participate in early education. In Tulsa, Oklahoma, with support from the George Kaiser Family Foundation and in conjunction with local community colleges, low-income parents participate in a workforce program that prepares them for high-demand jobs in nursing and health information technology positions.

As part of their participation in Career Advance, parents join peer support groups and have career coaches and life skills training. At the same time, their young children are enrolled in the Early Head Start and Head Start programs run by the Community Action Agency of Tulsa. Short-term longitudinal evaluations of Career Advance are ongoing, and findings will be reported in the next 5 years regarding the potential value of this approach (Chase-Lansdale & Brooks-Gunn, 2014).

Proposals to widen access to higher education, including through free community college education and postsecondary training for in-demand, well-paying job sectors, would reduce the prohibitive costs of higher education for many lower-income families. An important factor, however, is that access is only the first step; completing these programs is the goal. Given the competing demands in the lives of low-income families and limited resources to meet these demands, past decades of research on effective workforce development programs point to coaching and peer support as essential for attaining degrees and credentials and should be built into the programs, as in Career Advance.

Workforce development programs have not yet addressed the needs of low-income immigrant parents (Suarez-Orozco et al., 2015). Yet immigrant families and their children will constitute the majority of the future American labor force, and therefore, investment in their education and skills is in the country's self-interest.

One promising program is the Integrated Basic Education and Skill Training (I-BEST) in the state of Washington (Ross, 2015), which cultivates both English language and workforce-development skills at the same time. Students learn basic literacy skills (reading, writing, math) as well as receive vocational education. I-BEST also provides critical wraparound services to help parents navigate postsecondary education requirements and financial aid so they may pursue career pathways that provide good wages.

Allied programs that focus on adult education and English language literacy are in perpetual jeopardy for lack of funding, but they provide essential opportunities to increase the human capital of all low-income workers, especially immigrants who do not speak English but understand that English proficiency is a high priority for their economic mobility.

One critically important work sector that has been overlooked, with a few exceptions (Hong, 2011), are parent engagement programs in which there is a systematic career ladder in primary education for parents to start as classroom assistants with opportunities to gain access to postsecondary education, and over time to attain their bachelor's degrees and teacher certification. In spite of the demographic changes in the race and ethnicity of students, 82% of American teachers are White and 72% are female (Goldring et al., 2013). Teachers of color tend to be concentrated in certain areas such as New York City and the District of Columbia, where about half the teachers are African Americans.

The racial and ethnic diversity of the teaching workforce is desirable on its own merits. Studies indicate that teachers, regardless of their race and ethnicity, who care deeply and believe in the potential of their students make a difference for all children. But the diversification of the teacher workforce can send a powerful message to students about the value of education, provide role models, and shape their own aspirations for their future.

Primary schools can work with postsecondary education institutions in their communities to recruit, prepare, and support parents who are interested in teaching careers to attain the education required and then to become teachers in the schools. Career ladders that systematically prepare educators, from the teaching assistant to lead educator ranks, can lead to a more diverse teaching force with multilingual competence.

According to the U.S. census data, among children ages five to fourteen, 21.8% speak a language other than English at home (Ryan, 2013). Given the fact that about one-quarter of young children entering kindergarten speak a language other than English in their homes (Ryan, 2013), and research that indicates that strengthening the home language of children leads to better English proficiency in the primary grades, multilingual teachers are in high demand. Teacher preparation programs should prioritize the recruitment, selection, preparation, and support of such teachers.

About one-third of the staff in early learning programs are individuals of color, many able to speak the language of the children (Park et al., 2015) but who require further postsecondary education to qualify for lead teacher positions based on the bachelor's degree, now considered the gold standard for teachers (Allen & Kelly, 2015). Workforce-development programs that focus on diversifying the educator ranks in the primary school are highly desirable, in terms of both the students and the adults who are seeking to increase their economic mobility, but their outcomes have been mixed.

Hong (2011) documents a 2-decade-long effort to recruit and prepare parents from low-income communities to be teachers in neighborhood schools. Established in 1996, the Parent Mentor Program began in the Logan Square community in northwest Chicago, which is composed of low-income Latino families, including first-generation arrivals. The program is a partnership between a longstanding grassroots and community development agency—the Logan Square Neighborhood Association—the Southwest Organizing Project, and the schools to support parents to be advocates, leaders, and role models in their children's classrooms.

Using a career ladder approach, parents begin as classroom assistants with opportunities to attend postsecondary education and over time to attain their bachelor's degrees and teacher certification, if that is their goal. Fifty parents have become certified classroom teachers in a Grow Your Own teacher preparation program offered at Northeastern Illinois University.

The program is currently in 70 schools in the Chicago public schools and in districts outside that urban area. On a daily basis, parents are working in 600 classrooms serving 14,000 students. Replication of this program is occurring in Colorado, Michigan, Pennsylvania, Washington, West Virginia, and Wisconsin.

The jury is still out and will be for a number of years as these Two Generation 2.0 programs are evaluated over the course of 5 years or more. These 2.0 approaches address the either-or (family poverty or children's education) debates with an integrated social strategy that is informed by earlier attempts to connect investments in children with those in their families.

Whether this will be sufficient, given other important factors that shape children's life outcomes, remains to be seen. But it is a strategy for recruiting and systematically preparing teachers for classrooms in which they have a firsthand understanding of what it is like to grow up in the children's communities. These teachers may also be more likely to stay in schools serving dual-language learners, based on their commitment to their communities.

EMPOWER PARENTS TO BE ADVOCATES

Ever since the federal War on Poverty of the 1960s, reformers have struggled to find ways to share power among parents and educators in schools serving low-income families. Today, many schools serve children from low-income households who are newcomers to the United States or who represent the first generation of their family born in the United States. The experiences of immigrant parents with educational systems may be very different from those of their children attending U.S. schools. Cultural traditions, including languages for communicating between families and educators, can be diverse within a school. The tensions between the professional autonomy of educators and the time and commitment required to engage families meaningfully are formidable.

But the benefits can be worthwhile in fostering parents' sense of efficacy in influencing their children's educational prospects and its potential impact on their children's aspirations for their future. When parents move from their strong belief in the power of education to create better lives for their children to direct experience of shaping that education for their children, the norms for parent engagement are changed. Parents become strong advocates for their children's education at the school site, district, and state levels. They become participants in shaping the civic life of their communities. Partnership between school and families is no longer mere rhetoric.

Reaching common ground on how to educate all students well in a school should be a shared responsibility. It starts with a strong value system among educators—superintendents, principals, and teachers—that holds that parents must be an integral part of how schools are designed and education takes place, and ensuring that parent participation in these processes is authentic. Making this happen must be highly intentional, guided by values, and must involve key community partners and resources in moving toward a shared sense of influence in children's learning and educational success.

A case study of Earle Boyles Elementary School in Oregon (Williams & Garcia, 2015) describes how first-generation immigrant parents became advocates for their children's education and well-being, how this school changed over time to begin with pre-K and evolved into a community school, and perhaps most significant, how newcomer parents and families became invested in their children's schools through planning and advocating for changes they believed would better support their children's learning. From shaping, collecting, and analyzing data from community surveys to setting priorities, parents were involved as respected equals at the planning table with school staff. (See Resource 4.1.)

RESOURCE 4.1. DEEPER FAMILY ENGAGEMENT IN SCHOOLS: EARL BOYLES ELEMENTARY

Earl Boyles Elementary School in Portland, Oregon, has earned significant praise in recent years because it has approached its families as valuable partners who understand what their children need and have significant assets to support their educational success. But this is not casual work. While most educators, administrators, or researchers agree that family engagement is a critical way to support young learners—especially dual-language learners (DLLs)—there is considerably less agreement on what it looks like to implement it in a school.

That is, it is easy to say that schools should "engage with DLLs' families." But meaningful involvement is far more difficult. It is a give-and-take process that involves planning, discussing, revising, and careful implementation of new programs in a way that allows families input on the school's direction. This requires educators to offer ideas and guidance while also ceding some control of areas—from community events to school logistics and even unit planning—that have traditionally been exclusively the domain of professional educators.

While this kind of power sharing can be uncomfortable, when done right it is extraordinarily powerful. As Williams and Garcia (2015) describe in detail in their case study, Earl Boyles's "parents are not just engaged—they are empowered. They are setting an agenda for their involvement with the school, as well as expectations for themselves, their children's teachers, and the community" (p. 24). Teachers and administrators repeatedly express their appreciation both for the group's vitality and how it strengthens the broader school community.

But the parents' organization—Padres Unidos—did not spring forth spontaneously. It was part of an intentional strategy supported by shared values among the Children's Institute (refer to Resource 3.2), staff at Earl Boyles Elementary School, David Douglas School District administrators, the local nonprofit Metropolitan Family Services, and many others. In 2011, the Children's Institute reached out to these individuals and organizations to work, side by side, in creating an education system that begins with early learning and is integrated with primary schools.

From the beginning, the Children's Institute recognized that *families* needed to be a critical part of any new initiative. As the institute's site liaison, Andreina Velasco, says, "We really bring parents in as partners in every kind of setting: advocacy, planning and implementation." Williams and Garcia (2015) describe the meetings and activities that led to the establishment of a new pre-K program in a new wing called a community hub attached to the school, and the designation of Earl Boyles as a community school supporting families with health and social services. Families were involved at every stage of this journey, from collecting and analyzing needs assessment data from communities, advocating in the state capital for state funds for pre-K programs, planning the design of the new wing of the school, and volunteering in classrooms as part of their exploration to work toward becoming paid instructional assistants with a Child Development Associate (CDA) credential.

When a visitor walks into Earl Boyles Elementary School, he or she immediately encounters an entry area organized around a library of books and resources with an attractive seating area for reading and conversation. Smiling parents with Padres Unidos shirts are the first individuals a visitor sees as they welcome you to the school. This is just the door into a school where deeper parent engagement and power sharing are palpable.

For a detailed account of how parents are engaged in Earl Boyles, see Williams and Garcia (2015).

Source: Williams, C. P., & Garcia, A. (2015). *A Voice for All: Oregon's David Douglas School District Builds a Better Pre-K–3rd Grade System for Dual Language Learners.* Washington, DC: New America.

Not many schools at this time have the district and school leadership in place, or the partnership of a research and policy advocacy group such as the Children's Institute in Oregon (refer to Resource 3.2), to undertake the thoughtful, strategic work that has resulted in a primary school at Earle Boyles that begins with pre-K for 4-year-olds. It is not easy to replicate what has happened there in other districts without the district leadership and the commitment of a child advocacy group to sharing power with parents. But the Earle Boyles case study (Williams & Garcia, 2015) serves as an aspiration for those who believe it is possible to create a different kind of school that values the assets that parents bring to the table as educators seek to better meet the educational needs of children in their schools.

FOCUS ON CLASSROOM INSTRUCTION

The menu for parent and family engagement in a school can be extensive: volunteering in the classroom and chaperoning outside activities; organizing bake sales and other fund-raising activities; attending workshops, sometimes with teachers, on children's development and how to stimulate their children's learning; creating toy and book lending libraries; participating in healthy eating, yoga, and other wellness activities. These activities aim to engage parents with the schools and to share information about how their children are developing. Less attention is paid to involving parents in what their children are learning in the classroom and how parents can support them on a daily basis (McGhee et al., in press).

In her book *The Smartest Kids in the World: And How They Got That Way*, Amanda Ripley (2013) reported on a PISA study about how parents shape high-achieving children in 13 countries. She flips prevailing parent involvement practice in the United States on its head, by reporting that volunteering and bake sales are not related to higher achievement among students. She concludes that in the United States and in the other countries studied, parents who read to their children early on, engage in conversations about daily events, encourage critical thinking, and have authoritative parenting styles raise children who do better in school.

Ripley puts her finger on what researchers are finding: Across national borders parental focus on instruction and learning makes a difference in children's achievement. Just how much all this can do to narrow the achievement gap between rich and poor children in the United States is not yet clear.

American parents typically have limited information on what their children are learning in classrooms. Parent–teacher conferences, at best, take place two to three times a year and can be relatively brief, and teacher feedback to parents is often general rather than pointing to specific learning difficulties encountered by their children. To be fair to teachers, knowing what can be a large number of students in their classes is demanding, as, for example, when pre-K or kindergarten teachers teach two half-day sessions of 20–25 children each, or when teachers in Grades 1–5 can have 25–30 students in their classes.

Often, teachers and parents do not have a common language with respect to what children are expected to learn and how they are actually meeting those expectations. This lack of a common language to discuss children's learning is further exacerbated when families do not speak English, and teachers must communicate through translators, sometimes children themselves, if they are available (Li, Fung, Bakeman, Rae, & Wei, 2014).

Parents are often surprised to learn, based on standardized tests that tend to measure outcomes at the end of a grade, that their children have not learned what is expected at their grade level. In many cases, the information may be available too late for them to take appropriate action. A time-sensitive focus on what children are learning and how well, reported on an ongoing basis to parents, can be a powerful antidote to the existing information gap about children's progress in learning. Parents seek this information, which can help engage them more actively in their children's education.

Continuous diagnostic and assessment tools, such as Strategic Teaching and Evaluation of Progress (STEP), developed for early literacy and early math from pre-K–Grade 3 at the University of Chicago Urban Education Institute, provide one transparent system of formative assessment for tracking the learning progress in these two content areas (McGhee-Hassrick et al., in press). Teachers are trained to use STEP, which includes a way of assessing the literacy skills of pre-K through third graders. These 12 steps, ranging from pre-reading to high levels of reading comprehension, are informed by basic research showing the developmental progress of literacy and mathematical learning in young children (i.e., they are based on evidence or research).

Teachers are also provided with ways to adapt their instruction to what STEP assessments indicate an individual child needs to master. The goal is for students to reach at least 3 steps during a school year, and all 12 steps by the end of 3rd grade or earlier.

The new primary school should post STEP or similar formative assessments on student progress as part of the public record, showing where every child in every grade is based on a continuum of learning. Teaching and its results become shared and lead to in-depth conversations among principals, teachers, students, and parents on how to help each child to make steady progress. STEP data provide a common metric from pre-K to 3rd grade, from which all can work together to ensure that all children are learning, and that no child is left behind. The STEP metrics provide a common language for all adults—principals, teachers, and families—to talk in concrete ways about student learning.

The potential of STEP and similar continuous diagnostic tools is that formative assessment data based on monitoring of student learning not only drive teaching in the classroom; the public nature of the data can also generate shared accountability for children's learning. All participants in the school-as-learning-community—teachers, principals, families, and students—have access to the data, and all develop a stake in a child's literacy development. This joint responsibility for children's learning can be powerful in moving from the single heroic teacher's responsibility for students' learning to a genuine collaboration among teachers and with parents aimed at steady progress in children's learning day by day, and year by year (McGhee-Hassrick et al., in press).

TAP TECHNOLOGY FOR ENGAGING PARENTS

Smartphones and other devices are now being used to reach parents and provide examples of how parents can support their children's learning. Taking into account the time demands faced by most parents, the use of technology to communicate with families about their children's activities and progress in school should be carefully designed so that the constant tethering to digital communications is moderated. Meanwhile, parents must be good screeners of what information they need to support their children in school. Schools must be mindful of bombarding parents with texts and notices that parents may come to disregard.

Ariel Kalil (2012) makes a compelling case that technological advances create the venues for cost-effective interventions to improve both child and family literacy, which hence potentially contribute to narrowing the achievement gap between children from low- and from high-income families. She cites advances in low-cost devices such as smartphones, game consoles, e-book readers, and interactive toys. There are also intelligent tutoring systems that personalize instruction, and digital libraries with age-appropriate resources that can be used as learning tools.

Education apps such as Remind have untapped promise to ensure timely communications between parents and teachers. The days of reaching into the bottom of your child's backpack (fearful of what you might encounter) may soon be over. Remind can inform parents of student assignments and meetings, but it can be designed to communicate to parents about ongoing student learning in timely, meaningful detail to families and to offer a menu of ways in which parents can bolster the reading and math skills of their children.

The use of technology in supporting children's literacy can be a game changer for parent engagement. The nearly universal use of smartphones means that parents can access information about children's health, behavioral issues, and tips on how to support children's literacy. Based on successful efforts in the health prevention area, Stanford researchers created a text-messaging program designed to support parents of preschoolers to prepare them for kindergarten (York & Loeb, 2014). READY4K sends three weekly cell phone texts to parents whose children participate in the San Francisco Unified School District pre-K programs. Texts are sent in English, Spanish, and Chinese, with specific tips for supporting early literacy skills in the context of daily activities. These tips are aligned with the California preschool learning standards.

A randomized control trial of this program found that English- and Spanish-speaking parents who received the tips were more likely to do home literacy activities with their young children, such as telling stories, going over words that rhyme, and completing puzzles together. Results were less clear for Chinese-speaking families; researchers believe that some families may not have accessed the texts in Chinese, which required a further step on their smartphones.

Compared with children of parents in the control group, children of parents who received literacy text messages scored significantly higher on a literacy assessment. Control group parents received texts related to school announcements only. Significantly, the intervention also increased parental engagement in their children's classroom learning; parents in the text-message group were more likely to ask teachers questions about their children's progress in school than were parents in the control group. This suggests that parents gained efficacy and knowledge and thus became more active regarding their children's learning in classrooms. The lasting effects and relevance of this approach as children move from pre-K into kindergarten and the primary grades remains to be seen.

The focus of these technology-based interventions is to increase literacy and math achievement among children. However, it is worth examining how these interventions affect the intellectual or educational capital of parents, who may have low levels of education and are motivated to increase their own learning and skills (Suarez-Orozco, Yoshikawa, & Tseng, 2015) to improve the economic status of their families. These parents are themselves prime candidates for literacy, workforce development, and skills programs.

Another technology-enabled innovation fostering both child and family learning is the Familias en la Escuela program in Buenos Aires, Argentina, which could be replicated in low-income areas in the United States (Zinny, 2015) . Each student in that city is given an Internet-enabled laptop, which permits easier studying and better communication with families. The laptops also provide free online learning and tutoring for parents so that they can complete their secondary education. Thus the program addresses the lack of secondary degrees among many of the parents, and the lack of computers and Internet access by many of the children's families. Familias en la Escuelas may be scaled up from Buenos Aires to a national program. It is an idea worth trying in the United States with similar conditions.

RECOGNIZE CHANGING RELATIONSHIPS
BETWEEN CHILDREN AND FAMILIES

Relationships between children and their families change as children move from the pre-K years into Grades 1–5, roughly from age 3 to age

10. Designers of family engagement strategies recognize that as children grow older, their social and cognitive development requires correspondingly deeper levels of parental responsiveness. Higher levels of parental literacy in reading and math are also required as children grow. Helping with homework may reach its limits for some groups of parents, and this limit is not restricted to parents without higher education degrees. As one example, the requirements of the Common Core State Standards with its emphasis on problem solving and critical thinking have resulted in pushback even from well-educated "suburban moms."

As children grow older and are less dependent, parents can focus more energy on their own needs. Issues of timing—when it is optimal for parents to engage in their own continuing education and skills development in relation to their children's early education—have not received the attention they should. Programs like the residential Jeremiah Project provide child care and education for young children while their parents, mainly mothers, continue their education and training. While the costs of a residential program for mothers and young children limit large-scale expansion, it is an example of what it may take to provide a highly supportive environment for the families that includes housing; postsecondary education and training for parents; early education for the children; and life skills and employment services in a campus, residential setting.

Some program developers believe that early childhood is prime time for engaging parents in their own education, when they are inspired by what their young children are learning, and that this may be prime time to build on parents' hopes for their future (Chase-Lansdale & Brooks-Gunn, 2014). But early childhood is also a time when responsibilities for children can be at their peak, when parents are stretched for time, and when their earning power is low relative to their later years. Thus attention to and support of time-deprived parents, especially parents in workforce programs, is essential for good outcomes.

A new frontier for family engagement will be to address the alignment of child and parent development over time, specifically with respect to what children are learning in their classrooms. Shaping the learning interactions between parents and children during the early childhood years may evolve from its instructional focus to how parents can foster resiliency (Tough, 2009) to deal with difficult experiences in schools and neighborhoods. During adolescence, providing strong social support and peer networks that keep children on the path to postsecondary education and its completion move to the fore as children become more independent of their parents and more oriented toward their peers. Thus parents and families evolve from a child's first teacher to a hub or coordinator of a network of learning partners—teachers, siblings, friends, and peers.

Within this framework, families should be supported in building their networks with other adults—siblings, relatives, and others—who can be mentors to their children (Li et al., 2014) when they themselves are unable to be so because of work and other life circumstances. A shift from families themselves to building wider networks of individuals and organizations that can support children on their educational journeys should be considered, starting no later than the end of the primary school years (Carnegie Council on Adolescent Development, 1996) and ideally before. These networks become crucial as children consider high school and post-secondary education options.

EMBED DUAL-GENERATION STRATEGIES INTO THE PRIMARY SCHOOL

Children can't succeed on their own. Their families' social networks and economic assets, as well as their belief in lifelong learning, matter for their children's educational success. We have far to go in engaging families in schools, especially schools serving low-income families, to have effects not only on children's learning but also on the enhanced capacity of parents to provide for their families. Indeed, asking schools and educators to shift their perspectives regarding their roles vis-à-vis families toward dual-generation strategies is a game changer. This represents a profound cultural shift from a family-supportive orientation that focuses primarily on children's prospects to one that focuses on adult family members. This is a tall order and will not be easy to implement.

An example of a dual-generation program that focuses on families with children from birth to age 5, including pre-K, is the Briya Public Charter School in the District of Columbia (Garcia & Williams, 2015), located within a public school building and across the hallway from a primary school. Briya is not part of a pre-K–5 primary school, but it is a prime example of comprehensive supports for families, focusing on newcomers to the United States by connecting them with adult education and workforce development. Briya provides a model of the kinds of programs with which the new primary school can seek partnerships in its communities, when the school lacks the facilities to house such a program. Children's outcomes, as measured by the Teaching Strategies GOLD assessment system, indicate that when children leave Briya for kindergarten, their growth meets or exceeds expectations for children of a similar age (Sanchez & Garcia, 2015). (See Resource 4.2.)

In setting its priorities and allocating its resources, the new American primary school combines high-quality classroom learning for children with dual-generation family supports such as those provided by Briya

Public Charter School. The school leadership and teachers understand that better-educated and more economically stable families are able to provide their children with the advantages that are now contributing to wide gaps in educational performance and attainment (Sawhill & Rodrigue, 2015). Thus, educators in the new primary school embrace families not only in relationship to their children as learners but also as adult learners who seek to enhance their own education and skills to achieve a better life for themselves and for their children.

The main responsibility of schools and educators is to create rich learning environments that foster curiosity and exploration, encourage learning from fellow classmates as well as adults, and promote critical thinking. At the same time, schools, especially in low-income communities serving struggling families, must reach out and partner with community organizations and service agencies to support families in their quest for economic stability. Districts and schools should make these linkages a high priority and accordingly designate specific staff responsible for facilitating and supporting these partnerships. Examples of community-wide approaches include community schools (Blank, Melaville, & Shah, 2003), Promise Neighborhood approaches inspired by the Harlem Children's Zone (Tough, 2009) and described in the East Side San Antonio Promise Neighborhood (Williams, 2015), and Beacon Schools with before- and after-school services for children and families (Kirp, 2013).

In schools serving low-income families, assistance with tax preparation, housing referrals and other social services, health clinics, family literacy and GED classes, English language classes, job searches, and family counseling are offered. In these community schools, which assist both students and their families, schools are designed as hubs, often called "full-service schools," to facilitate access to services that families require but may otherwise be difficult to obtain because of costs, language barriers, and accessibility outside their neighborhoods (Dryfoos & MacGuire, 2002). In too many low-income neighborhoods, schools are frequently the only community service centers in operation and thus play a vital role in supporting families.

Families and children live in a broader society beyond their neighborhoods and schools. How well families are integrated socially and economically into other institutions in their communities, indeed their sense of safety, acceptance, and belonging, influence how their children think of their own futures. As children grow older, their aspirations, and their calculations about reaching these aspirations, loom large in the daily choices they make regarding their own educations. Staying on course requires the self-regulation that they acquired in primary schools and deepened in the upper grades. And as children grow older, their struggles to keep on course

RESOURCE 4.2. DEVELOPING HUMAN CAPITAL OF PARENTS AND CHILDREN: BRIYA PUBLIC CHARTER SCHOOL

Briya Public Charter School is the only public school in the District of Columbia to offer a dual-generation, family literacy approach to serving dual-language learners (DLLs). Family literacy is centered around four components: early childhood education, adult education, parenting, and Parent and Child Together Time (PACT). As part of a dual-generation model, the school offers infant/toddler care, a public pre-K program, and an adult education program. Families are offered social and health services via a partnership with Mary's Center, a community health center.

Briya, whose name comes from the Spanish word *brillar*, or "to shine," serves primarily low-income immigrant families who are beginning to learn English. The parents of the majority of Briya's students are enrolled in adult education programs with two components: family literacy and workforce development. The first program includes classes in English for Speakers of Other Languages (ESOL), computer literacy, and parenting. Workforce development programs include working toward the Child Development Associate (CDA) credential, registered medical assistant training, or study toward earning a high school diploma. Some of Briya's early childhood teachers and assistants completed the CDA and ESOL programs. Those enrolled in the medical assistant program receive on-site training at the Mary Center's health clinics, and some are later hired to work there.

While the parents are in school, their infants, toddlers, and pre-K children participate in project-based learning programs. Briya's infant and toddler programs are much more than "day care," asserts Lisa Luceno, director of early childhood education. They are part of a robust parent-engagement model, where parents are seen as valuable contributors to their children's development and are provided with a range of supports to become involved in their children's learning. Parent classes focus on how they can develop literacy and language skills with their children, by choosing age-appropriate books and strategies for reading these books to their children. Parents also participate in PACT, where they spend time in classrooms and apply what they have learned in their own classes.

Ninety-three percent of the children in Briya's early childhood programs are DLLs. Most DLLs speak Spanish, but many other languages are represented, including Bengali, Vietnamese, Amharic, Arabic, and Mandarin. Having bilingual teaching staff allows children to receive substantial home-language support. Pre-K classrooms have two teachers, one who provides instruction in English and one who provides instruction in Spanish. Each classroom also has a special education teacher. Briya's early education programs are aligned to the Common Core State Standards and DC's Early Learning Guidelines.

Student outcomes suggest that Briya's family literacy model is having a significant impact on kindergarten readiness. The pre-K program for 3- and 4-year-olds uses the Teaching Strategies GOLD assessment system and tests students when they enter the program and when they leave. GOLD is an early childhood assessment instrument teachers use to track students' development across a range of areas such as gross motor skills, fine motor skills, and language development. It uses national data sets to create benchmarks of what children should know at different ages and be able to do across all domains of development. Many of Briya's pre-K students enter the program performing below expectations for their age, but are meeting age expectations or exceeding them when they leave for kindergarten.

Source: Garcia, A., & Williams, C. P. (2015). Stories from the Nation's Capital: Building Instructional Programs and Supports for Dual Language Learners from Pre-K–3rd Grade in Washington, DC. Washington, DC: New America.

are influenced by how they and their families view the alignment of their aspirations and the possibilities of attaining them. The greatest threat is an erosion of the hope that learning matters for their future well-being.

Social policies that extend beyond the education sector—policies addressing health care, as well as tax policies that support work, affordable housing, food security, minimum wage increases, and workplace support—can give families reason to hope that they and their children will be given a fair chance and that their lives will be better in the future. Boosting employment, making work pay through increasing the minimum wage and Earned Income Tax Credit, assistance for child care, and paid work leave are key policy levers that can support working families, especially those who are low income and of modest means (Sawhill & Rodrigue, 2015). We are more likely to see a narrowing of education gaps if we make stronger connections between these employment and tax policies and efforts to transform schools.

Social and economic mobility remain critical values in the American Dream. There is bipartisan consensus that these values are under siege. As always, pundits disagree about what to do. To restore the dream, investments in children must be tightly linked with investments in their families' well-being. When this linkage is made, children's outcomes may be greater than with an exclusive focus on the school and children themselves, which is the overwhelming norm today. While this complicates our efforts, dual-generation strategies recognize that there is no single or simple solution to narrowing social and economic inequalities. A good education—for children and for their families—opens doors and equips individuals with the skills they need, but much more effort will be required to attain this goal.

CHAPTER 5

How Do We Create a
New Primary School?

If we are to muster the vision and the will to meaningfully change education—to bring teaching and learning into closer alignment with the contemporary world as it really is—one of the leaps we need to make is to understand that the currently dominant educational model was not, in fact, inevitable. It is a human construct. It evolved along a certain pathway; other pathways were also possible.

—Salman Khan, *The One World Schoolhouse*

The American public education system was created over a century ago in response to social and economic conditions at that time. The fact that this system remains largely unaltered when those conditions have changed markedly—including through technological advances and related economic globalization—is arresting (Khan, 2012). There is an urgent need for the constructive disruption of a broken, out-of-date set of practices. Reimagining and then creating new American primary schools constitutes one such action.

Recognizing the decentralized character of American education, the new American primary school will take different forms, depending on local conditions and stakeholders. But we must keep in mind a set of nonnegotiables that will always remain at the center of these efforts.

For instance, the creation of these primary schools will require a new infrastructure of organized supports to integrate pre-K into the first level of American schooling. And that will require new norms, expectations, and incentives to support that integration. This means field building, which includes the creation of new professional networks of innovators working in schools, districts, and states to allow the sharing of experiences on a regular basis. When such networks become part of existing organizations or are established as freestanding organizations, the new primary school will have arrived.

Successful field building requires institutions that provide the intellectual capital for these networks, programs in higher education to prepare educators for new roles, new teacher credentialing and licensing, and researchers to generate knowledge about how these schools are faring and how they continue to improve. And field building must include the adoption of federal, state, and local policies that support the new primary school, not make it so dependent on heroic, creative individuals to achieve, as it is at the present time.

This chapter describes what must take place for a new primary school to be created and who will be responsible. As such, it is a guide, not a checklist, for broader implementation. I start with the school as the unit of innovation and as the most important locus of learning for children, and then move up the organizational and governance chain to the role of district offices; state and federal governments; and the private sector, especially the philanthropic one. I conclude with an agenda for policymaking and advocacy, which is based on new primary schools as the organizing principle.

In so doing, I invert the usual pyramid (Mehta, 2013) for thinking about education transformation as top down, but firmly adhere to the necessity of a social strategy aimed at reaching the most children possible. It was Julius B. Richmond (Richmond & Schorr, 1992), the first director of Head Start, who never ceased to point out that any effort directed toward improving children's well-being must aim, from its inception, to reach, not just a few children, but all of them.

WHAT SCHOOLS CAN DO

Schools and districts will, for the foreseeable future, be at the front lines of creating the new American primary school. Some pre-K programs are already located in primary schools or on their grounds. As the number of programs slowly increases, many are being located in public schools as well as in community-based organizations. In 2014, the state of Hawaii made history by deciding to locate its state-funded pre-K programs only in its public schools.

While it cannot be assumed that colocation (or even adjacent location) leads to closer alignment between pre-K and the rest of the primary grades, the rise of the pre-K–3rd approach is focusing more attention on how primary schools can better work with pre-K programs (Ritchie & Gutmann, 2013). Head Start programs as well as community-based programs can also be partners in this approach. A deft and informed school principal will be necessary to bring these two galaxies into a common space (NAESP, 2014).

The primary school is where children are educated each day, and where teachers, allied staff, and principals matter most for children's outcomes. However, local conditions vary widely. Some schools are in large districts with more than 1 million students (New York City); others, in small rural districts with less than 100 students. Some school sites have considerable autonomy, while others are subjected to more steering from the district office. The work of principals and teachers is shaped by these district policies and by union contracts, which will be addressed later in this chapter.

At the school level, there are three core nonnegotiables for creating the new primary school:

- *Provision of full-day pre-K and kindergarten in hours equal to those of the rest of the primary grades (Bornfreund et al., 2014).* This is necessary for pre-K and kindergarten teachers to provide an educational experience that offers deep learning and alignment with, as a start, Common Core State Standards. A 2.5- or 3-hour pre-K or kindergarten can no longer give children time to acquire both the content knowledge and the social and self-regulatory skills required for being well-educated.
- *Strong principal leadership, providing instructional and managerial direction that enables all staff from pre-K to Grade 5 to work together to create a learning continuum from pre-K through the primary grades.* As pointed out in Chapter 3, the National Association for Elementary School Principals (2015) is a leader in articulating the importance of this continuum and in issuing guides and resources to assist school principals in this work. Giving principals authority and responsibility for pre-K programs is an important step in institutionalizing the connections between pre-K and the rest of the primary grades. This was one of the key strategies used in the San Francisco Unified School District as part of its pre-K–3rd implementation (Nyhan, 2015).
- *Regular time necessary for teachers to work with each other within and across grades to develop aligned curriculum, improve instruction, and conduct formative assessments that inform their ongoing instruction.* This collaborative work should take place within the regular school day and on a daily basis and be considered part of the core responsibility of teachers.

There are other significant actions schools can take to create the new primary school. Principals and staffs can work with families to encourage them to keep their children in the same school from pre-K until at least 3rd grade, communicating clear rationales for the importance of a stable, consistent primary education. This continuity can be especially critical for children who are learning a second language. Trusting relationships with families to gain their support and loyalty to the school must be nurtured. Admittedly, this can be challenging, given the economic and housing factors that often force families to move, including during the school year itself. But the staff can mitigate some of this stress by talking with parents about the importance of the continuity of an educational experience for their children and the importance of regular attendance, thus creating a community of families and educators who share responsibility for the education of the children.

WHAT DISTRICTS CAN DO

Superintendents are critical catalysts in forging strong connections between early learning programs and the existing primary grades (Marietta, 2010a; Marietta & Marietta, 2013; Ritchie & Gutmann, 2013). The number of superintendents who are leaders in creating the new primary school is increasing (Children's Institute, 2014). There are currently, however, few incentives for superintendents to lead in this area, given the work demands they already face. One of the compelling rationales for creating new primary schools is that pre-K will no longer be seen as an "extra" responsibility that superintendents can choose to take on but a required one, and one for which superintendents have authority and responsibility.

The growing recognition that strong early learning programs can strengthen outcomes in the K–12 grades for which superintendents are currently accountable can be an incentive for districts to partner with early learning programs. The recent communications campaigns to establish early learning or pre-K programs as sound investments in youth and adult outcomes—especially the visibility of economists as messengers (Bartik, 2014; Heckman, 2013) regarding returns on investments—has encouraged some superintendents to attend to what happens before kindergarten. However strong these messages have been, they have not yet influenced superintendents in any significant numbers, suggesting that other policy and organizational incentives are required.

School boards can play a critical leadership role in adopting district policies that support superintendents in making strong connections between early learning and the rest of the primary grades. However, it is still rare that school boards attend to pedagogical considerations in the schools. In other districts under mayoral control, mayors play an important leadership role, as they have demonstrated in Denver, the District of Columbia under several mayors, San Francisco, Seattle, San Antonio, and New York City.

Prime examples of superintendents recognizing the critical importance of early learning—even though it is not mandated—include Sandy Sanger in Union City (NJ) (described in Kirp, 2013), and Bette Hyde, formerly in Bremerton (WA) and Jerry Weast in Montgomery County (MD) (described by Marietta, 2010b). Improved outcomes for students are an incentive for superintendents who recognize the value of early learning, but policy-based incentives will be required for more widespread acceptance and implementation of school systems that begin with pre-K. The December 2015 reauthorization of ESEA—now the Every Student Succeeds Act (ESSA)—provides more direction to do so than in previous legislation. (See Resource 5.1.)

Districts can institute policies that recognize the importance for children of establishing stable pathways between school- and community-based early learning programs and the primary grades. Districts can also develop policies for the recruitment of children into their pre-K programs by informing parents why it is important that their children should attend the same school from pre-K onward. District policies can also permit children to stay in the same schools even though their families relocate within the district—especially during the course of a school year—but also in future years. Finally, a school district with a common curriculum that is implemented in all its schools, for example, Union City (Kirp, 2013), will benefit children whose families must move within the district because of economic and related housing issues, which are part of the unstable lives of many low-income families.

Districts can signal the importance of pre-K by funding it full day, making use of new ESSA provisions that encourage using Title I funds for pre-K programs in schools. This policy is also likely to help ease the scheduling burden on working families and therefore contribute to reducing the high rates of absenteeism in pre-K and kindergarten (University of Chicago Consortium on Chicago Schools Research, 2014). While many factors contribute to these rates, the fact that pre-K and, in most districts, kindergarten are not part of the compulsory education system gives families a sense of complacency about the importance of these early years. Efforts to engage families in the regular attendance of their young children in pre-K and kindergarten can be beneficial to both students and their teachers, who must instruct children with different exposures to the curriculum (Attendance Works & Healthy Schools Campaign, 2015).

At the present time, children attend pre-K programs in a public school with no assurance by the school—and often no intention of the

RESOURCE 5.1. POTENTIAL ALLY IN CREATING NEW PRIMARY SCHOOLS: THE EVERY STUDENT SUCCEEDS ACT

The Every Student Succeeds Act (ESSA), signed into law in December 2015, provides opportunities to create the new American primary school. Within the 1,000-plus pages of this legislation are encouraging provisions that can help to establish a primary school that connects early learning programs with the early grades.

- Title I of the Elementary and Secondary Education Act, now called ESSA, has always allowed states to fund programs for children from birth. However, less than 5% of the funds are actually used for early learning programs. ESSA reiterates that states can use their funds to support early learning programs, including pre-K programs. Forward-looking districts have always turned to Title I to support their pre-Ks.
- The law includes language that clearly states that Title II funds to prepare and train educators can be used for early educators and for teachers and principals in the early grades to learn about creating smooth transitions to primary schools. Joint professional development activities that address instructional and assessment strategies from early learning programs into K–5, including participation by staff from pre-K programs, are allowable. While these are encouraging, they are suggested activities: States and districts do not have to engage in connecting pre-K and the early grades of the primary school.
- States are required to demonstrate alignment between K–12 academic standards and early learning standards, potentially leading to better coordination between pre-K and kindergarten learning experiences than exists at this time. Continuity in educational experiences, including pedagogy and assessment, are supportive of children's learning (Zellman & Kilburn, 2015).
- Title II also includes a new program that focuses on literacy instruction, from birth through the 12th grade, providing the potential for instruction to be made on evidence-based developmental trajectories in children's literacy.
- A new Preschool Development Grant (PDG) program will be housed in the U.S. Department of Health and Human Services and jointly administered by the secretaries of education and of health and human services. This PDG program will help states improve collaboration between existing early education programs from birth to 5 in a mixed delivery system. It will also aim to support children's transitions from pre-K programs to kindergarten.

> While ESSA has more potential to support the creation of a new American primary school than its predecessors, this law explicitly empowers the individual states to address the educational needs of the vulnerable and low-income children targeted by this law. Thus, ESSA is likely to contribute to the inequalities between the states in providing a sound primary education for low-income children. Some states with the appropriate leadership and conditions will develop more effective policies and practices. Others will take advantage of the opportunities to connect their early learning programs to create a birth-to-age-18 learning system. Still others will continue to adhere to the two galaxies of early learning and K–12 grades. The ball is squarely in the state-playing field, and the final scores will emerge from the school districts.

families—that they will continue into the K–5 grades in that school. Districts can change this practice so that children can benefit from schools that are organized to provide a seamless continuum of learning from pre-K into the primary grades. Such a practice will also help build more enduring bonds between families and school staff. Districts such as the San Francisco Unified School District and Minneapolis Public Schools have instituted such policies to create more stable pathways from their pre-K programs into later grades. However, what might seem to be low-hanging fruit has not proved easy to put into place. Outdated ideas do not change quickly.

District offices can also designate staff to work with schools in creating pathways from neighborhood-based early learning centers, also called feeder community-based centers, to specific primary schools. Principals of these schools can include staff from these programs in joint professional development activities, including sharing curriculum, and provide data to the feeder programs about how their children are doing. Districts such as Bremerton (WA) (Sullivan-Dudzic et al., 2010) and Montgomery County (MD) (Marietta, 2010b) have established such partnerships to the benefit of all involved.

It is important to make the distinction between what innovative district leaders do and what they are required to do regarding community-based pre-K programs, including Head Start. In most school districts, superintendents do not have responsibilities for pre-K programs, unless the programs are state funded and located in public schools or the district is a designated agency for running Head Start programs. Furthermore, it is unlikely that aspiring administrators receive any exposure to early childhood programs in their training, since pre-K is not yet considered part of the public education system except in a few states.

This situation is changing slowly with special institutes aimed at engaging superintendents and principals in pre-K and early learning programs (described later in this chapter). For example, the CAYL Institute professional development for principals focuses on connecting pre-K with the rest of the primary grades. The National P–3 Center at the University of Washington College of Education provides professional development to principals and to school district teams.

Another example are the statewide institutes in New Jersey for school administrators organized by Advocates for the Children of New Jersey. Participants focus on ways in which they can lead in connecting their districts and schools with pre-K programs (Rice & Costanza, 2011). These institutes provide an important contribution to strong connections between pre-K programs and the rest of the primary grades but are not addressing this connection in the preparation of educational leaders.

Another important action that school districts can take is negotiate with teacher unions to ensure that teachers have the time for planning and collaborating with other teachers during the school day. As I pointed out earlier, according to the OECD, American teachers spend the most time in classrooms with students compared with their peers in developed countries, who spend 20–40% of their work time outside the classroom, preparing for classes, working with other teachers on curriculum and improved instructional practice, and engaging in other professional development activities. This out-of-class time occurs regularly, and in some places on a daily basis (Green, 2014), reflecting the importance and the regularity of teachers' collaborating and having time to reflect on their practice and ways to be more effective. Such time can strengthen instruction when teachers are in classrooms with students.

The American way of teaching assumes that the classroom teacher best spends his or her time in the presence of students. What is clear from classroom observational studies and international comparisons is that this does not necessarily result in more time for actually teaching students (Ripley, 2013). In fact, time can be spent on classroom management, routines, and administrative matters instead of on instruction.

In forward-thinking school districts, the teacher's day is extended to include a daily time before or after school to focus on classroom instructional planning, feedback from peers, and review of student progress as a basis for future instruction. In other districts like Pittsburgh (PA), contract hours specify common prep periods for teachers teaching the same content/subject matters, which can reduce the time teachers spend working independently and without professional support from their colleagues. These innovations that build professional development into the daily work of teachers can strengthen their effectiveness to the benefit of their students. (See Resource 5.2.)

Resource 5.2. School Districts with Integrated Pre-K–5: Common Elements

New America and the Foundation for Child Development have issued profiles or case studies of school districts that construct pathways for integrating pre-K programs with their primary grades K–5. Based on these narratives, aimed to inspire and inform initiatives in other districts, nonnegotiable or essential elements can be identified. What these profiles also offer are insights on what is desirable, but they are not sufficient to create new primary schools.

Here are the lessons learned. The nonnegotiables for designing new primary schools at the district level include the following:

- *Superintendent leadership.* Whether the district is large, with 150,000 students (Montgomery County, MD); of medium size, with 10,000 (Union City, NJ); or small, with 5,000 (Bremerton, WA), superintendents working successfully with their school boards and unions are essential. They provide the vision, alliances with community and political leadership, and authority to support principals to reach out and work with pre-K and early learning programs in the schools and community.
- *Principal leadership.* At the school site, principal leadership is essential to engaging school- and community-based pre-K programs in joint professional development among educators to implement coherent curricula and institute feedback loops about how children are progressing in schools to the feeder early education programs (NAESP, 2014; Sullivan-Dudzic et al., 2010). Giving principals the responsibility and authority for pre-K programs in their schools is an important step that the San Francisco Unified School District instituted as part of its pre-K–3rd strategy (Nyhan, 2015).
- *Joint professional development.* Within schools, pre-K, kindergarten, and Grades 1–5 teachers and other staff are continuously engaged within and across grade levels to implement curricula and instruction that build on previous student learning and what is expected for students in the future. When schools do not have pre-K programs and are connecting with community-based programs, teachers and staff from these programs are full and regular participants in joint professional development with the schools. In negotiating for professional work conditions, teacher unions can build in time to support teachers' participation in ongoing professional development.

If these are the nonnegotiables, what is up for negotiation?

- *School-based pre-K programs.* While it is logistically easier to connect with pre-K programs if they are housed within the school site, colocation does not automatically lead to essential connections. Pre-K programs can be located in the communities surrounding the schools, and provided by non-profit and for-profit providers. When they are, superintendent and principal leadership is critical to initiating and sustaining genuine partnerships between community-based programs and the schools (NAESP, 2014). Likewise, directors of early education programs in communities must be committed to work with K–5 schools to provide a coherent, continuous learning experience for their students. Union City and the Chicago Child-Parent Centers are prime examples that, with the appropriate leadership and staff, connecting K-5 schools with community-based pre-K programs can be achieved.
- *Family engagement focused on instruction.* When teachers and families have a shared sense of how children learn and how that learning can be supported in the classroom and home, children are likely to be the big beneficiaries. Parent education programs that include both parents and teachers to learn about how children develop provide common language for understanding of and communication about students, as well as an opportunity to develop partnerships on children's behalf (McGhee-Hassrick et al., in press).

WHAT TEACHER UNIONS CAN DO

Teacher unions are potentially a powerful force in changing the American system of education to support and reward optimal learning for teachers and their students. With 3.3 million teachers in 50 states, educational transformation cannot occur without the engagement of teachers and their union leaders. The anti-teacher rhetoric of the past 5 decades has led to unfortunate outcomes, specifically the shortage of well-prepared teachers in some states, and to demoralization in the teaching ranks.

The American education system cannot depend on individual, heroic teachers. Instead, it must find ways to support all teachers to be strong instructional leaders who work with others to create the instructional infrastructure of shared responsibility for student outcomes (McGhee-Hassrick et al., in press). Building professional capital (Hargreaves & Fullan, 2012) must be a higher priority on union agendas.

Successful districts and their superintendents who find ways to work collaboratively with teacher unions produce stronger outcomes for students as a result (Kirp, 2013; Marietta 2010b). Union-district partnerships focused on common goals and continuous teacher improvement are critical in improving student learning, especially among the students who are often left behind.

Teacher unions can play a constructive role in the new primary school by putting into practice ways of reducing teacher turnover, especially in schools serving low-income children, and stabilizing teams of teachers in a school to create strong professional learning communities. One strategy is to give principals the responsibility of hiring and retaining teachers in their schools, and to abolish the practice of seniority, all other factors being equal, in hiring teachers (Bornfreund et al., 2014).

Teachers have favored seniority rights, because that practice has allowed them to move from more challenging schools to those where teaching conditions are considered to be better. But it is time for unions to shift from seniority rights toward better working conditions and collaborative partnerships in all schools. If unions move in this direction, the results might be a better distribution of experienced teachers in schools serving low-income children. Currently, such distribution is not the case. Children who could benefit the most from experienced and competent teachers are least likely to have them. That itself is the basis for civil rights action.

Principals should be given the authority to assemble their own teams of teachers who are committed to working together to enhance student learning in each school. Consistent with practices in effective organizations, leader-managers should be able to select their own teams. Current practice results in having pockets of effective teachers in schools, not a strong team of teachers. This result is unfortunately the case in most schools serving the most vulnerable children and is very likely a factor in low achievement rates among those children.

Teacher unions can also bargain to institute working conditions that provide the opportunity and time to develop teaching skills on a continuous, if not daily, basis (Hargreaves, 2014). Moving from a trade-union to a professional-association model that focuses on creating conditions to support professional development and practice is a change that is long overdue.

As noted above, contract hours can include time at the beginning or end of each school day when teachers can have time to plan and work with other teachers and staff to hone their skills and improve their effectiveness during the time they are in the classroom. The increasing recognition of this time factor, both by teachers themselves and by those who design stronger instructional practices (Goldman & Pellegrino, 2015), is an encouraging sign. When planning and reflection are activities outside the work hours, their value is diminished, and the cost of burnout to the teachers cannot be justified.

WHAT STATES CAN DO

The size of student populations in a state varies greatly. For example, by population California qualifies as a nation and by gross national product as a top-ten world economy and could be divided into several states or regions. Both California and Texas have 1,000 school districts. The alignment of state, district, and school policies is made more difficult not only by size but also by how a state organizes its education regionally. In California, several school districts are clustered into county school districts. In Washington State, districts are organized into Educational Service Districts (EDS). Nowhere in the world is there such a multilayered education system as exists in the United States. Thus, the local control principle of *subsidiarity* (those closest to the action should be the decisionmakers), which is being implemented in California, should be monitored closely as it is implemented.

There is only one state in the country—Hawai'i—in which the entire state is one school district. Even districts that have come under state control, like Newark (NJ), are now requesting that local autonomy be restored. It is exceedingly difficult for state departments of education to steer the work of local districts, especially in the larger states like California, Texas, and Florida, and in large urban districts, which may also choose to grant local autonomy to individual schools. Not only is scale an issue, but the resources of state departments of education relative to school districts is also a factor (Cross, 2014), reflecting limits of a state department of education's authority over local school districts.

However, state departments of education remain important as first-line implementers of federal and state education laws and providing technical assistance and professional development to districts. It is likely that the role of state departments of education will change as student populations grow and we enter a period of increased local control, led by ESSA of 2015. Federal initiatives will continue to flow through states and governors, although that flow of funds could also change.

States, however, can make a crucial difference for the new primary school in two ways. First, state laws and state education funding formulas should consider pre-K as the beginning of the state's public education system and fund pre-K at the same level as K–12 grades, as is the case in Oklahoma (Bornfreund et al., 2014).

All teachers, including pre-K teachers, should have the same qualifications, including a bachelor's degree and other appropriate credentials, and be compensated with the same salary schedules, health insurance, and retirement benefits. Pre-K should be a full-day program with similar hours as those of kindergarten and the rest of the primary grades. Revising state constitutions and laws related to children's basic rights to education are critical to ensure that these nonnegotiables are in place.

Second, states have their most important influence on the requirements for the preparation and credentialing of teachers, principals, and superintendents. These requirements drive what happens in educator preparation programs in the state's higher education institutions and other teacher preparation organizations, and dictate who can work as a teacher or school leader. As I discussed in Chapter 3, there is strong consensus that the teacher education system in the United States needs to be overhauled. The changes that have occurred already, including growth in Teach for America and teacher residency programs in several locations, are currently insufficient to improve the educational experience of most students.

States also have an important role in defining qualifications for teachers and staff working in early learning programs serving children from birth through kindergarten. Those qualifications now vary from a high school diploma to college degrees (Whitebrook, 2014). Depending on the state, qualifications for early learning programs serving children from birth to kindergarten entry may be governed by an agency other than the state education system. Rules and regulations in state agencies are related to federal funding streams and laws governing child care and early learning programs. Head Start bypasses state agencies in most states, and funding flows from the federal to the local agency levels.

This extreme lack of coherence in the early learning field (Goffin, 2013), combined with 50 states specifying K–12 teacher qualifications in some 2,000 teacher education institutions, makes for a dizzying array of educator requirements (Allen & Kelly, 2015; Whitebrook, 2014). With the new primary school as an organizing principle, all teachers in pre-K programs would have the same qualifications as the rest of the K–5 primary grades. As noted earlier, this is usually the case when pre-K programs are located in public schools. But it is a mixed bag when pre-K programs are located in other settings, where most of these pre-K programs now are.

As I explained in Chapter 3, the following changes in educator credentialing at the state level are key in supporting the new primary school:

- Creating a pre-K–3rd or pre-K–5th teaching credential that prepares teachers to teach any grade from pre-K to at least 3rd grade. Such a credential was recently highlighted in a report of the California Commission of Teaching Credentialing and Licensure, to acknowledge the importance of pre-K programs as the beginning of a pre-K–12 educational system. Pre-K–3rd credentials exist in other states such as New York and New Jersey.
- Restructuring the credentialing system so that there is one research-based credential for the pre-K–5 years instead of multiple, overlapping, and confusing credentials, as is the case now (Allen & Kelly, 2015). Many states have both a K–5 credential and a pre-K–3rd credential, leading prospective teachers to choose the K–5 credential in order to be more attractive hires for typically higher compensation potential in the K–5 grades.
- Requiring principals and other school leaders to receive preparation and training in early education so that they are better able to lead schools with pre-K programs and to supervise and mentor teachers with responsibilities for younger children. As New York City has worked to create a universal pre-K program, there is concern that principals are not prepared to evaluate pre-K teachers whose classrooms are more activity-based, hands-on sites than those of the other primary grades.

State departments of education can also organize pre-K–3rd units, or primary education units that include pre-K, to provide resources and guidance to districts in the state, as has recently taken place in California. Currently, state departments of early learning may be part of the state department of education, but that is no assurance that they are integrated into the K–12 system. States vary in the extent to which such integration is occurring, and early learning agencies are also located in governors' offices or in other state agencies such as health and labor. When that occurs, another layer is added and building bridges to the education department can be more difficult.

WHAT THE FEDERAL GOVERNMENT CAN DO

The federal government has played many roles in educational reform over time, and those roles change with presidential administrations and their attendant education agendas (Cross, 2014). Traditionally, the federal role has been to support research and evaluation in education, to collect education statistics from the states, and to stimulate changes that are in the national interest, especially when directed by congressional action.

Federal education policies can range from national security and world dominance in the post-Sputnik era to equal protection under the law in the civil rights era. Today the focus is on leveling the playing field for children who live in poverty, have disabilities, speak a language other than English, and encounter discrimination as a result of their race, ethnicity, or gender. However, the 2015 reauthorization of the Elementary and Secondary Education Act (ESEA), now known as the Every Student Succeeds Act (ESSA), weakened the federal role. Combined with declining federal funding of education (Hahn, 2015), the capacity of the U.S. Department of Education to support innovation and to enforce civil rights protections consistent with laws already in place is likely to decline.

Administration of Early Learning Programs

Depending on the president's interest in education, federal agendas can steer education reform during an administration in specific directions. In 2012, the Obama administration established a Department of Early Learning in the Division of Elementary and Secondary Education in the U.S. Department of Education, with a deputy assistant secretary for early learning. This was the first administration in which early learning (with the exception of special education for children from birth to 5, which has long been mandated under the Individuals with Disabilities Education Act) has had a presence in a federal agency that primarily focuses on K–12 and higher education.

Early learning has been layered onto the existing K–12 elementary and secondary division. This early learning division manages grants to states to improve access to and the quality of programs serving children from birth to 5, including the Early Learning Challenge Fund and the Preschool Development grants. Under ESSA, these functions will move into the U.S. Department of Health and Human Services. This shift reflects the intent of the U.S. Congress not to expand the U.S. Department of Education's role in early education.

The Obama administration defined early learning as spanning the years from birth to age 8. ESSA signals that federal policy for birth-to-5 programs, which are primarily in the U.S. Department of Health and Human Services, and K–12 (i.e., elementary and secondary) education, which is part of the federal education agency, will shift into the U.S. Department of Health and Human Services, although the law specifies joint administration between the two agencies. Special education programs for children from birth to 5 are under the Office of Special Education Programs in the Department of Education, as well as early education programs funded by

Title I of ESSA. The overlap of K–3 in the early learning and the elementary education divisions has not been addressed.

ESSA specifies that federal policy regarding the connection between early learning and primary education can be used to plan for "transition" to kindergarten and beyond. The Preschool Development grants to the states incentivized states to make those connections in their own ways, and that will continue under ESSA, giving states wider latitude than previously. Such policies are now in development. But the grants are few and far between. Not all states received these grants, and their long-term sustainability is in question.

Other federally funded early education and child care programs are administered by the U.S. Department of Health and Human Services. Thus, early learning programs are located in two federal agencies, whose responsibilities for children from birth to 5 are the result of the history of congressional action and different authorizing and appropriation committees in each house of Congress. Each of these programs in each of these two federal agencies has different funding streams, rules and regulations, technical assistance, and accountability requirements. Calls for bringing all or some of the programs into the U.S. Department of Education are unlikely to be answered (Bornfreund et al., 2014), given entrenched interest groups and leadership. While such recommendations are reasonable and likely to be beneficial to children, previous attempts to bring Head Start from the Department of Health and Human Services into the Department of Education have been unsuccessful, and no change is in sight.

Another federal department, the Department of Defense (DOD), has developed a highly respected child care program over the past few decades, reversing its reputation for less than adequate services. DOD also runs a K–12 educational system located near military bases throughout the world.

Little is known about DOD's efforts to connect their child care programs with their educational system, although consistent with the early learning definition of the U.S. Department of Education, early education in the DOD goes up to Grade 3. As a closed system with a clear chain of command significantly different from the rest of the American educational system, the DOD could easily integrate its early learning programs and K–12 grades if the leadership required it.

While advocates have pointed to DOD as an example of a quality early education and care system (National Women's Law Center, 2000) with well-paid teachers (Whitebrook et al., 2014), it is not easily replicated in the decentralized nonmilitary sector that exists in stark contrast to DOD's chain-of-command system.

Distribution of Federal Funds for Education

The federal agencies distribute a declining proportion of discretionary funds for education that are narrowly targeted at specific programs. This creates constraints on any kind of fundamental change. Whatever new funds the federal government has supports small pilots of demonstration programs that have limited capacity to grow in an era where discretionary funds for children in the federal budget are small (about 7.8% in 2015) and likely to decline because of the increased needs of nondiscretionary programs such as Social Security and Medicare (Hahn, 2015). The alternative of reallocating existing funds to be used in different ways presents a political minefield; it is unlikely to occur unless there are major changes in political leadership in Congress and the White House.

The federal government can stimulate innovation and replication of pre-K–3rd approaches to creating new primary schools. In the third round of competition for the Early Learning Race to the Top grants, the U.S. Department of Education for the first time recognized pre-K–3rd as an innovative strategy and placed a priority on state proposals to connect early learning programs with primary education (Race to the Top will no longer exist after this third round). Approximately 10 grants to states were made in 2015; these will provide opportunities for states and districts to shape their efforts with federal support. Since the earliest start of these state efforts will take place in 2015–2016, it will be a few years before the influence of this federal stimulus becomes known. However, it is an important signal 40 years after Project Follow Through, a small federal initiative to build on Head Start programs in K–3, of the importance of building on the gains made from effective pre-K programs. These efforts will continue under ESSA with greater latitude to the states.

In 2011, in a federal grant competition called Investing in Innovation (I3), the Chicago Child-Parent Centers (CPC) were awarded an expansion grant to implement and evaluate the CPC approach in several sites in St. Paul (MN) and Normal, Evanston, and Chicago (IL) (refer to Resource 2.2). This is the first federal grant to support an explicitly pre-K–3rd approach serving children from 3 to 8 years of age in public school settings and one of the few to draw on Title I funds since the 1960s. Early evaluation findings are promising, but it will be several years before the long-term impacts are reported.

The federal government plays a central role in supporting research and development in education through federal grants. In the current budget gridlock, research funds have not kept pace with needs, and there is a shift toward reliance on private sources, including foundations, in supporting mission-driven research that was once the sole responsibility of federal research support agencies.

That being said, funds for early learning and for K–12 educational research are still located in separate agencies, making it difficult for researchers who wish to conduct needed research that follows children from pre-K into the primary grades to obtain funding for even short-term longitudinal studies. Evaluation of the CPC expansion is one bright exception, but its funding source is limited to a few years. The role of a few foundations in support of the research field has been crucial, but is insufficient to make up for what federal agencies can potentially invest.

Use of Title I Funds for Young Children

Although Title I of the Elementary and Secondary Education Act allows for funds to be used for children from birth to 5, less than 4% of this federal pot of $14.4 billion (2014–2015) is currently being spent on that age group. An education law that has existed for 50 years naturally has entrenched interest groups who have a stake in the current allocation of Title I funds to longstanding programs. Thus, provisions to increase the allocation of new funds to early learning programs for low-income children has encountered strong opposition. Even in the case that states and districts are given more flexibility in how they spend Title I funds, much will depend on gubernatorial and local district leadership to steer more funds toward pre-K. ESSA explicitly states that Title I funds can be used for pre-K programs.

I and others (Zigler, 2011) have argued that, given Title I's goals aimed at improving the achievement of low-income students, its lackluster record of achievement since its inception in 1965, and evidence for the efficacy of quality early education programs, a much larger percentage of its funds should support early learning programs. Some creative school districts like Montgomery County (MD) decided to allocate new infusions of Title I funds to the district's early learning programs. That is a practice that other districts could emulate with the right leadership. The flagship pre-K–3rd approach of the Chicago Child-Parent Centers has been funded with Title I from its inception in 1967. The use of Title I funds for pre-K programs is highly dependent on local leadership, specifically innovative superintendents with support of school boards.

Funding of Higher Education for Educators

The federal government also supports the preparation of educators through the Higher Education Act. Any potential effort to support the education costs of individuals preparing for teaching should include pre-K teachers. Title II of ESSA clearly states that funds can be used to prepare and train early educators and principals and other school leaders. Congress should also consider increased investments in the higher education of all teachers as a national economic security issue. A democratic society with undereducated members is a dangerous place.

The funding of higher education for the training of the allied health professions such as doctors and nurses, particularly those who promise to work with underserved groups, can be a model for investments in educators who intend to teach in schools serving low-income children. Loan forgiveness programs, such as exist for public interest lawyers, should also be considered for educators who are underpaid, given their education attainment compared with those in other professions both in the United States and in other countries (OECD, 2014).

Public–Private Funding Partnerships

Finally, since there is unlikely to be further significant federal investment in early learning during the last year of the Obama presidency (2016), his use of the bully pulpit to continue to raise the visibility of early learning will be valuable. President Obama promised to host a White House summit on pre-K during his first year in office in 2008. In December 2014, the summit was held, with the announcement of a $1 billion investment in birth-to-5 programs, of which $330 million is from private sources.

In the short term, public–private partnerships can increase access to and the quality of pre-K programs. The long-term consequences of such a partnership for the prospects of pre-K as beginning of public education (i.e., a public good for all children) cannot be easily predicted. What is indisputable is that private funding can never be a stable source for financing pre-K programs.

WHAT THE PHILANTHROPIC SECTOR CAN DO

Foundations can provide the seed capital to stimulate educational innovation and social entrepreneurial activity (Nyhan, 2015). If focused and strategic in their grantmaking, foundations can have a significant impact in nurturing new programs and in changing educational trends. For example, the role of the Carnegie Corporation of New York, specifically the late vice president Barbara D. Finberg, in supporting longitudinal studies of children enrolled in the Perry Preschool Project has been critical. This research demonstrated the lifelong influence of a high-quality pre-K program on low-income African American children in the small segregated town of Ypsilanti, next to Ann Arbor (MI) (Weikart, 2004). Alan Pifer, a former president of Carnegie, was instrumental in providing the seed capital for *Sesame Street* and stimulating the public radio and television systems (Lagemann, 1989).

A small number of foundations such as the Walton Family Foundation and the Bill and Melinda Gates Foundation have played significant roles in the growth of charter schools, including in their teacher training, support organizations, and leading advocacy organizations (Klein, 2014). Alternative teacher preparation programs, such as Teach for America and teacher residency programs, as well as principal academies, are also beneficiaries of philanthropic investments. While the numbers of individual teachers, principals, superintendents, and students affected is relatively small, given the size of the public system, the visibility of these investments is disproportionately high. The challenge of influencing how some 3.3 million teachers educate students in some 15,000 school districts remains daunting.

Foundation grant-making programs tend to mirror the existing education system in that they follow existing structures such as early learning or pre-K, primary, middle and high school reform, or higher education. Until recently, pre-K or early learning was not considered part of traditional education grant-making; instead it was considered part of the children, youth, and families portfolio. This is still the situation in the majority of foundations that fund the education sector. But these boundaries are slowly shifting.

Thus, it is noteworthy that a small group of foundations—albeit all interested in children and early learning—sought to span the two galaxies, and in so doing, are contributing to the emergence of the new primary school. These foundations—Foundation for Child Development, W. Clement and Jessie V. Stone Foundation, Bill and Melinda Gates Foundation, the McCormick Foundation, the New School Foundation (merged with the League of Education Voters in Washington state), and the W. K. Kellogg Foundation—had to convince the K–12 education funders in education philanthropy that pre-K was more than an add-on and could actually be a new beginning for public education. As in the world outside education philanthropy, making that case continues to be a struggle. The galaxies of early learning and K–12 education in education grantmaking remain worlds apart. The above foundations have been able to establish a beachhead on the shifting sands of education reform by working together for a decade. Their longer-term influence, as their leaders and boards change and priorities shift, is uncertain.

Together in different co-funding partnerships, these foundations supported five waves of professional education institutes for state and district teams working on pre-K–3rd approaches as part of professional development and building local capacity to implement the approach. A cluster of foundations also supported the development of a framework to guide the implementation of pre-K–3rd approaches at the local level (Kauerz & Coffman, 2013). This framework is being used to guide schools and districts as they consider ways to integrate early learning into their K–12 education systems.

Some foundations are also supporting the development of STEP, a continuous diagnostic and assessment tool described in Chapter 4. It is used by teachers starting in pre-K and through the 3rd grade. STEP is based on scientific findings of the cognitive trajectories shown by children as they learn to read and do math, and allows for different rates of learning among children. Essential to the alignment of curriculum, instruction, and assessment is such a tool that provides a stepwise trajectory for assessing student learning and for adapting instruction to where a student is and needs to move (McGhee-Hassrick et al., in press). Other tools for formative assessments are increasing in use, part of the backlash against excessive high-stakes testing in the past decades under No Child Left Behind, a predecessor to ESSA.

Other foundations, including community foundations like Marin Community Foundation and Silicon Valley Community Foundation, are working with school districts in their California counties to provide professional development and school leadership institutes to enhance the capacity of their educators to better connect early learning programs to their primary schools toward the goal of narrowing achievement gaps by the end of 3rd grade. The McKnight Foundation and Evelyn and Walter Haas, Jr. Fund are leading pre-K–3rd efforts in the Twin Cities (MinnCAN, 2014) and San Francisco (Nyhan, 2015), respectively. An emerging initiative for pre-K–3rd in Nebraska is supported by the Buffett Early Childhood Institute at the University of Nebraska.

McKnight focuses on pathways to early literacy in the pre-K–3rd grades in Minneapolis, St. Paul, and Brooklyn Center public schools, and in one charter school. Educators in these schools, as well as district office administrators, participate in professional development focused on literacy instruction, and in cross-school and district leadership teams (Lieberman & Bornfreund, 2015).

The Haas, Jr. Fund supported strategic planning in the San Francisco Unified School District to include pre-K programs in its vision, and an internal assistant superintendent for early education as part of the district leadership team (Nyhan, 2015). (See Resource 5.3.)

RESOURCE 5.3. EFFECTIVE PHILANTHROPY IN DISTRICT-LED PRE-K-3RD: WHAT A FOUNDATION CAN DO

In 2007, the Evelyn & Walter Haas, Jr. Fund approached the San Francisco Unified School District, the city, and other state foundations about forming a public–private partnership that would support pre-K–3rd alignment in the city's public schools.

The partnership's clear goal was systemic change. Its vision was to remake the city's public primary schools into places where curriculum, instruction, professional development, and assessment would be aligned from pre-K through 3rd grade, with a focus on early and bilingual literacy, math, and social-emotional development. The schools would engage families and be aligned throughout the district, including with after-school and summer programs.

The Haas, Jr. Fund served as a catalyst for aligning pre-K with K–3. Instead of laying out how this should be accomplished, the fund brought ideas, partners, and resources to the school district, supported its planning, and raised funds for its work. At the same time, the fund created joint learning opportunities for the district, city, and funders about the research and rationale behind pre-K–3rd to recruit champions within the district and a core of supportive funders.

The fund cultivated the ground for a pre-K–3 system in the following ways:

- Sent a cross-sector team from the district and city to a Harvard University professional development institute on pre-K–3rd approaches
- Sponsored sessions with speakers from across the country so that local educators and policymakers learned about the latest ideas, lessons, and pre-K–3rd approaches, which they then used to develop their own district plan
- Launched what became a 5-year focus of the district's pre-K–3rd work: educating and encouraging district leaders to make pre-K–3rd a priority and devote resources to it

These efforts paid off as the idea gained traction among district leaders, who began developing their own vision of a pre-K–3rd system. Their strategy created the context within which foundations could play supportive or additive roles, which aligned with their own grant-making priorities. "We understood that the district needed to own and lead this effort," said Sylvia Yee, vice president of programs at the Haas, Jr. Fund. "The district hired the talented staff, developed the strategy and the plan. We followed their lead, but we held them accountable."

Early on, by studying successful pre-K–3rd efforts around the country, the fund learned an important lesson about connecting pre-K with the rest of primary education: Have patience. This work was going to take at least a decade, because it was not implementing a simple program model, itself a complex endeavor. The fund referred to its investment as "patient capital," which meant giving the district enough time to research, plan, build partnerships, learn, and produce results, such as higher average scores on 3rd- and 4th-grade standardized English language and math tests among children at risk for poor outcomes.

The second defining lesson from these early stages was the importance of a genuine partnership with a superintendent, Richard Carranza (and at the beginning of this work with his predecessor, Carlos Garcia), with a strong commitment to pre-K–3rd and funders.

In recent education reform efforts, funders have approached school districts with clear views of what the work should look like and how money should be spent. In San Francisco, funders encouraged and supported an idea and broad vision, but clearly put the district in the driver's seat. The district defined the ambitious agenda and implementation, which allowed funders and other partners to support parts of the agenda that fit their own priorities. The Mimi and Peter Haas Fund, for example, was most interested in pre-K, while the Lucile and David Packard Foundation focused on transitional kindergarten (TK), but together both were contributing to broader pre-K–3rd goals.

To read the complete case study, go to www.newamerica.org.

Source: Nyhan, P. (2015). *The Power of a Good Idea: How the San Francisco School District is Building a Pre-K–3rd Grade Bridge.* Washington, DC: New America.

The influence of private philanthropy has increased as foundation assets have grown. However, any philanthropic investment is small relative to public dollars that now fund education, and it has to be used strategically to have any chance at generating change. Consider the well-publicized example of the $100 million that Facebook co-founder Mark Zuckerberg gave to Newark, New Jersey, in 2010 to be spent over a period of 5 years (Russakoff, 2015). Most of those funds were used for teacher merit increases, teacher-led projects, consultants, and community engagement efforts. Yet during the 5 years when Zuckerberg's donation was being distributed, the annual budget of the Newark schools exceeded $600 million.

Through funding partnerships, two small foundations, the Foundation for Child Development and the W. Clement and Jessie V. Stone Foundation, established the Early Education Initiative at the New America Foundation (now New America) to be a new voice for pre-K–3rd issues. New America has diversified its funding base and the issues it covers spanning early and primary education. It has played a significant role in highlighting pre-K–3rd issues through its policy research, reports, blog postings, and conferences, and it deserves credit for branding pre-K–3rd and being a national communications center for pre-K–3rd efforts.

The foundations also supported several professional development institutes (mentioned earlier) for district and state teams working to implement pre-K–3rd approaches in their communities at the Harvard Graduate School of Education. Teams from school districts and states applied for participation in these institutes, bringing key stakeholders from the districts and states, including foundation staff and board members, to begin joint planning. The institutes are now continuing at the University of Washington College of Education. They provide opportunities for teams from school districts and from states to work in teams to plan for the implementation of pre-K–3rd approaches in their localities.

Within its organization, the Foundation for Child Development also established a communications unit, which focused on generating resources based on the work of grantees and others, to engage and inform educators interested in pre-K–3rd approaches. In addition, the foundation created a series of practical guides highlighting the work of effective districts to provide models for other districts hoping to initiate and implement their own efforts. Over a period of 10 years, a rich source of information aimed at educators to support their work was created (see www.fcd-us.org). This unit has been disbanded, but the resources are still available, especially at New America (see www.newamerica.org).

A 10-year commitment to pre-K–3rd by a small foundation is unusual. Whether the Foundation for Child Development or other foundations will seek to sustain or continue to build this movement is unclear at this time. What is clear is that the idea of pre-K–3rd has permeated federal law, exemplified by provisions in ESSA. As noted earlier, in the final round of Race to the Top states were selected to try to make stronger links between early education and the primary grades. At the same time, there are districts and states that, given the expansion of their pre-K programs, are seeking to create their own ways of connecting and aligning early childhood programs and K–12 education (Ritchie & Gutmann, 2013).

Building on the ideas and approaches of pre-K–3rd, foundations could broaden the base of this fledgling field by contributing to the establishment of an infrastructure that can nurture and sustain local efforts. Field build-ing—creating communities of research, policy, and practice—would in-clude establishing networks of sites working on pre-K–3rd approaches so that there can be regular and mutual exchanges and learning, both face to face and online.

Forums and conferences for innovators can also create a sense of mo-mentum and community for those engaged in difficult work. Foundations can fund new research and policy centers in higher education institutions and think tanks that are interested in pursuing ideas and supporting indi-viduals who can be the future leaders as these efforts increase.

Foundations can have a significant impact if they focus their resources on transforming the educator preparation system, not only for the pri-mary school but also for the entire public education system, as the Bill and Melinda Gates Foundation has begun to do for the K–12 grades. Foundations have played a pivotal role in creating several teacher resi-dency programs, but their contribution will be broader if they take on the mainline teacher education programs that produce most of America's educators (Goldstein, 2014).

As more children participate in pre-K (with 51% of 3- and 4-year-olds participating in full-day programs in 2013), teachers in the post-pre-K grades face children with different skills and experiences in their K–5 classrooms. Earlier I discussed the instructional ramifications of effective pre-K programs in the grades that follow. Foundations can assist school districts and educator preparation programs in addressing this important issue regarding post-pre-K curriculum and instruction that is slowly being acknowledged as critical to sustain gains from pre-K programs.

The idea of a new primary school is an intentional strategy to build from a few promising exemplars and to highlight them as ways to trans-form how education now begins for American children and what needs to change in the primary grades (Ritchie & Gutmann, 2013). As I have shown, such primary schools exist throughout the country, but most schools have not taken advantage of the opportunity to create a more coherent educa-tional experience for children out of the elements that are already in place. And whether more coherence makes a difference for student achievement is an open question. A RAND evaluation of implementation of pre-K–3 demonstrated modest but statistically significant increases in scores on a state reading proficiency test (Zellmann & Kilburn, 2015).

The role of foundations, combined with the federal government's sup-port through the third round of its Early Learning Challenge Fund, can tip the scale in the direction of a pre-K–3rd approach. Right now, that base is small and is highly dependent on individual innovators operating with-out enabling policies. The new provisions in ESSA provide policy levers to support pre-K–3rd implementation. Foundations that fund advocacy for policy change can make a significant difference in building the field and putting into place policies to support implementation. One such organization funded by several foundations—aiming to connect practice to policy—is the Children's Institute in Oregon (refer to Resource 3.2)

WHAT ADVOCACY ORGANIZATIONS CAN DO

In Hans Christian Andersen's "The Emperor's New Clothes," it was a child who called attention to the fact that the emperor was naked. The adults, in contrast, averted their eyes and avoided the reality before them. The moral that applies here is that advocacy for early learning programs has skirted core issues that undermine the provision of quality programs, and overlooked the fact that children living in concentrated disadvantage have the least access to these programs, undoubtedly contributing to educational inequality.

Core Issues to Address

The difficult conversations about these issues must now begin.

First, advocates must address adequate, sustained financing of quality programs. This involves issues of not only more funding but also how the funding will be generated and used. Advocates, including the leading economists among them (Friedman, 2005; Heckman, 2013; Kleinbard, 2014; Stiglitz, 2010), who point to early education as part of solutions to reduce inequality, should lay out alternative scenarios to finance what they are recommending.

There are signs that changing corporate taxes to support expansion of federally funded pre-K programs as proposed by Senator Robert Casey (D-Pennsylvania) and expansion of pre-K in New Jersey as well as taxation of financial transactions by investors (Bernstein, 2015) are finally being put on the table. While it is not likely that these financing proposals will pass the Congress in the near future, they represent a beginning in breaking through the policy ruts in which financing mechanisms for early education have languished.

When advocates call for quality programs, they must also note that the current funding for existing programs is not adequate. I agree with my colleagues at New America who concluded in their 2014 assessment of the state of pre-K–3rd, "It is wrong to call for broad increases in quality and access without recognizing the costs" (Bornfreund et al., 2014).

The new primary school with its 2 years of full-school-day pre-K education, and its full-school-day provision for kindergarten, will cost more than what the United States is now spending on pre-K–5 education. The pre-K provision is not typically part of education budgets. Efforts to expand kindergarten as a full-school-day program for about 25% of the 5-year-olds who are in part-day programs will continue to be a struggle. Thus a strong campaign for building public will must be launched to support what constitutes a long-overdue expansion of public education. Education financing, long off the table in recent decades, must return as a policy priority for reformers, including in the use of the courts to argue violations of children's civil rights to an equal education.

Alternatively, restructuring of the current K–12 system and reallocating of existing funds to the earlier years, while formidable, should be on the advocacy agenda. As one example, the reimagining of primary education is connected with the reimagining of high school education, the latter once again in the news with funding from a philanthropist, Laurine Powell Jobs. As I pointed out in Chapter 1, if student choices for the current high school years are diversified to include early college attendance, career academies, and apprenticeship programs, costs of high schools may be shifted to other sources such as businesses and to higher education. These shifts could provide more funds for the grades at the beginning of the education system.

Any serious proposal to expand pre-K must have a sustainable financing scheme to support it. Thus advocates and researchers who advocate for more pre-K programs must address the funding issues, especially in terms of longer school days (also referred to as "dosage") and higher teacher salaries and benefits. As noted earlier, these typically are lower for pre-K programs than public school salaries and benefits and often require staff to access public benefits for health care, food, and housing (Whitebrook et al., 2014).

Minnesota is poised to fund quality over access as it expands its scholarship fund for pre-K by raising the per pupil cap on program slots, which may result in smaller numbers of children served, while scholarship funds allocated by the state legislature have increased. What is clear from the Minnesota experiment is that these funds are insufficient to raise the quality of the programs, one of the goals of the scholarship approach.

As I have emphasized throughout this book, in the new primary school, pre-K and kindergarten grades should be funded at the same per pupil costs as Grades 1–5, with the same school-day hours, and should be staffed by teachers with the same qualifications as K–5 teachers. These criteria are requirements for the Preschool Development grants of the U.S. Department of Education. However, what is not addressed is how pre-K will be funded to meet these criteria, and how revenue will be generated to support these programs on a sustainable basis. Funding for pre-K should be part of the state education formula and based on actual enrollments without caps, effectively integrating pre-K into a state-funded public education system. A promising number of states are moving in this direction (Bornfreund, 2015), and more should follow.

Second, advocates must address the disturbing fact that the children who could benefit the most from quality pre-K programs are the least likely to participate in them. Supported by research on the benefits of pre-K programs, advocates have made substantial progress in the past 2 decades in building a strong case for the benefits of good pre-K programs (Yoshikawa et al., 2013). Research is playing a role in forming a deeper understanding of what effective programs are like (Yoshikawa et al., 2013).

There is strong consensus that not all programs serve children in ways that are consistent with the well-evaluated programs and that the quality of most pre-K programs must be improved, especially the programs attended by low-income children. But below the surface of that consensus, fundamental disagreements persist and, most important, frame the debates and undermine that consensus.

Third, advocates must address the possibility that quality pre-K, even 2 years of it, may not be sufficient to attain its promised outcomes. Most central to this book is the underlying argument that it is not necessary to attend to what happens to children after their pre-K experience. Pre-K, many advocates claim, fortifies children in mysterious ways that are not well understood so that they continue through K–5 grades of varying educational quality and emerge as career and college ready by the end of high school. Many people wrongly assume that we will see long-term pre-K benefits without any changes to what happens in the K–12 public education system. This is the rhetoric and narrative of leading advocates (Bartik, 2014; Heckman, 2013).

Their views fail to consider and address the quality of learning occurring in the K–5 grades and how these experiences contribute to building on and augmenting pre-K gains (see, however, McGhee-Hassrick et al., in press). Given the highly mixed results of various educational initiatives in primary education, it is easier to avoid addressing changes in how children are educated in these grades. But placing all the bets on pre-K is wishful thinking.

The evaluation of the Tennessee pre-K programs provides the most recent example of how pre-K gains were found not to be sustained in the K–3 grades (Lipsey, Farran, & Hofer, 2015). Legislators interpret these findings in two ways: Pre-K programs should not be funded because they do not lead to promised outcomes, or attention should be focused on what is being learned in the primary grades to sustain pre-K gains.

   Fourth, advocates, largely within the early education field, must agree on the qualifications and preparation of pre-K teachers and supporting staff. There is consensus that the quality of teachers matters, but there is disagreement about what makes a quality teacher and specifically what qualifications should be required. Chapter 3 focused on this issue at some length. Here, suffice it to say that experts remain divided over how teachers should be prepared, including whether or not training should occur separately from K–5 teachers and whether a bachelor's degree should be required.

   The long-awaited National Academies of Science, Engineering, and Medicine report on the early childhood workforce (birth to age 8) recommended a bachelor's degree for lead teachers and directors of early childhood programs (Allen & Kelly, 2015). However, that is a recommendation that will need to be adopted state by state, and most would agree that achievement of that recommendation is far into the future, especially in programs outside the public school system. Raising teacher qualifications means raising their compensation and, therefore, the costs of programs. The coupling of teacher qualifications and compensation has been a central approach-avoidance issue in the pre-K debates.

Roots of Advocate Disunity

At the heart of unease about, if not opposition to, the new primary school is that American children will be subjected to the more formal instructional practices of public schools at a too early age. Debates elicit hot-button images: babysitting in full-day kindergartens, paying for children to play to their hearts' content supported with public funds while mothers do yoga. Related to this unease is the position, often articulated by early educators, that since the public schools have not done a good job for children, they are unsuitable for educating young children.

   An interesting twist to this argument is why, then, is there little attention among early educators to working with primary schools to improve the quality of children's learning after pre-K? Some see the role of public education in early learning as increasing members for the teacher unions, which are characterized as "self-interested" advocates in their calls for increasing access to pre-K programs. To be fair, primary school principals and teachers are not building bridges to early educators in significant numbers. The clear losers in this adult standoff are children who are denied access to educational programs that could change their life prospects. For too many, the consequences can be tragic.

These largely unspoken, but I believe widely shared, beliefs among advocates prevents any viable coalition for pre-K as part of a public education system (Stevens, 2015). Support for this position is based in the array of nonprofit, for-profit, and religious-based programs that serve most of the children in pre-K programs and their fear that they will lose children (and revenue) to the public schools and be forced to close or to serve younger children who are more costly to serve because of higher staff-child ratios.

Truth be told, no expansion of publicly funded pre-K programs has yet eliminated or weakened this private provider sector. Community-based programs are most often a large part of the programs that benefit from expansion, especially since public schools do not have space for additional pre-K programs. And while the evidence is still being collected, it is likely that the quality of the programs, based on standards and other requirements of the state-funded or city pre-K programs, have increased the quality of children's learning experiences overall, including small changes in the key issue of adequate compensation of teachers and staff in the programs.

Most important, the expansion of publicly funded programs has benefited families in which a fifth or more of their incomes could be spent on early care and education programs. Thus in the United States, public investment, similar to what has long been the case in other countries, has the potential to build a strong political constituency for these programs. Polling results indicate that public support is indeed building.

Call for United Advocacy

In their report on the compensation of the early childhood force, Whitebrook and colleagues (2015) made the following observation:

> It is worth recognizing that it took kindergarten teachers nearly 100 years to be considered the equal of other teachers in public school systems. Their task, while challenging, was made easier because they mostly were employed in public schools already, and were seeking inclusion in a relatively uniform coherent system of services for which there was widespread public support. Most importantly, kindergarten in most states, is financed similarly to the higher grades. (p. 79)

That statement is one of the best rationales for a new American primary school that begins with pre-K as the starting line for public education. As I pointed out earlier, if pre-K teachers are considered part of a public education system, their compensation should be the same as the rest of the system. When pre-K is provided in public schools (e.g., New York City), compensation is aligned that of with K–12 teachers. However, teachers with similar qualifications in the community-based pre-K programs in New York City's universal pre-K do not earn the same salaries or have the same benefits as their counterparts in public school settings.

The new primary school does not address programs that serve children younger than the age of 3. I propose that programs for children from birth to age 3 be targeted toward the most vulnerable (i.e., not universally available) and be provided largely outside the public schools, but with connections to neighborhood primary schools being highly desirable. A few superintendents in school districts see connecting with infant-toddler programs as part of a pre-K–3 approach, but such programs are still rare.

I further propose that Head Start 2.0 focus on vulnerable children below the age of 3, to reflect the growing research on the early origins of inequality in learning opportunities for many low-income children prior to age 3 (Allen & Kelly, 2015). These are the children who are truly underserved, as Early Head Start reaches less than 5% of the eligible children. Starting with age 3, pre-K programs should be universally available and state funded, but remain voluntary until kindergarten, when attendance is compulsory.

This proposal is not original. In fact, many countries already have implemented such a scenario in their social policies for children. In France, for example, the year prior to universal pre-K in the *école maternelle* at age 3 is provided to children living in low-income neighborhoods only. Even in countries where compulsory education begins in Grade 1, most of the children have attended pre-K programs for 2 or more years before. Americans who do not support public funding for pre-K point to the late beginning of compulsory education in these countries, conveniently overlooking the widespread provision of early education prior to that time.

In the United States, however, the status quo is not easily disrupted. Big-systems change is not likely, given the current advocacy agendas, which tend to be narrowly focused and incremental on increasing participation in programs and improving quality of learning experiences for children. Given restricted resources for these programs, achieving better quality is likely to result in reduced access to these programs, under current tax and budget policies. Proposed changes in Head Start to become full-day programs equivalent to the 180-day school year, as a prime example, are likely to reduce the number of children served.

"Tinkering at the margins" best describes the current state of advocacy for early education. As advocates begin to address financing issues, they will encounter powerful opposition to reforming tax and budget policies, which is required to generate funds to support both access and quality that our children deserve (Bernstein, 2015), even though the impact is on a few individuals and the levies very small. It is not too soon to develop and advocate for restructuring the financing of early education. Better still, linking this extended struggle to the financing of the K–12 education system is an integral part of the rationale for the new American primary school.

The coming decades for advocacy could be even more tumultuous than the previous decades, when cultural wars over the primacy of families versus government in early learning raged (Karch, 2013). Those cultural wars, which emerge from time to time, are now largely background. Demographic changes in American families, the great divides in family economic resources, and the large numbers of families who cannot finance pre-K education for their children but recognize its value will hopefully be influential in future debates.

Bipartisan support for pre-K education is very strong (Stevens, 2015). But financing these programs is the big elephant in the room. That is where advocates can begin to build bridges across the divides described in this book. Joining forces with efforts to finance adequately funded public education in general should be seriously considered.

Indeed, should advocacy shift to challenging the distribution of wealth embodied in current tax policy—even though at very minimal levels—it will take bipartisan leadership and unified public support to enact change (Bernstein, 2015; Steuerle, 2013). At the time of this writing, there are few signs that these conditions are present in American civil society. Sadly, polarization and social divides characterize our times. Continuing to avert our eyes from this reality is perilous.

THE NEW AMERICAN PRIMARY SCHOOL: EMERGING PATHWAYS

The new American primary school can be a game changer. It will move the starting line for publicly supported education for all children from 5- or 6-years-old to the age of 3. It will offer the same hours of learning time to pre-K and kindergarten as older children now receive. It will equalize the compensation of pre-K and kindergarten teachers to the same levels as K–12 teachers.

And, in so doing, it can potentially provide children with more time for learning from an earlier age with well-qualified, better-compensated teachers than is now the case. Children can learn in a more continuous fashion, as teachers build on their previous experiences as well as what will come after. Evidence from the Midwest Child-Parent Center expansion indicates that this approach is one that can have highly beneficial outcomes for participating low-income children, especially African American and Hispanic children, in terms of academic outcomes (Reynolds et al.,

2014). The promise of pre-K–3rd approaches in the early literacy development of English learners and dual-language learners is also untapped (Olsen, 2014).

Establishing a new primary school, funded as part of our public education system, also allows us to shift and to target more federal resources to vulnerable children between birth and age 3. Currently, there is a huge and troubling gap between our knowledge about the development of children during the critical first 3 years of life and the lack of support for programs that can address the inequalities in learning opportunities that have their origins during this early period of life. The starting line for early intervention for vulnerable children is no longer 3 or 4, as it has been for most of a half century. Not to address the opportunity for early intervention—defined as birth to 3—is inconsistent with what we know and is socially irresponsible.

If public education available to all were to begin at 3 years of age, children who are at risk for poor educational outcomes could receive home visiting and parent engagement programs as well as center-based experiences to support their learning during their first 3 years of life. Their parents and other adult members of their families could be involved in dual-generation workforce development programs to increase the economic mobility necessary for providing living conditions and resources for the healthy development that is essential in supporting their children's learning.

Creating a new American primary school will be slow and arduous. There will always be district and local innovators who understand that starting early and connecting early learning to the K–12 grades make sense. Indeed, we know that such schools are educating their students well (Kirp, 2013). These schools and districts are now on the fringes of reform, and it is not clear whether they will be able to survive and flourish, especially when key political and educational leadership in the district changes.

These schools are not yet the norm. And educators are not to blame. The lack of the crucial instructional infrastructure to support coherent connections between educational goals, curricula, how students are taught and assessed, and how teachers are prepared and supported in their roles results in suboptimal conditions for ambitious instruction (Cohen, 2011; Cross, 2014; McGhee-Hassrick et al., in press). Thus, the core operating principle of alignment between standards, curriculum, instruction, and assessment—so central to pre-K–3—must be relentlessly re-created in each school (McGhee-Hassrick, et al., in press) until the time when school and district policies can better support that alignment than is now the case.

CHAPTER 6

FIRST THINGS FIRST!
IF NOT NOW, WHEN?

The moral arc of the universe is long, but it bends towards justice.

—Martin Luther King Jr.

Now is the time to reimagine primary education (pre-K–5) in the United States.

The idea of the American primary school, starting with pre-K for children at least at 4 years of age, is close to a century old. National education leaders such as George Stoddard in the 1930s, U.S. commissioner of education Harold Howe II in the 1960s, and American Federation of Teachers leader Al Shanker in the 1970s, among others, predicted that all young children would be attending pre-kindergarten in public schools by the beginning of the 21st century. In 2016, the United States is only halfway there, while other countries surge ahead, achieving universal, voluntary participation of their young children (Economist Intelligence Unit, 2012; European Commission, 2014).

None of these men could have predicted America's faltering progress toward their vision. None would have predicted the wide inequalities in access based on family resources or, most important, the immoral inequalities in the quality of early learning experiences in American primary schools that can start all children on a path to good life. Now is the time to push for a 21st-century agenda in education to create a first level of public education—the new American primary school—that addresses inequalities right from the start. Creating this school is the civil and human rights issue of our times.

Four actions are proposed in this book. First, we must reimagine how primary education in America can be designed for children from 3 to 10 years of age when it is rooted in the science of how children learn, as described in Chapter 1. Second, given the decentralized governance of education in the United States, we must learn from well-documented local innovations that are now creating America's new primary schools, as profiled in Chapters 2–4.

Third, we must carefully reflect on these local innovations, take note of their commonalities and site-specific features, and identify where legal or statutory reform is needed to institutionalize and support them on a sustainable and broader scale in school districts, states, and across the nation (NAESP Taskforce on Early Learning, 2012). Fourth, we must be aware that tax and budget reforms will be necessary to create the possibility of increasing the public investments, currently inadequate, given the need, that will be required to support children and for new primary schools to flourish (Atkinson, 2015; Steuerle, 2013). And reform should also be focused on simplification of the myriad rules and regulations that have sought over decades to provide quality education in a fragile and underfunded delivery system (Bornfreund et al., 2014; Sunstein, 2013).

A cross-cutting theme of these four calls to action is challenging the status quo in American education, especially in early learning as it has evolved since the 1960s (Karch, 2012). Breaking the silence on some inconvenient truths will be necessary to get us out of our current stagnation and crippling mindsets that are barriers to reaching the goals we seek: a sound, strong foundation for lifelong learning for every child.

REIMAGINE PRIMARY EDUCATION IN AMERICA

Most education reformers have neglected primary education, because they see it as teaching fundamental skills in reading, writing, and mathematics (Wagner, 2008). They assume that the time for fostering skills for thriving in a global economy is during the middle and high school years, when building on these so-called basic skills established during the primary grades occurs. Robust evidence from the early childhood years challenges these outdated views (Allen & Kelly, 2015).

Common Core State Standards focused on deeper learning (fostering critical thinking, analysis, and problem solving) have moved into primary schools and promise to focus more attention on these early grades. Indeed, the ideal early learning programs have always aimed to foster creativity, deep engagement in learning, social skills, self-direction, intentionality, and reflection, which are valued global education goals. So common ground is potentially achievable if early educators and K–5 educators are willing to move beyond their territories and their misgivings about each other.

However, all available evidence challenges the assumption that primary schools are doing just fine. According to our nation's report card, the congressionally mandated National Assessment of Educational Progress

(NAEP, 2015), two-thirds of all American children are not proficient in reading and mathematics by the end of the 3rd grade. Less than three-quarters of low-income children, including those who are children of color and dual-language learners, are reaching proficiency in these two areas by the end of 3rd grade.

The stubborn flatline of education achievement since the 1970s leads to a clear conclusion: The American primary school deserves our urgent attention now. However, everywhere we look, we see that the American public is primarily concerned about the education of their own children, but not the children of others (Putnam, 2015). One telling indicator of this disinterest is the number of store shelves devoted to books about raising one's own children versus those related to public education issues.

How to engage the public to care for the future of other people's children—our joint future on which the quality of life in our communities and nation depends—will be increasingly challenging, given the demographics of the child population and the fact that children below the age of 18 living in families are now less than 20% of all American households. Between 1970 and 2012, the share of households with married couples with children below the age of 18 halved, from 40% to 20% (Vespa et al., 2012).

In our era of quick fixes and short timelines, especially in education reform, attention is more likely to remain focused on reimagining high schools than on reimagining primary schools. Solid evidence from many fields and disciplines challenges this focus and urges policymakers and reformers to focus instead on the first decade of life as an opportunity to reduce inequality (Bradbury et al., 2015).

The science of children's development during the first decade of life has flourished in the past half century (Allen & Kelly, 2015). This knowledge requires a more nuanced balance between ensuring the safety of children and nurturing their enormous learning potential, which responds to rich relationships with others and stimulating surroundings. The capacities of infants and toddlers to learn from their environment and relationships with significant others, as well as research-based interventions to alter the trajectory of learning, are a robust source of knowledge about the factors that support children's learning from an early age. We ignore this science of children's potential to learn at our peril.

What is missing within the education reform movements is the imagination to connect this knowledge with policy and practice on a broader scale than currently exists. Coupling imagination with the urgency of re-designing the beginning of public education is needed. Some steps and concrete ideas to rectify this situation were offered in this book and should be more seriously debated.

In the book I have connected this knowledge base to redesigning the American primary school starting at age 3. Such a school not only successfully develops literacy in reading, writing, and oral communications, but also is integrated with science, mathematics, and social studies. Such a school also draws on the curiosity and imagination that are the hallmarks of the early childhood years and infuses them into the learning of content. Such a school begins to nurture the critical thinking and problem solving abilities of young children and supports children's social skills so they may work respectfully and productively with others. The "soft skills" for life (Heckman, 2013) are actually core skills, or what the U.S. Department of Education is calling "skills for success." These not only are shaped during the first decade of life but also are critical to the development of deep learning that should be nurtured starting with the primary grades (Tooley & Bornfreund, 2014).

The new American primary school develops both core skills and content skills from the very beginning of primary education, starting at age 3. There is no good reason to separate these until middle school. Such a school combines the best of traditional early education, with its focus on supporting curiosity, imagination, discovery, and self- and social regulation, with the best of primary education with its focus on subject matter or content.

Either-or divisions are no longer productive in terms of children's lives and, most important, how we know they actually learn. An integrated early education and primary school, described in Chapter 2, exemplifies this approach by putting children and what we know about how they develop and learn at the center. Effective primary schools demonstrate how this integration already is taking place and why we must work to create more of them. (See Resource 6.1.)

LEARN FROM LOCAL INNOVATION

In the United States, education is a state and local matter. The federal government currently provides about 12.5% of education funding, and this level has been declining in recent years (Hahn, 2015; Takanishi, 2015). The traditional federal role is to promote equality of educational opportunity in the context of the primary responsibility of states for educating all their children. All federal funds are targeted toward low-income students, as in the case of Title I and children in poverty, an example being Head Start, and to all children who are defined as disabled, as defined in the provisions of the Individuals with Disabilities Education Act (IDEA). The decline in federal investments in K–12 education serves as a serious

RESOURCE 6.1. HOW WELL CAN PRE-K–3RD WORK?
A COMPREHENSIVE EVALUATION

From 2009 to 2014, the RAND Corporation conducted the first evaluation of the implementation of a contemporary comprehensive pre-K–3rd reform in five sites in Hawai'i and reported student outcomes indicating a modest but statistically significant narrowing of gap in reading scores (Zellman & Kilburn, 2015). This evaluation also examined changes in state-level policies resulting from the work of the initiative. Zellman and Kilburn concluded that without continuing funding, the sustainability of the changes made at the school and classroom levels remain to be seen. However, the policy achievements at the state level are likely to continue to have an impact on practice.

The following is a modified excerpt from the brief of the report (www.rand.org/t/RB9866):

With support from the W. K. Kellogg Foundation, the Hawai'i P-20 Partnerships for Education—a collaborative overseen by state leaders in early, K–12, and higher education—launched the state's P–3 initiative in 2007, one of the first comprehensive P–3 initiatives in the country. The goal was for every child in Hawai'i to read at grade level by 3rd grade in 2012. Five demonstration sites (four on the island of Oahu and a rural site on the Big Island, Hawai'i) were selected to implement the initiative in urban, suburban, and rural areas of the state. All the schools selected had poor achievement records and served low-income children, some of whom were immigrants.

The P-20 organization also undertook state-level work to raise awareness of the potential value of early learning among state policy leaders, to align early learning standards with K–12 standards, and to prepare teachers to work in P–3 schools. Zellman and Kilburn (2015) note that state-level outcomes of the initiative are likely to endure: Hawai'i Early Learning and Development Standards, the PK–3 Graduate Certificate program based at the University of Hawai'i, and professional development courses on early childhood education that primary school staff can complete for salary credits.

Pre-K and primary school leaders in the demonstration sites signed agreements to work in the following areas:

- Improve access to early learning opportunities
- Work together to align standards, curriculum, instruction, and assessment from pre-K to Grade 3
- Implement observations of teachers to continuously improve their instruction

- Work with schools and parents to support transitions from pre-K experiences into kindergarten
- Support parents as their children's first teachers and to engage them in their children's classroom learning

Through interviews and document reviews from 2009–2014, Zellman and Kilburn (2015) concluded that most of the elements of what was then understood as a pre-K–3rd approach had been implemented. There were variations from site to site, based on the initiative's design to enable each site to select activities that best met the shared areas of focus. Each of the five sites implemented P–3 for different lengths of time.

The evaluators found that, compared with primary schools not involved in the initiative, more years of participating in the initiative raised reading scores modestly but significantly and increased the likelihood of scoring proficient on the Hawai'i State Assessment reading test. They note, "although activities other than P–3 were occurring in the sites that may have contributed to these impacts, the findings are encouraging in showing a narrowing of the reading score test gap by the end of the P–3 initiative. The impact is comparable to estimates of the effects of nine additional weeks of schooling and is higher than an estimate of the average effect size for elementary school interventions for mainstream students" (p. 3).

Zellman and Kilburn (2015) identified six implications for future pre-3rd initiatives and evaluations:

- Determine in advance the appropriate balance between standardization and site-specific needs and resources, rather than relying on one-size-fit-all approaches
- Consider contracts that specify outcomes rather than activities—increasingly recognized as a valuable approach for education and social service contracting
- Establish measurable, standardized outcomes for the work to enable monitoring and suggest midcourse corrections if the sites are not producing expected outcomes
- Plan explicitly for unanticipated changes in policy and personnel
- Consider sustainability from the inception
- Require explicit agreements between high-level early education and K–12 administrators to engage in the collaborative work between the two sectors

For the full report of the evaluation, go to www.rand.org/t/RR1100.

Source: Gail L. Zellman and M. Rebecca Kilburn. (2015). *How Well Did P–3 Work? The Hawai'i Preschool–Third Grade Education Reform Initiative.* Santa Monica, CA: RAND Corporation.

warning that vulnerable children—those who live in low-income families, are disabled, or speak a first language other than English—will not receive the resources and support to which they are entitled under existing laws. This scenario includes currently inadequate resources to meet current and projected needs of children and their families.

Even the Obama administration, which has been characterized as increasing the federal influence in education, provides grants to states to develop their own standards and assessment systems in early learning. Thus, state and local control of education is largely sustained in some 15,000 school districts and 100,000 schools in the United States.

School districts and a few states have moved to begin public education at age 3 or 4. The role of mayors of major urban cities should not be overlooked. In the pre-K–3rd space, innovation occurs mainly in local school districts (Ritchie & Gutmann, 2013). Learning from these local innovations, in the context of federal and state policies, will be essential to expanding the new American primary school, and points to an approach to education research and evaluation that is based on a close examination of and reflection on local practice (Mehta, 2013). An analysis of what can be learned from local innovations thus far will be valuable for other school districts that are contemplating similar change. Diversity of approaches within common operating principles is the American way.

But we cannot stop at supporting and learning from local implementation. The United States is a large, diverse, and decentralized country, characteristics best exemplified in its education and child investment policies that intersect with family values. The majority of investments in children come from state coffers, largely for their K–12 education and for health care (Hahn, 2015). This division of responsibilities for children contributes to wide inequalities between states in their support for children (O'Hare, 2012) that must be addressed in a nation founded on principles of equality of opportunity.

States, as well as the federal government, have a responsibility to level the playing field for children. Historically, addressing inequalities has been the role of the federal government, but there are encouraging signs that states such as California are directing local education agencies to allocate education funds based on the backgrounds of children, including family resources, race and ethnicity, disabilities, and linguistic backgrounds. Early studies of resource allocation in California's districts, however, are raising questions about whether funds are being used for their intended purposes. And at the federal level, current levels of funding are not adequate to meet current needs under existing laws.

Unfortunately, provision of pre-K education is not one of eight priorities for consideration by California's state education agency, and by implication pre-K is not considered in law and in practice as an important factor in leveling the playing field in education. Given what we know about pre-K as a key contributor to reducing racial/ethnic and economic disparities, access to pre-K as a civil and human right should be high on a social justice agenda that targets educational inequalities and the reduction of poverty.

PURSUE STATUTORY CHANGE IN BASIC RIGHTS TO EDUCATION

Strategies to pursue statutory change in basic rights to education should be sought at the state level to provide a legal framework for ensuring children's rights to public education starting at age 3. This is a long-term strategy and therefore should ensue without delay. Other strategies described in this book should also be pursued.

Compulsory attendance at age 5 in kindergarten should be given serious consideration based on what we know about children's capacities to learn from an early age, as reviewed in Chapter 1. In most states, this change would move the age of entry into compulsory education from Grade 1 to kindergarten. The recent veto by Governor Jerry Brown of California of legislation to make kindergarten compulsory indicates that elected officials are reluctant to increase state responsibilities and consequently funds for another year of education, regardless of the evidence base for it. At the same time, the state of Hawai'i, with a new pilot program of pre-K education, has instituted kindergarten as the beginning of compulsory public education.

The role of the federal government should be to continue to hold the states accountable for leveling the learning field, especially gaps in opportunities to learn among students. That role has been steadily eroded by declines in federal education funding (Hahn, 2015). The federal government, in its research support role, can also foster interstate learning based on local innovation in primary education and hopefully advance shared standards and regulations that cross state borders (Bornfreund et al., 2014). These regional associations are promising, but it is too early to predict their growth and their influence.

Changes in law do not necessarily lead to desired outcomes. Unfunded mandates like the Individuals with Disabilities Education Act (IDEA) is a prime example. However, such a law does provide a framework and grounds for pursing funding for services that do not now characterize early learning, which remains very vulnerable to economic conditions and political cross-currents. IDEA established a legal entitlement of children with special needs to an appropriate education. A similar entitlement to early learning should also be pursued to provide a stronger basis on which sustained funding can occur.

With a few exceptions such as in New Jersey (*Abbott v. Burke*) and in New York (Campaign for Fiscal Equity), advocates have not pursued legal strategies, including access to pre-kindergarten education, for good reasons. Such a strategy requires a long-term commitment, as in *Abbott v. Burke*, which took 25 years, followed by continuing court battles to shape implementation of quality programs for low-income children. But taking a historical perspective, 25 years is not long compared with ideas espoused over several decades that have achieved weak traction as a result of public campaigns and child advocacy (Gormley, 2012). Advocates have also pointed to changes in the composition of courts at all levels, including the Supreme Court, as a reason for not pursuing legal action, but that is no justification for inaction.

Legal advocacy, as well as communications and constituency-building strategies, should be strengthened in the future. Specifically, civil rights lawsuits should be initiated in states where there is good evidence that children have unequal access to quality pre-K programs. The courts may be our only recourse in the coming years.

REFORM TAX AND BUDGET POLICY

As noted above, the passage of laws does not necessarily lead to desired outcomes. The inadequacy of public funds to implement laws continues to be a formidable barrier to fulfilling legal obligations even if they are in place. Clearly, reform of tax and budget policy at the federal (Atkinson, 2015; Hahn, 2015; Steurele, 2013) and state levels will also be required in order to generate the funds necessary for public investments in the new primary school, as well as other programs for children. The United States is one of the few nations in the world that invests less in low-income children's education than it does in that of more advantaged children.

Future proposals for financing education should begin with pre-K education. The image of Oliver Twist begging, "Can I have more, sir?" is apt. Right now and in the foreseeable future, there is not much more to invest in children without changes in tax and budget policies (Hahn, 2015). Raising the sales tax (Denver and San Antonio) and approving dedicated levies for programs (Seattle) do provide for models that could lead to expansions for more children. Much more is required.

In Minnesota, the scholarship fund approach, instituted about 20 years ago, still serves less than 10% of the income-eligible children and has done little to increase the quality of programs (Lieberman & Bornfreund, 2015). And Georgia, the flagship state for universal pre-K funded by the state lottery (Raden, 1999), is seeking to broaden its funding base for early learning as program costs and competition for lottery funds for higher education scholarships increase.

Avoiding financing issues or denying that they exist only increases the frustration among advocates, as well as educators, who must continue to work with inadequate resources for programs and for staff. Many children, eligible for means-tested programs, remain unserved, and compensation for well-prepared staff—a leading indicator of quality programs—remains at abysmal levels (Whitebrook et al., 2015), even forcing staff to turn to public benefit programs to survive. We should no longer leave these issues off the table.

It is time to raise the question of whether the federal and state governments invest adequately in early education. From all available data, including international comparisons, the answer is clear: not at all. Future efforts must address the disparities across states in the funding of early education, including attention to the costs of the programs in the private sector.

As noted in Chapter 1, in New York City in 2015–2016, the per pupil cost of its universal pre-K program is about $10,239 for a full-day, full-school-year program. Comparable costs in private schools in the city range up to $40,000 per child, a sum financed entirely by families. Both New Jersey and the District of Columbia invest more per child than New York City does. At the same time, pre-K investments in Florida, one of the few states with a universal pre-K provision, are about $2,238 per child (NIEER, 2015).

These wide inequalities in investments in the early education of young children, both within the public sector and between the public and the private sectors, must be addressed. Combined with the strong scientific consensus about the opportunities we have to alter the life course of the majority of American children, the use of the courts once again to reduce social inequalities must be renewed. As I finish writing this book, the U.S. Congress is increasingly gridlocked. It is highly unlikely that any major federal legislation to address these inequalities will pass. A few state legislatures may continue to invest relatively small amounts in increasing access to pre-K programs. Cities, under the leadership of mayors, can provide more programs.

The outlook is grim: inequalities in access to programs based on the economic resources of families and inequalities in the quality of educational experiences for children in the existing programs. Children who can benefit most from good primary education—those living in concentrated disadvantage, including the minimal economic resources of their families; who have special needs; whose home language is not English—are least likely to be in these programs. The courts increasingly are our only re-course for the foreseeable future.

Advocates and education reformers must recognize that they have been fighting for declining resources for several decades (Steiner, 1981), and the situation is not likely to improve under current conditions (Hahn, 2015). In fiscal year 1996, discretionary funds were about 34%of the fed-eral budget, with about 7% of that discretionary spending allocated to education. In fiscal year 2015, discretionary investments made up about 29% of the federal budget, with about 6% of that discretionary funding allocated to education. In the face of inaction, of sticking our heads in the sand, which is the status quo, increased investment in children will be small to meager, and likely none at all.

The courage to address tax policy, especially revenue generation and corporate tax policies in a global economy (Atkinson, 2015; Piketty, 2014), is required. Turning the debate from deficit reduction to human capital investments that have the potential to contribute to a more pro-ductive society with less inequality is directly relevant to the need for in-creased education investments (Stiglitz & Greenwald, 2014). I see a few encouraging signs that this is occurring, but certainly no groundswell.

There is public consensus that education is one of the sectors that must be targeted to reduce inequality in America, and that greater invest-ments in public education are needed (Sawhill & Rodrigue, 2015). And that consensus coexists with the recognition that the American education system is itself contributing to inequality (Porter, 2015) by working only for a few (Kristof, 2014). Calls for greater investments must be coupled with calls for adequate financing of education, especially primary educa-tion. That will entail difficult disruptions of the status quo.

CHALLENGE THE STATUS QUO

The early learning field faces a crossroads in its evolution as a field. It can continue to struggle to create new systems out of what has evolved over 50 years from deeply entrenched, competing institutional and organiza-tional interests (Karch, 2012). It can seek to streamline and simplify the massive numbers of regulations and accountability requirements that seek to bolster an inadequately funded sector, as is currently the case for Head Start with its 1,000-plus regulations. It can continue to accommodate to (or ignore) declining public investments and be satisfied with small gains. And it can continue to think about ways to strengthen itself without en-gaging with powerful allies to work toward common ground and shared goals, including addressing where the funds to support these investments will come from. It is time to challenge this status quo.

This book aims for change on a large scale. The question is, What would such change look like? At its inception, pre-K–3rd can be considered a stealth strategy to connect the two galaxies of early education and existing primary education. The victories thus far have been limited, and many of the achievements remain outside debates about educational transformation. Intergalactic connections remain a black hole.

What we have learned is that this strategy—by whatever name—faces an uphill battle in the context of available funds to expand pre-K provision at any scale without changes in education codes and children's rights to early education, not to mention significant increases in public investments. One of the lessons of pre-K–3rd thus far is that good intentions, public campaigns, and creative and committed leaders are not enough.

Equally daunting is the continuing existence of two camps in education—early education and K–12 public education. While pre-K–3rd efforts have had some traction, for the most part, their success is dependent on committed, energetic, creative, savvy educators at the local level who are leveraging what they have in their arsenal to forge effective connections between the two camps (Kirp, 2013; Marietta, 2010a; Marietta, 2010b; Nyhan, 2015). They are the pioneers whose achievements are considerable in the districts and schools in which they are working. Truth be told, they are working in and across two chaotic sectors in which common learning standards, curriculum, and assessment must be reinvented at the local level, often by individual teachers working in isolation. The work is long and hard and highly dependent on local leadership and innovators. This should not be the case.

Their efforts will be isolated and likely unsustainable without attention to three formidable barriers:

- Existing educational policy provisions regarding when basic rights to education begin
- The funding mechanism that is based on those provisions
- Changing the culture and practice that rests on the first two

To return to the analogy from architecture, form shapes function.

Calls of moral imperatives for fairness and equal opportunity to address early inequalities in learning opportunities may increase, if the country continues to address economic inequalities and their consequences for social cohesion (Stiglitz, 2010). Early education is increasingly evoked as part of the solution for economic inequalities, with little understanding of what it will take for early learning to make a meaningful contribution to narrowing learning gaps and to developing workplace skills (Heckman, 2015).

Economists focus on outcomes and sometimes on inputs, leaving the critical connection between the two as a black hole of what actually takes place between educators and students to produce the outcomes we seek. What happens in the primary school, as described in this book, matters fundamentally for greater social equality.

The divide between rhetoric and reality is vast. And it will be part of a much larger solution that includes not only the transformation of American education into a pre-K–lifelong learning system but also how the United States chooses to address economic and social inequalities outside its schools.

The dominant economic framework or case for pre-K education has reached its limits. This framework has advanced the cause for early learning more than previous ones based on social justice (Gormley, 2012). A new narrative must now be crafted, combining the gains made by the economic case and lifting the social and moral case for children's human rights to a basic quality education from the start (Marmot, 2015).

As I pointed out in Chapter 1, in 2015 the United Nations put in place the Sustainable Development Goals (SDG), successor to the 2000 Millennium Development Goals. Reaffirming longstanding international commitments to universal primary education, the SDG now includes attaining universal access to pre-primary education by 2030. For the first time, the United Nations has recognized the critical value of educational programs prior to compulsory primary education, typically at Grade 1. It is time for the United States to do the same.

Educating all children right from the start is the civil and human rights issue of the 21st century. In the 20th century, we fought successfully for civil rights based on race, gender, and language of instruction. Today, we must address inequalities in access to early education based on economic resources of families and in the uneven quality of educational experiences of their children.

We must marshal the scientific evidence, employing its influence—as was done in *Brown v. Board of Education*—to argue that the vast potential for learning is being squandered from an early age, before kindergarten, to launch every child on a successful pathway to a good and productive life. Neglecting to do so will lead to a nation of individuals inadequately educated for a global world and result in continuing and widening social divides in the United States itself.

We now have the opportunity to design a 21st-century primary school that is rooted in America's founding principles of fairness and the pursuit of happiness. This book proposes a framework that is offered in hopes of challenging the status quo, combating inertia, and provoking a sense of urgency about lost opportunities not only for children but also for the nation.

Talent and potential are universally distributed, and so must be opportunities to develop that potential. The reauthorization of ESEA, now the Every Student Succeeds Act (ESSA), provides an opportunity to reimagine a new American primary school.

It will be up to us to visualize what the future for children's primary education will be, and how we get there. We have the responsibility to create powerful pathways to lifelong learning starting with the early childhood years. What will be our powerful and convincing narrative? If not now, when?

REFERENCES

Allen, L., & Kelly, B. (2015). *Transforming the workforce for children birth through age 8: A unifying foundation*. Washington, DC: National Academies Press.

Alexander, K., & Entwisle, D. (2014). *The long shadow: Family background, disadvantaged urban youth, and the transition to adulthood*. New York, NY: Russell Sage Foundation.

Alliance for Excellent Education. (2005, August). Teacher attrition: A costly loss to the nation and to the states. Retrieved from nctaf.org/wp-content/uploads/TeacherAttrition.pdf

Aragon, S. (2016). Teacher shortages: What we know. Denver, CO: Education Commission of the States.

Atkinson, A. (2015). *Inequality: What can be done?* Cambridge, MA: Harvard University Press.

Attendance Works & Healthy Schools Campaign. (2015). *Mapping the early attendance gap: Charting a course for school success*. Retrieved from www.attendanceworks.org/wordpress/wp-content/uploads/2015/07/Mapping-the-Early-Attendance-Gap-Final-4.pdf

Bartik, T. (2014). *From preschool to prosperity: The economic payoff to early childhood education*. Kalamazoo, MI: W. E. Upjohn Institute.

Bassok, D., Fitzpatrick, M., Loeb, S., & Paglayan, A. S. (2013). The early childhood care and education workforce from 1990 through 2010: Changing dynamics and persistent concerns. *Education Finance and Policy, 8*(4), 581–601.

Bassok, D., & Rorem, A. (2015). Is kindergarten the new first grade? (EdPolicyWorks Working Paper Series, No. 20). Retrieved from curry.virginia.edu/uploads/resourceLibrary/20_Bassok Is_Kindergarten_The_New_First_Grade.pdf

Beatty, B. (1995). *Preschool education in America: The culture of young children from the colonial era to the present*. New Haven, CT: Yale University Press.

Bernstein, J. (2015, July 22). The case for a tax on financial transactions. *New York Times*. Retrieved from www.nytimes.com/2015/07/22/opinion/the-case-for-a-tax-on-financial-transactions.html

Björklund, A., & Salvanes, K. G. (2011). Education and family background: Mechanisms and policies. In E. Hanushek & F. Welch (Eds.), *Handbook of the economics of education* (Vol. 3, pp. 201–247). Amsterdam, Netherlands: North Holland.

Blank, M. J., Melaville, A., & Shah, B. P. (2003). *Making the difference: Research and practice in community schools.* Washington, DC: Coalition of Community Schools.

Boots, S. W. (2015). New ways of creating opportunities for families in poverty. In First Focus, *Big ideas—Pioneering change: Innovative ideas for children and families* (pp. 1–13). Washington, DC: First Focus.

Bornfreund, L. (2015, June 17). New federal focus on building skills for success. *EdCentral.* Retrieved from www.edcentral.org/new-federal-focus-building-skills-success

Bornfreund, L., Cook, S., Lieberman A., & Loewenberg, A. (2015). *From crawling to walking: Ranking states on birth–3rd grade policies that support strong readers.* Washington, DC: New America.

Bornfreund, L., McCann, C., Williams, C., & Guernsey, L. (2014). Beyond subprime learning: Accelerating progress in early education. Retrieved from static.newamerica.org/attachments/743-beyond-subprime-learning/Beyond_Subprime_Learning_by_Bornfreund-et-al_New_America_Jul2014.pdf

Bradbury, B., Corak, M., Waldfogel, J., & Washbrook, E. (2015). *Too many children left behind: The U.S. achievement gap in comparative perspective.* New York, NY: Russell Sage Foundation.

Brown, K., Squires, J., Connors-Tadros, L., & Horowitz, M. (2014). Preparing principals to support early childhood teachers. Retrieved from ceelo.org/wp-content/uploads/2014/07/ceelofast content/uploads/2014/07/ceelo_fast_fact_principal_prep.pdf

Burchinal, M., Vandergrift, N., Pianta, R., & Mashburn, A. (2010). Threshold analysis of association between child care quality and child outcomes for low-income children in pre-kindergarten programs. *Early Childhood Research Quarterly, 25,* 166–176.

Butler, L., & Markman, E. (2012). Preschoolers use intentional and pedagogical cues to guide inductive inferences and exploration. *Child Development, 83*(4), 1416–1428.

Carnegie Council on Adolescent Development. (1996). *Great transitions: Preparing adolescents for a new century.* New York, NY: Carnegie Corporation of New York.

Cascio, E. U., & Schanzenbach, D. W. (2014, June 19). Expanding preschool access for disadvantaged children. Retrieved from www.brookings.edu/research/papers/2014/06/19-expanding-preschool-access-disadvantaged-children-cascio-schanzenbach

Chase-Lansdale, P. L., & Brooks-Gunn, J. (2014). Two-generation programs in the twenty-first century. *The Future of Children, 24*(1), 13–39.

Cherlin, A. (2014). *Labor's love lost: The rise and fall of the working-class family in America.* New York, NY: Russell Sage Foundation.

Child Trends Databank. (2015). *Head start.* Retrieved from www.childtrends.org/?indicators=head-start.

Children's Institute. (2014). Building blocks: How two Oregon communities built early learning facilities using public funds. Retrieved from www.childinst.org /images/Building-Blocks- Fall2014.pdf

Cohen, D. (2011). Teaching and its predicaments. Cambridge, MA: Harvard University Press.

Cohen, D., & Moffitt, S. (2009). The ordeal of equality: Did federal regulation fix the schools? Cambridge, MA: Harvard University Press.

Cohen, D., Stern, V., Balaban, N., & Gropper, N. (2016). Observing and recording the behavior of young children (6th ed.). New York, NY: Teachers College Press.

Coleman, James S. (1966). Equality of educational opportunity study. Washington, DC: U.S. Department of Health, Education, and Welfare.

Crosnoe, R., Bonazzo, C., & Wu, N. (2015). Healthy learners: A whole child approach to reducing disparities in early education. New York, NY: Teachers College Press.

Cross, C. (2014). Political education: Setting the course for state and federal policy (2nd ed.). New York, NY: Teachers College Press.

Darling-Hammond, L. (2010). The flat world and education: How America's commitment to equity will determine our future. New York, NY: Teachers College Press.

Dell'Antonia, K. (2014, December 10). "Invest in us," and our parents, too. New York Times. Retrieved from parenting.blogs.nytimes.com/2014/12/10 /invest-in-us-and-our-parents-too.

Diamond, J. (2008). Welcome to the aquarium. A year in the lives of children. New York, NY: Free Press.

Dow, S. (2014). Testimony to the New York City Council. Retrieved from media .wbur.org/wordpress/11/files/2014/02/0220_prek-testimony.pdf

Dryfoos, J., & Maguire, S. (2002). Inside full-service community schools. Thousand Oaks, CA: Corwin Press.

Duncan, G., & Chase-Lansdale, P. L. (Eds.). (2001) For better and for worse: Welfare reform and the well-being of children and families. New York, NY: Russell Sage Foundation.

Duncan, G., & Murnane, R. (2013). Restoring opportunity: The crisis of inequality and the challenge for American education. Cambridge, MA: Harvard University Press.

Economist Intelligence Unit. (2012). Starting well: Benchmarking early education across the world. Retrieved from graphics.eiu.com/upload/eb/Lienstartingwell .pdf

Education Commission of the States. (2013). Access to kindergarten: Age issues in state statutes. Retrieved from mb2.ecs.org/reports/Report.aspx?id=32

Education Commission of the States. (2014, March). Children must attend kindergarten. Retrieved from ecs.force.com/mbdata/mbquestRT?rep=Kq1403.

Spero, F. (2015, October 22). When schools and teachers don't reach out to families, it's bad for everyone. Education Post. Retrieved from educationpost.org/when -schools-and-teachers-dont-reach-out-to-families-its-bad-for-everyone

Epstein, J. (2011). *School, family, and community partnerships: Preparing educators and improving schools* (2nd ed.). Boulder, CO: Westview Press.

European Commission/EACEA/Eurydice/Eurostat. (2014). Key data on early childhood education and care in Europe. 2014 Edition. Retrieved from eacea.ec.europa.eu/education/eurydice/documents/key_data_series/166EN.pdf

First Five Years Fund—2015 Poll. (2015). Retrieved from ffyf.org/2015-poll/

Friedman, B. (2005). *The moral consequences of economic growth*. Cambridge, MA: Harvard University Press.

Fromberg, D. (2003). Professionalism in early childhood teacher education in an era of elevated standardization and minimalist testing. *Journal of Early Childhood Teacher Education, 24*(2), 103–109.

Gadsden, V. (2013). *Family engagement in pre-K–3*. New York, NY: Foundation for Child Development.

Gallup. (2014, September 8). In U.S., 70% favor federal funds to expand pre-K education. Retrieved from www.gallup.com/poll/175646/favor-federal-funds -expand-pre-education.aspx

Galston, W. A., & McElvein, E. (April 2015). *Institutional innovation: How it happens and why it matters*. Washington, DC: Brookings Center for Effective Public Management. Retrieved from www.brookings.edu/research /papers/2015/04/22-institutional-innovation-galston-mcelvein

Garcia, A., & Williams, C. P. (2015). *Stories from the nation's capital: Building instructional programs and supports for dual language learners from pre-K– 3rd grade in Washington, DC*. Washington, DC: New America.

Genesee, F., & Lindholm-Leary, K. J. (2011). The education of English language learners. In K. Harris, S. Graham, & T. Urdan (Eds.), *APA education psychology handbook* (Vol. 3, pp. 499–526). Washington, DC: American Psychological Association Press.

Gilliam, W. S. (2008). *Implementing policies to reduce likelihood of preschool expulsion*. FCD Policy Brief No. 3. New York, NY: Foundation for Child Development.

Goffin, S. (2013). *Early childhood education for a new era: Leading for our profession*. New York, NY: Teachers College Press.

Goldin, C., & Katz, L. F. (2010). *The race between education and technology*. Cambridge, MA: Belknap Press of Harvard University Press.

Goldman, S., & Pellegrino, J. (October 2015). Research on learning and instruction: Implications for curriculum, instruction, and assessment. *Policy Insights from the Behavioral and Brain Sciences, 2*(1), 33–41.

Goldring, R., Gray, L., & Bitterman, A. (2013). *Characteristics of public and private elementary and secondary school teachers in the United States: Results from the 2011–12 Schools and Staffing Survey* (NCES 2013-314). Washington, DC: National Center for Education Statistics. Retrieved from nces .ed.gov/pubs2013/2013314.pdf

Goldstein, D. (2014). *The teacher wars: A history of America's most embattled profession*. New York, NY: Doubleday.

Gopnik, A., & Wellman, H. M. (2012). Reconstructing constructivism: Causal models, Bayesian learning mechanisms, and the theory theory. *Psychological Bulletin, 138*(6), 1085.

Gordon, E. W., & Rajagopalan, K. (2016). *The testing and learning revolution: The future of assessment in education.* New York, NY: Palgrave Macmillan.

Gormley, W. (2012). *Voices for children: Rhetoric and public policy.* Washington, DC: Brookings Institution Press.

Green, E. (2014). *Building a better teacher: How teaching works (and how to teach it to everyone).* New York, NY: W. W. Norton.

Greenberg, J., Walsh, K., & McKee, A. (2015). 2014 Teacher prep review: A review of the nation's teacher preparation programs. Retrieved from www.nctq.org/dmsView/Teacher_Prep_Review_2014_Report

Guernsey, L., Bornfreund, L., McCann, C., & Williams, C. (2014). *Subprime learning: Early education in America since the great recession.* Washington, DC: New America.

Guernsey, L., & Mead, S. (2010). A Next Social Contract for the Primary Years of Education. Retrieved from www.newamerica.org/education-policy/a-next-social-contract-for-the-primary-years-of-education

Guttmacher, A. (2012). Nature, nurture, and the research agenda at NICHD. In IOM (Institute of Medicine) and NRS (National Research Council), *From neurons to neighborhoods: An update: Workshop summary* (pp. 10–13). Washington, DC: The National Academies Press.

Hahn, H. (2015). Federal expenditures on children: What budget policy means for children's policy. *Social Policy Report.* Retrieved from www.srcd.org/sites/default/files/documents/vol_29_1.pdf

Hamilton, S. (1990). *Apprenticeship for adulthood: Preparing youth for the future.* New York, NY: Free Press.

Hargreaves, A. (2014). Teachers are not a problem: They are an opportunity. Retrieved from blogs.edweek.org/edweek/finding_common_ground/2014/05/teachers_are_not_a_problem_they_are_an_opportunity.html.

Hargreaves, A., & Fullan, M. (2012). *Professional capital: Transforming teaching in every school.* New York, NY: Teachers College Press.

Heckman, J. (2013). *Giving kids a fair chance.* Cambridge, MA: MIT Press.

Henderson, A. T., Mapp, K. L., Johnson, V., & Davies, D. (2007). *Beyond the bake sale: The essential guide to family-school partnerships.* New York, NY: The New Press.

Hong, S. (2011). *A cord of three strands: A new approach to parent engagement in schools.* Cambridge, MA: Harvard Education Press.

Horowitz, F. D., Darling-Hammond, L., & Bransford, J., with Comer, J., Rosebrock, K., Austin, K., & Rust, F. (2005). Educating teachers for developmentally appropriate practice. In L. Darling-Hammond & J. Bransford (Eds.), *Preparing teachers for a changing world: What teachers should learn and be able to do* (pp. 88–125). San Francisco, CA: Jossey-Bass.

Kalil, A. (2012). *A dual-generation strategy: Using technology to support learning for children and for families.* New York, NY: Foundation for Child Development.

Karch, A. (2013). *Early start: Preschool politics in the United States.* Ann Arbor, MI: University of Michigan Press.

Katz, M. (1990). *The undeserving poor: From the war on poverty to the war on welfare.* New York, NY: Pantheon Books.

Kauerz, K., & Coffman, J. (2013). *Framework for planning, implementing, and evaluating pre-K–3rd approaches.* Seattle, WA: College of Education, University of Washington.

Kelly, D., Xie, H., Nord, C. W., Jenkins, F., Chan, J. Y., & Kastberg, D. (2013). *Performance of U.S. 15-year-old students in mathematics, science, and reading literacy in an international context: First look at PISA 2012* (NCES 2014-024). Washington, DC: National Center for Education Statistics. Retrieved from http://nces.ed.gov/pubs2014/2014024rev.pdf

Khan, S. (2012). *The one world schoolhouse: Education reimagined.* New York, NY: Twelve Books.

Kirp, D. (2013). *Improbable scholars: The rebirth of a great American school system and a strategy for America's schools.* New York, NY: Oxford University Press.

Klein, J. (2014) *Lessons of hope: How to fix our schools.* New York, NY: Harper.

Kleinbard, E. (2014). *We are better than this: How government should spend our money.* New York, NY: Oxford University Press.

Kostelnick, M. J., & Gracy, M. L. (2009). *Getting it right from the start: The principal's guide to early childhood education.* Thousand Oaks, CA: Corwin.

Kotlowitz, A. (1991). *There are no children here: The story of two boys growing up in the other America.* New York, NY: Doubleday.

Kristof, N. (2014, October 26). The American Dream is leaving America. *New York Times*, p. SR13.

Lagemann, E. (1989). *The politics of knowledge: The Carnegie Corporation, philanthropy, and public policy.* Middletown, CT: Wesleyan University Press.

Lee, V., & Burkam, D. (2002). *Inequality at the starting gate: Social background differences in achievement as children begin school.* Washington, DC: Economic Policy Institute.

Li, J., Fung, H., Bakeman, R., Rae, K., & Wei, W.-C. (2014). How European American and Taiwanese mothers talk to their children about learning. *Child Development, 85,* 1206–1221.

Libassi, C. J. (2014). *Raising Arizona: Lessons for the nations from a state's experience with full-day kindergarten.* Washington, DC: New America.

Lieberman, A., & Bornfreund, L. (2015). Building strong readers in Minnesota: Pre-K–3rd grade policies that support children's literacy development. Retrieved from www.edcentral.org/wp-content/uploads/2015/09/Building-Strong-Readers_Final-.pdf

Lieberman, A., & McCann, C. (2014, September 5). The third rail: Funding reform for early learning programs—EdCentral. Retrieved from www.edcentral.org/third-rail-funding-reform-early-learning

Lindholm-Leary, K. (2015, March 9). *Sobrato Family Foundation, Early Academic and Literacy Project, after five full years of implementation. Final research report.* Cupertino, CA: Sobrato Family Foundation.

Lipsey, M. W., Farran, D. C., & Hofer, K. G., (2015). *A randomized control trial of the effects of a statewide voluntary prekindergarten program on children's skills and behaviors through third grade* (Research Report). Nashville, TN: Vanderbilt University, Peabody Research Institute.

Maeroff, G. (2006). *Building blocks: Making children successful in the early years of school.* New York, NY: Palgrave Macmillan.

Marietta, G. (2010a, September). Pre-K–3rd: How superintendents lead change. *FCD pre-K–3rd Policy and Action Brief.* New York, NY: Foundation for Child Development. Retrieved from fcd-us.org/sites/default/files/FCDSuperintBrief.pdf

Marietta, G. (2010b, December). Lessons for pre-K–3rd from Montgomery County Public Schools. *FCD Policy Brief.* New York, NY: Foundation for Child Development. Retrieved from fcd-us.org/sites/default/files/FINAL%20MC%20Case%20Study.pdf

Marietta, G., & Bookover, E. (June 2011). Effectively educating pre-K–3rd English language-learners (ELL) in Montgomery County Public Schools. *FCD Case Study.* New York, NY: Foundation for Child Development. Retrieved from fcd-us.org/sites/default/files/FCDCaseStudyMntgmryCtyELLS.pdf

Marietta, G., & Marietta, S. (2013). *Pre-K–3rd's lasting architecture: Successfully serving linguistically and culturally diverse students in Union City, New Jersey.* New York, NY: Foundation for Child Development. Retrieved from fcd-us.org/sites/default/files/FCDCaseStdyUnionCity(2).pdf

Marmot, M. (2015). *The health gap: The challenge of an unequal world.* London, England: Bloomsbury.

McEwen, B. (2012). The role of stress in physical and mental health. In IOM (Institute of Medicine) and NRC (National Research Council). *From neurons to neighborhoods: An update: Workshop summary* (pp. 14–18). Washington, DC: The National Academies Press.

McGhee-Hassrick, E., Raudenbush, S. W., & Rosen, L. (in press). *The ambitious elementary school: Its conception, design, and contribution to educational equality.* Chicago, IL: University of Chicago Press.

Mead, S. (2011). Pre-K–3rd: Principals as crucial instructional leaders. Retrieved from fcd-us.org/sites/default/files/FCDPrincipalsBrief7.pdf

Mead, S. (2014). Renewing Head Start's promise: Invest in what works for disadvantaged preschoolers. Retrieved from bellwethereducation.org/sites/default/files/Bellwether_Head-Start_July2014.pdf

Mehta, J. (2013). *The allure of order: High hopes, dashed expectations, and the troubled quest to remake American schooling*. New York, NY: Oxford University Press.

Mehta, J., & Teles, S. (2014). Professionalism 2.0: The case for plural professionalism in education. In M. Q. McShane & F. M. Hess (Eds.), *Teacher quality 2.0: Toward a new era in education reform*. Cambridge, MA: Harvard Education Press.

Minnesota Campaign for Achievement Now (MinnCAN). (2014). Starting strong: Pre-K–3rd success stories from across Minnesota. Minneapolis, MN: Author. Retrieved from www.minncan.org/sites/minncan.org/files/MinnCAN -StartingStrong-WEB.pdf

Mourshed, M., Chijioke, C., & Barber, M. (2010). How the world's most improved school systems keep getting better. Retrieved from www.mckinsey.com /client_service/social_sector/latest thinking/worlds_most_improved_schools

Muschkin, C., Ladd, H., & Dodge, K. (2015). Impact of North Carolina's early childhood initiatives on special education placements in third grade. *Educational Evaluation and Policy Analysis, 37*(4), 478–500.

NAESP Foundation. (2011). Transforming early learning in grades pre-K–3. Retrieved from www.naesp.org/naesp-foundation/early-childhood-task-force

NAESP Task Force on Early Learning. (2012). *Building & supporting an aligned system: A vision for transforming education across the pre-K–grade three years*. Alexandria, VA: NAESP Foundation.

National Association of Elementary School Principals (NAESP). (2014). Leading pre-K–3 learning communities: Competencies for effective principal practice. Retrieved from www.naesp.org/sites/default/files/leading-pre-k-3-learning -communities-executive-summary.pdf

National Commission on Excellence in Education. (1983). *A nation at risk: The imperative for educational reform: A report to the nation and the secretary of education, United States Department of Education*. Washington, DC: Author.

National Commission on Teaching and America's Future. (2007). Policy brief: The high cost of teacher turnover. Retrieved from nctaf.org/wp-content /uploads/2012/01/NCTAF-Cost-of-Teacher-Turnover- 2007- policy-brief.pdf

National Council for the Accreditation of Teacher Education. (2010). *The road less traveled: How the developmental sciences can prepare educators to improve student achievement—policy recommendations*. Washington, DC: National for the Accreditation of Teacher Education.

National Institute for Early Education Research (NIEER). (2015). *The state of preschool 2014*. New Brunswick, NJ: Author.

National Task Force on Early Childhood Education for Hispanics. (2007). *Para nuestros niños: Expanding and improving early education for Hispanics; Main report*. Tempe, AZ: National Task Force on Early Childhood Education for Hispanics. Retrieved from fcd-us.org/sites/default/files/PNNExecReport.pdf

National Women's Law Center. (2000). Be all that we can be: Lessons from the military for improving our nation's child care system. Retrieved from nwlc .org/wp-content/uploads/2015/08/military.pdf

The New Teacher Project (TNTP). (2015). The mirage: Confronting the hard truth about our quest for teacher development. Retrieved from tntp.org/assets /documents/TNTP-Mirage_2015.pdf

Nortes, M., & Barnett, S. (2014). *Access to high quality early care and education: Readiness and opportunity gaps in America* (CEELO and NIEER Policy Report). New Brunswick, NJ: Center on Enhancing Early Learning Outcomes. ceelo.org/wp-content/uploads/2014/05/ceelo_policy_report_access_quality _ece.pdf

Nyhan, P. (2011). The power of pre-K–3rd: How a small foundation helped push Washington State to the forefront of the pre-K–3rd movement (FCD Case Study). New York, NY: Foundation for Child Development. Retrieved from fcd-us.org/sitesdefault/files/FCDCase StudyWashington.pdf

Nyhan, P. (2015). The power of a good idea: How the San Francisco School District is building a pre-K–3rd grade bridge. Retrieved from static.newamerica .org/attachments/3403-the-power-of-a-good-idea/The Power of a Good Idea .1bbfe312ed6d419d98c582c2d80747d6.pdf

Ochshorn, S. (2015). *Squandering America's future: Why ECE policy matters for equality, our economy, and our children.* New York, NY: Teachers College Press.

OECD. (2013). Country note: PISA results from PISA 2012. Retrieved from www .oecd.org/pisa/keyfindings/PISA-2012-results-US.pdf

OECD. (2014). Education at a glance 2014: OECD indicators. Retrieved from www.oecd.org/edu/Education-at-a-Glance-2014.pdf

O'Hare, W. (2012). Analyzing state differences in child well-being. Retrieved from fcd-us.org/sites/default/files/Analyzing State Differences in Child Well -Being_0.pdf

Olsen, L. (2014). *The SEAL model: Powerful language learning.* Cupertino, CA: The Sobrato Family Foundation. www.sobrato.org

Ortiz Oakley, E., & Burdman, P. (2015, May 29). Community colleges sending too many into remedial math. *San Francisco Chronicle.* Retrieved from www .sfchronicle.com/opinion/article/Community-colleges-sending-too-many-into -remedial-6293307.php

Park, M., McHugh, M., Batalova, J., & Zong, J. (2015). Immigrant and refugee workers in the early childhood field: Taking a closer look. Retrieved from www.migrationpolicy.org/research/immigrant-and-refugee-workers-early -childhood-field-taking-closer-look

Pew Center on the States. (2010). *Tapping Title I: What every school administrator should know about Title I, pre-K, and school reform* (Federal Policy Series). Washington, DC: Pew Charitable Trusts

Pew Research Center. (2014, February 11). The rising cost of not going to college. Retrieved from www.pewsocialtrends.org/2014/02/11/the-rising-cost-of-not-going-to-college

Piketty, T. (2014). *Capital in the twenty-first century* (A. Goldhammer, Trans.). Cambridge, MA: Belknap Press of Harvard University.

Porter, E. (2015, September 22). Education gap between rich and poor is growing wider. *New York Times.* Retrieved from www.nytimes.com/2015/09/23/business/economy/education-gap-between-rich-and-poor-is-growing-wider.html

Putnam, R. (2015). *Our kids: The American dream in crisis.* New York, NY: Simon and Schuster.

Raden, A. (1999). Universal prekindergarten in Georgia: A case study of Georgia's lottery-funded pre-K program. Retrieved from fcd-us.org/sites/default/files/Universal pre-K in Georgia.pdf

Raden, A. (2002). *Achieving full-day kindergarten in New Mexico: A case study.* New York, NY: Foundation for Child Development. Retrieved from fcd-us.org/sites/default/files/Achieving%20Full-Day%20Kindergarten%20in%20New%20Mexico.pdf

Raudenbush, S. W., & Eschmann, R. D. (2015). Does schooling increase or reduce social inequality? *Annual Review of Sociology, 41,* 443–470.

Reardon, S. F. (2011). The widening academic achievement gap between the rich and the poor: New evidence and possible explanations. In R. Murnane & G. Duncan (Eds.), *Whither opportunity? Rising inequality and the uncertain life chances of low-income children* (pp. 91–116). New York, NY: Russell Sage Foundation.

Reynolds, A., Hayakawa, M., Candee, A. J., & Englund, M. M. (2016). *CPC P–3 program manual.* Minneapolis, MN: University of Minnesota.

Reynolds, A., Richardson, B., Hayakawa, M., Lease, E. M., Englund, M. M., Ou, S., Candee, A. J., Smerilo, N. E., & Giovanni, A. (2015, October). Midwest expansion of the child-parent center preschool to third-grade program: Year 1 preschool findings from Chicago. Paper presented at the Human Capital Research Collaborative National Invitational Conference "Sustaining Early Child Gains," Minneapolis, MN.

Reynolds, A., Richardson, B., Hayakawa, M., Lease, E. M., Warner-Richter, M., Englund, M. M., & Sullivan, M. (2014). Association of a full-day vs. part-day preschool intervention with school readiness, attendance, and parent involvement. *JAMA, 312*(20), 2126–2134.

Reynolds, A. J., & Robertson, D. L. (2003). School-based intervention and later child maltreatment in the Chicago Longitudinal Study. *Child Development, 74*(1), 3–26.

Reynolds, A. J., Temple, J. A., Robertson, D. L., & Mann, E. A., (2001). Long-term effects of an early childhood intervention on educational achievement and juvenile arrest: A 15-year follow-up of low-income children in public schools. *Journal of the American Medical Association, 285*(18), 2339–2346.

Rice, C., & Costanza, V. (2011). Building early learning leaders: New Jersey's pre-K–3rd leadership training. Retrieved from acnj.org/downloads/2011 03 01 Prek3TrainingReport.pdf

Richmond, J., & Schorr, L. (1992, June 23). Every child can have a Head Start: This program works and can easily be expanded; being prepared for school isn't a middle-class birthright. *Los Angeles Times*. Retrieved from articles .latimes.com/1992-06-23/local/me- 782_1_local-head-start.

Ripley, A. (2013). *The smartest kids in the world: And how they got that way.* New York, NY: Simon and Schuster.

Ritchie, S., & Gutmann, L. (2013). *FirstSchool: Transforming pre-K–3rd grade for African American, Latino, and low-income children.* New York, NY: Teachers College Press.

Robinson, K., & Aronica, L. (2015). *Creative schools: The grassroots revolution that's transforming education.* New York, NY: Penguin.

Rose, E. (2011). Prekindergarten in Oklahoma. In E. Zigler, W. S. Gilliam, & W. S. Barnett (Eds.), *The pre-K debates: Controversies and issues* (pp. 188–191). Baltimore, MD: Brookes.

Ross, T. (2015). *The case for a two-generation approach for educating English language learners.* Washington, DC: Center for American Progress.

Rothstein, R. (2004). Class and the classroom: Even the best schools can't close the race achievement gap. *American School Board Journal, 191,* 16–21.

Russakoff, D. (2009, December 23). Schooling low-income parents in helping students. *Los Angeles Times*. Retrieved from articles.latimes.com/2009/dec/23 /opinion/la-oe- russakoff23-2009dec23.

Russakoff, D. (2015). *The prize: Who's in charge of America's schools?* New York, NY: Houghton Mifflin Harcourt.

Ryan, C. (2013). Language use in the United States: 2011. Retrieved from www .census.gov/prod/2013pubs/acs-22.pdf

Sabol, T., & Chase-Lansdale, P. L. (2015). The influence of low-income children's participation in Head Start on their parents' education and employment. *Journal of Policy Analysis and Management, 34*(1), 136–161.

Sahlberg, P. (2014). *Finnish lessons 2.0: What can the world learn from educational change in Finland?* (2nd ed.). New York, NY: Teachers College Press.

Sanchez, I., & Garcia, A. (2015). Briya public charter school: A dual generation approach to pre-K. In A. Garcia & C. P. Williams, *Stories from the nation's capital: Building instructional programs and supports for dual language learners from pre-K-3rd grade in Washington, D.C.* (p. 13). Washington, DC: New America.

Sandler, L. (2015, May 18). Taking care of our own: Paid leave goes from progressive pipe dream to political reality. Retrieved from newrepublic.com /article/121822/paid-leave-goes-progressive-pipe-dream-political-reality

Sarason, S. (1996). *Revisiting "The culture of the school and the problem of change."* New York, NY: Teachers College Press.

Sastry, N., & Pebley, A. (2010). Family and neighborhood sources of socioeconomic inequality in children's achievement. *Demography, 47*(3), 777–800.

Sawhill, I., & Rodrigue, E. (2015, November 18). An agenda for reducing poverty and improving opportunity. Retrieved from www.brookings .edu/research/papers/2015/11/campaign-2016-presidential-candidates -poverty-and-opportunity

Schaenen, I. (2014). *Speaking of fourth grade: What listening to kids tells us about school in America.* New York, NY: The New Press.

Schulman, L. J. (2000). Teacher development: Roles of domain expertise and pedagogical knowledge. *Journal of Applied Developmental Psychology, 21*(1), 129–135.

Schulte, B. (2014). *Overwhelmed: Work, love, and play when no one has the time.* New York, NY: Sarah Crichton Books.

Searcey, D., Porter, E., & Gebeloff, R. (2015, February 22). Health care opens stable career path, taken mainly by women. *New York Times.* Retrieved from www.nytimes.com/2015/02/23/business/economy/health-care-opens-middle -class-path-taken-mainly-by-women.html

Shonkoff, J., & Phillips, D. (2000). *From neurons to neighborhoods: The science of early child development.* Washington, DC: National Academy Press.

Sizer, T. (2013). *The new American high school.* San Francisco, CA: Jossey-Bass.

Steiner, G. (1981). *The futility of family policy.* Washington, DC: Brookings Institution.

Steuerle, C. E. (2013). *Dead men ruling. How to restore fiscal freedom and rescue our future.* New York, NY: The Century Foundation.

Stevens, K. (2015, September 1). Pre-K isn't enough: Don't let political actors hijack the early learning agenda. Retrieved from www.usnews .com/opinion/knowledge-bank/2015/09/01/early-childhood-learning-is -about-more-than-universal-pre-k

Stiglitz, J. (2010). *Freefall: America, free markets, and the sinking of the world economy.* New York, NY: W. W. Norton.

Stiglitz, J. (2012). *The price of inequality: How today's divided society endangers our future.* New York, NY: W. W. Norton.

Stiglitz, J. (2014, June 27). Inequality is not inevitable. Retrieved from opinionator .blogs.nytimes.com/2014/06/27/inequality-is-not-inevitable/

Stiglitz, J., & Greenwald, B. (2014). *Creating a learning society: A new approach to growth, development, and social progress.* New York, NY: Columbia University Press.

Suarez-Orozco, C., Yoshikawa, H., & Tseng, V. (2015). *Intersecting inequalities: Research to reduce inequality for immigrant-origin children and youth.* New York, NY: W. T. Grant Foundation.

Sullivan-Dudzic, L., Gearns, D., & Leavell, K. (2010). *Making a difference: 10 essential steps to building a pre-K–3 system.* Thousand Oaks, CA.: Corwin.

Sunstein, C. (2013). *Simpler: The future of government.* New York, NY: Simon & Schuster.

Superville, D. (2015, August 19). Rookie principals' group sheds light on early-career challenges. *Education Week*. Retrieved from www.edweek.org/ew/articles/2015/08/19/rookie-principals-group-sheds-light-on-early-career.html

Takanishi, R. (2010). Pre-K–third grade: A paradigm shift. In V. Washington & J. D. Andrews (Eds.), *Children of 2020: Creating a better tomorrow* (pp. 28–31). Washington, DC: Council for Professional Recognition, National Association for the Education of Young Children.

Takanishi, R. (2011). Transforming America's primary education system for the 21st century: Integrating K–12 education with prekindergarten. In E. Zigler, W. S. Gilliam, & W. S. Barnett (Eds.), *The pre-K debates: Current controversies and issues* (pp. 181–184). Baltimore, MD: Brookes.

Takanishi, R. (2015). Federal expenditures on children: What budget policy means for children's policy. Inconvenient Truths. *SRCD Social Policy Report*, 29(1). Retrieved from www.srcd.org/sites/default/files/documents/vol_29_1.pdf

Talbot, M. (2014, December 10). The talking cure. *New Yorker*. Retrieved from www.newyorker.com.magazine/2015/01/12/talking-cure

Thompson, K. D. (2015, August 25). English learners' time to reclassification: An analysis. *Education Policy*, 1–34.

Tooley, M., & Bornfreund, L. (2014). Skills for success: Supporting and assessing key habits, mindsets, and skills in pre-K–12. Retrieved from www.newamerica.org/downloads/11212014_Skills_for_Success_Tooley_Bornfreund.pdf

Tough, P. (2012). *How children succeed: Grit, curiosity, and the hidden power of character*. New York, NY: Houghton Mifflin Harcourt.

Tough, P. (2009). *Whatever it takes: Geoffrey Canada's quest to change Harlem and America*. Boston, MA: Mariner Books.

Tucker, M. (2011). *Surpassing Shanghai: An agenda for American education built on the world's leading systems*. Cambridge, MA: Harvard Education Press.

Tucker, M. (2016, March 6). Why education research has so little impact on practice: The system effect. *Education Week*. Retrieved from blogs.edweek.org/edweek/top_performers/2016/03/why_education_research_has_so_little_impact_on_practice_the_system_effect.html.

Tyack, D., & Cuban, L. (1997). *Tinkering toward Utopia: A century of public school reform*. Cambridge, MA: Harvard University Press.

University of Chicago Consortium on Chicago School Research. (2014). Preschool attendance in Chicago public schools: Relationships with learning outcomes and reasons for absences. Retrieved from consortium.uchicago.edu/sites/default/files/publications/Pre-KAttendanceReport.pdf

U.S. Department of Education. (2014). Higher Education Act Title II Data Collection. Retrieved from title2.ed.gov/Public/Home.aspx

U.S. Department of Education, Institute of Education Sciences, National Center for Education Statistics, National Assessment of Educational Progress (NAEP). (2013). *The Nation's Report Card: Trends in academic progress 2012* (NCES 2013 456). Retrieved from nces.ed.gov/nationsreportcard/subject/publications/main2012/pdf/2013456.pdf

U.S. Department of Education, Institute of Education Sciences, National Center for Education Statistics, National Assessment of Educational Progress (NAEP). (2015). *The Nation's Report Card: 2015 mathematics and reading assessments.* Retrieved from nces.ed.gov/pubsearch/pubsinfo.asp?pubid=2015136

U.S. Department of Education, Institute of Education Sciences, National Center for Education Statistics. (2014, October). Profile of undergraduate students: 2011–2012. Retrieved from nces.ed.gov/pubs2015/2015167.pdf

Vespa, J., Lewis, J., & Kreider, R. (2013). America's families and living arrangements: 2012. Retrieved from www.census.gov/prod/2013pubs/p20-570.pdf

Wagner, T. (2008). *The global achievement gap: Why even our best schools don't teach the new survival skills our children need—and what we can do about it.* New York, NY: Basic Books.

Wagner, T., & Dintersmith, T. (2015). *Most likely to succeed: Preparing our kids for the innovation era.* Cambridge, MA: Harvard Press.

Watson, S. (2011). The right policy and at the right time: The Pew prekindergarten campaign. In E. Zigler, W. S. Gilliam, & W. S. Barnett (Eds.), *The pre-K debates: Current controversies and issues* (pp. 9–20). Baltimore, MD: Brookes.

Weikart, D. (2004). *How High/Scope grew: A memoir.* Ypsilanti, MI.: High/Scope Press.

West, M. R. (August 2012). Is retaining students in the early grades self-defeating? Retrieved from www.brookings.edu/research/papers/2012/08/16-student-retention-west

Whitebook, M. (2014). *Building a skilled workforce: Shared and divergent challenges in early care and education and in grades K–12.* Seattle, WA: Bill and Melinda Gates Foundation.

Whitebook, M., Phillips, D., & Howes, C. (2015). Worthy work, STILL unlivable wages: The early childhood workforce 25 years after the National Child Care Staffing Study. Retrieved from www.irle.berkeley.edu/cscce/wp-content/uploads/ 2014/11/ReportFINAL.pdf

Williams, C. P. (2015). *Boomtown kids: Harnessing energy and aligning resources for dual language learners in San Antonio, Texas.* Washington, DC: New America.*pre-K*

Whitehurst, G. J., & Klein, E. (2015). Do we already have universal preschool? Washington, DC: Brookings Institution. Retrieved from www.brookings.edu/research/papers/2015/09/17-do-we-already-have-universal-preschool-whitehurst-klein

Williams, C. P., & Garcia, A. (2015). *A voice for all: Oregon's David Douglas School District builds a better pre-K–3rd grade system for dual language learners.* Retrieved from static.newamerica.org/attachments/10363-a-voice-for-all/Voice-For-All.bda14b99676c40ccb3186fbc6a33ad58.pdf

York, B., & Loeb, S. (2014). One step at a time: The effects of an early literacy text messaging program for parents of preschoolers. *NBER Working Paper No. 20659.*

Yoshikawa, H., Weiland, C., Brooks-Gunn, J., Burchinal, M., Espinosa, L., Gorm-ley, W., & Zaslow, M. (2013). *Investing in our future: The evidence base on preschool education.* New York, NY: Society for Research in Child Development and Foundation for Child Development.

Zellman, G. L., & Kilburn, M. R. (2015). *How well did P–3 work? The Hawai'i preschool–third grade education reform initiative.* Santa Monica, CA: RAND Corporation. Retrieved from www.rand.org/pubs/research_reports/RR1100.html

Zigler, E. (2011). Redirecting Title I. In Zigler, E., Gilliam, W., & Barnett, W. (Eds.), *The pre-K debates: Current controversies and issues* (pp. 184–186). Baltimore, MD.: Paul H. Brookes.

Zigler, E., & Muenchow, S. (1992). *Head Start: The inside story of America's most successful educational experiment.* New York, NY: Basic Books.

Zigler, E., & Styfco, S. (2010). *The hidden history of Head Start.* New York, NY: Oxford University Press.

Zimmerman, J. (2014, December 4). Why is American teaching so bad? *New York Review of Books, 61,* (19). Retrieved from www.nybooks.com/issues/2014/12/04/

Zinny, G. (2015, April 9). Reforming education from the bottom up in Buenos Aires, Argentina. Retrieved from www.brookings.edu/blogs/education-plus-development/posts/2015/04/09-reform-education-argentina-zinny

Index

ABOUT THE AUTHOR

Ruby Takanishi is senior research fellow in the Early and Elementary Education Policy division at New America in Washington, DC. She received her PhD from Stanford University and taught at UCLA; Teachers College, Columbia University; Yale University; and Bank Street College. Takanishi was the president and CEO of the Foundation for Child Development, a grant-making philanthropy that launched the pre-K–3rd movement in 2003, and executive director of the Carnegie Council on Adolescent Development of Carnegie Corporation of New York, which issued landmark reports on middle school reform, youth development in out-of-school settings, and adolescent health. She chaired the National Academies of Sciences, Engineering, and Medicine consensus committee on the education of dual-language learners from birth to age 18. She has received awards from the American Psychological Association, the American Sociological Association (Division of Children and Families), and the Society for Research in Child Development in recognition of her contribution to connecting research with public policies. The American Education Research Association honored her with its 2014 Distinguished Public Service Award.